En

The Story of a Girl and Her Family Hijacked by Anorexia

LINDA MAZUR, JOHN MAZUR,
Emilee Mazur

Published by JACLIN PRESS

Rochester, New York

Copyright 2019 Linda & John Mazur

This story is based on actual events. Though we have attempted to recreate events, locales, and conversations from our memories, in order to maintain anonymity in some instances, some names and identifying details have been changed to protect the privacy of individuals.

[handwritten inscriptions]

Eva — You are an angel on earth. God bless, John

Eva, Thank you so much for sleeping yes! You are in our hearts. Thank you for all you do and for giving Emilee the peaceful passing — and with love + dignity — and so many people caring for all of us. Eternally grateful, Linda Mazur

Thank you, Kathe Healy, for sharing your wisdom, your counsel, and your compassion with our family.
You live on in our hearts.

"If there is a book you really want to read, and it hasn't been written yet, then you must write it."

Toni Morrison

"What is a soul? It's like electricity-we don't really know what it is, but it is a force that can light a room."

Ray Charles

Linda, John, and *Emilee* Mazur

"Amazingly profound! *Emilee: A Girl and Her Family Hijacked by Anorexia* is a must-read."

--Erica R. Fragnito, LMHC

* * * * *

"The Mazurs have written a beautiful story filled with compassion, clarity, and tenderness. Their daughter Emilee's journey through anorexia nervosa and substance use disorder reveals not only the extraordinary torments that patients and families go through, but also highlights the serious problems of a medical system both unfamiliar with and ill-equipped to provide optimal care for those with eating disorders. I am so grateful to see Emilee come alive in these pages; they honor her remarkable gifts and her equally remarkable suffering."

--Jennifer L. Gaudiani, MD, CEDS-S, FAED,
Founder & Director, Gaudiani Clinic, author of *Sick Enough*

* * * * *

"Emilee...provides a riveting view of how the eating disorder anorexia nervosa can hijack a person's life and the lives of family members, loved ones, friends, and colleagues who care about the person suffering from the disease.

Emilee's compelling story, told by tightly interwoven recollections of illustrative incidents—that both define the illness—and defy logic—from the perspective of her mother, her father, and Emilee herself, makes for captivating reading.

This book does not provide answers to questions such as "what causes" or "how to treat" anorexia nervosa. Nor is it a self-help book for individuals with anorexia nervosa—or for their parents--with simple solutions to complex problems. However, this book provides insights into how anorexia nervosa can "disconnect" an affected individual from one's self, from one's parents and other loved ones, in particularly destructive ways that threaten connections parents have with each other. It also provides insights on how loving parents can stay "connected" benefitting the parents as well as the child.

Most important, in very unexpected ways, this book powerfully illustrates the importance of parents NEVER giving up hope when they have a child with persistent and enduring anorexia nervosa."

--Richard E. Kreipe, MD, FAAP, FASHM, FAED

* * * * *

"Linda and John Mazur aptly describe the gradual onset of anorexia nervosa (AN) against the backdrop of Emilee's everyday experiences of becoming a young woman. Their journey poignantly illustrates how AN, capitalizing on their daughter's anxiety, achievement orientation, and inner critic, insidiously disconnects her from herself and those she loved. This memoir reveals how love of family and friends, though powerful and necessary, are not enough to overcome the devastating effects of AN. Emilee's parents call on the medical community and insurance companies to increase their knowledge about eating disorders and to support patient, family, practitioner, and school partnerships that promote early identification, intervention, and comprehensive, coordinated, and continuous care. The Mazurs' memoir underscores the importance of connection, communication, and collaboration in the eradication of these deadly illnesses that can lead to disconnection, physical and mental deterioration, spiritual despair, and the loss of the will to live."

--Mary Tantillo, PhD, PMHCNS, BC, FAED,
   co-author of *Understanding Teen Eating Disorders...*

"Do not be afraid to open your mind and your heart and let this book touch your soul. The inspiring words of John and Linda Mazur, leap off the page and flow like a stream of love down a long and winding river. *Emilee: The Story of a Girl and Her Family Hijacked by Anorexia* is a courageous narrative that urges you to listen, understand, and perhaps help someone you know who is suffering."

--Vickijo Campanaro, psychotherapist and co-founder of The Assisi Institute

Linda, John, and *Emilee* Mazur

The name *Emilee:*

Graceful, intelligent, kind, creative, and strong.

If you know an *Emilee*
You're in the presence of greatness.
She is good at everything and so very humble.
She has an unbelievable beauty that radiates
everywhere she goes.
Her kindness has no boundaries.
Her energy is infectious, which makes everyone
want to be around her.

The Baby Name Wizard

Linda, John, and *Emilee* Mazur

Contents

CHAPTER ONE • CRAZY

LINDA

It's difficult for me to remember what I'm supposed to do next. Having been assigned a small metal locker I remove my coat and scarf, take off my jewelry, empty my pockets, and carefully place everything, including my oversized leather purse, inside the small, square space. A police officer hands me a tiny silver key attached to a coiled plastic cord, and I'm instructed to wear it around my wrist. My hands tremble, and my usually sturdy legs feel like they are made of unraveling twine. The walls buzz in a low tone, and the entire room seems to vibrate and close in around me. *Breathe, Linda,* I think as I fumble with the key. *You can do this.* When I finally hear the metallic click of the lock I exhale, slowly and deliberately.

"Hey, lady," the officer says. "You have to stand over there before you can go into the visitation area." He gestures toward a line of men and women that has formed to my right. Three men wearing shiny suits and silk ties are ushered to the front of the line. I notice their well-coiffed hair and expensive leather briefcases. *Attorneys*, I surmise. I watch and wait as an officer in a starched blue uniform passes an electronic wand over everyone in front me, to be sure no one is hiding anything that could be used as a weapon inside the facility.

Eventually, it's my turn, and I walk to the designated space. "Spread your arms and legs," the officer says.

The last few months have been excruciating, and this day is no exception. There have been so many unexpected twists and turns over the last few years, nothing should surprise me. Yet each one has. The officer tells me to move along. I bump forward slowly, feeling jostled and out of place.

Visitors are corralled into one large room with long plastic tables and uncomfortable-looking chairs. The walls are a dismal shade of green. Ironically, I remember reading about a jail that had painted its walls in shades of bright reds and pinks—ostensibly, to lift the spirits of those incarcerated. Unfortunately, after the inmates became disruptive and aggressive, the walls were repainted the original drab green. Peace was restored, and the aggressive behavior was no longer an issue. So, of course, I think this color is appropriate.

After a short time, a heavy metal door opens and bodies shuffle into the visitation area, each inmate wearing a jumpsuit and plastic shoes. I notice varying degrees of hardness on some of the faces, and inscrutable sadness etched on the faces of others.

My daughter is almost unrecognizable, but there she is— standing across the room from me—the saddest, most malnourished inmate there. Looking much more like a sick and dying child than a thirty-year-old woman, her red jumpsuit is enormous and only emphasizes her skeletal frame and pale skin. Her arms hang like ropes at her sides, exposing bony elbows, and as the line inches closer I notice the gray circles under her eyes. Somehow, I manage a shaky smile. We're allowed only a quick embrace before we are, once again, separated by a thick, clear partition about 12 inches high. As we move towards the tables and chairs on either side of the barrier, I think about how small and frail she looks. It's a miracle she's alive. Once seated I spread my fingers against the clear partition, and she does the same thing on her side, our hands lining up almost perfectly. After a moment she closes her eyes, and tears begin to trickle down her cheeks. I want to hold her in my arms.

"It's going to be okay," I tell her.

Because, at that point, I honestly believed it would.

CHAPTER TWO • MY BABY

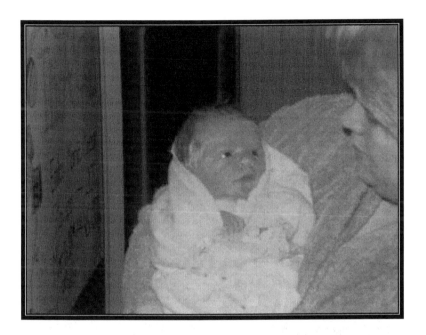

LINDA

It all started easily enough. In the weeks leading up to the birth of our daughter, Jack and I decide on an old-fashioned name with an unconventional spelling—and when we see her, the name fits. Presenting with bright blue eyes and porcelain skin, Emilee is born with a full head of thick, wavy blonde hair.

"She looks perfect!" Jack says, kissing my forehead while a nurse whisks our daughter away to be cleaned, measured, and weighed.

Physically and emotionally exhausted from a long, strenuous labor and delivery, I watch anxiously from across the room as the medical team examines Emilee. All of a sudden, I feel strange. Shaky. I can feel a vibration move throughout my entire body, and suddenly both of my legs begin to convulse involuntarily. I've never read about or heard about any other woman experiencing this, and I'm scared. When I call out for help, a nurse rushes over and covers me with a warm blanket.

She smooths the linens under my knees. "Those are labor shakes," she says. "For nine months your body nurtured, protected, and housed that little person from the time she was just a few cells. Giving birth is extremely hard on your body; these are like after-shocks, displacing all that energy."

I squeeze Jack's hand. "How long will it take for the shaking to stop?"

"It will stop," the nurse says. "I promise."

After medication and time, my legs gradually stop shaking. I am relieved and grateful when, after what seems like an eternity, the nurse brings our newborn back to us.

"Emilee's APGAR score is ten!" she announces, placing the baby in my arms.

"Is that good?" Jack questions.

"It's great! It means she's in the best possible condition."

Swaddled in a pink blanket and tiny knit cap, Emilee's blue eyes are riveted on our faces. No one could have prepared either of us for the depth of love and protectiveness we immediately feel for this child.

We're discharged two days later, and we place Emilee into a brand new car seat, checking and double-checking to make sure she is securely buckled in. Jack drives carefully the entire way home. As we approach the familiar weathered red barn on the corner of our road, two old horses walk slowly toward us, watching through the fence as we drive by.

Our cozy ranch welcomes the three of us, and we're delighted to see an oversized sign in bright pink lettering hanging from the front porch railing announcing – IT'S A GIRL! My mother, Dorothy, stands in the front picture window, smiling and waving at us. I am close to both my parents, and my mother has always been there for me whenever I've had a problem or needed to talk. She listens intently and non-judgmentally, always the calm voice of reason.

Though her nature is quiet, she is warm, compassionate, and kind. To me, she is pure love. My parents live one hour away in the small city of Geneva, New York, located on the northern end of Seneca Lake, known for its award-winning wineries, as well as Hobart and William Smith Colleges. My mother has taken time off from her job at the college to help us out for a few days, and get to know her first grandchild. My father, Carmen, is a barber. Colorful, naturally gregarious, and fun to be around, he makes people feel instantly comfortable and possesses an innate ability to make people laugh.

It's great to be home. I lay Emilee on the couch, and my parents watch me unbundle the baby. Clearly, they're mesmerized by their little granddaughter. They take turns holding her and kissing her rosy cheeks. I take Emilee on a tour of our home, her little body nestled in the crook of my arm. I talk to her softly as we walk down the hallway to the nursery. I love this room—scenes of happy children playing on a sandy beach cover the walls. I show her Jack's and my bedroom, where she'll sleep for the first few months. In the corner an antique white wicker bassinette, passed down on my mother's side through the generations, waits patiently to hold the newest baby in the family: Emilee.

Eventually, we join the rest of the family in the living room. "The firstborn is the experimental child," my father says, holding his granddaughter's little hand. My dad, now fifty-two, reminds us that he, too, was an 'experimental' child. The oldest of six children, he is a natural with babies. I look around the room and think to myself, *how fortunate I am to have grown up with family all around me.* All four of my grandparents lived close by. My father's parents lived just down the street from us, in a modest two-story home. My mother's parents moved from their small farm in the country to an apartment a few miles away. A few aunts, uncles, and cousins resided nearby, and those who moved away came to visit often. Like my father I am the eldest child in my family, three years older than my sister Ellen and eight years older than my brother Mark.

Our family has always been close, and on the day our daughter is born I feel blessed that Jack and I have added the very first member of the next generation of our family.

Before I had Emilee, I was a full-time hairstylist at Donald's Intercoiffure Salon. I had enjoyed working at the prestigious salon located in Rochester, New York. I was fond of the owner and the other stylists, but the moment I learned I was pregnant being a mother became my first priority. I made plans to leave my full-time job and open my own hair salon as an in-home business. Jack and I remodeled the lower level of our home to accommodate the salon, which allows me the flexibility to set my own hours and work around Jack's schedule. And, as a result, reduce the hours of daycare we need for our baby.

Six weeks after Emilee is born I begin working again, and when my baby is awake I bring her into the salon and proudly introduce her to my clients. As I open their gifts, I'm struck by their thoughtfulness and generosity. When I'm with clients Jack takes care of Emilee, and when he's not available our grandmotherly neighbor or a few experienced teens help out. I'm happy to run upstairs and check on Emilee if there is an issue, or whenever there is time between clients. I feel I have the best of both worlds: being able to work at home, set my own hours, be close to my baby, and contribute financially. It's an ideal arrangement, and I'm grateful.

Emilee is agile and strong and has a good appetite. Other than experiencing some minor reflux and a few ear infections, she is a curious, happy, and healthy baby. She's so expressive—her laugh is contagious, and I love the way my daughter's little face lights up whenever I walk into the room! In my entire life, I've never felt so fulfilled. We are attached with the Velcro of love.

CHAPTER THREE • FATHERHOOD

JACK

Growing up as an only child, I had no prior experience with babies. But fatherhood comes naturally and easily with Emilee. When I don't have to work the next day, I get up in the middle of the night to give my daughter a bottle so Linda can sleep. I change Emilee's diapers, and I enjoy seeing her reaction when we introduce new foods into her diet. As Em grows older, I'm thrilled to be able to participate more in her daily routine. She laughs through bath time, splashing and slapping the water with delight. I think everything she does is brilliant. I delight in each new accomplishment and praise her lavishly.

From the beginning, bedtime is a challenge for Emilee. No matter how much we rock or walk her, she fusses and takes a long time to settle in. And when she finally falls asleep, the littlest sounds rouse her. Linda and I experiment with all kinds of things. Eventually we realize our daughter likes music, so we put a radio in her room, tuned to soft, soothing music for background noise, and that helps her to sleep more soundly. We notice that Emilee becomes especially distressed when she is separated from Linda. Everyone, including Emilee's pediatrician, whom we like and trust, tells us all this is normal, a stage she's going through, and that she'll be fine.

As a pharmacist, I typically work a twelve-hour shift followed by a day off. Other than middle-of-the-night feedings, much of my "together time" with Emilee occurs in the mornings before I go to work. I relish the hours I spend with my daughter, happy to be with her every chance I get. The two of us go to the bank, the grocery store, the pharmacy where I work, and the mall. I especially enjoy taking her to the Oshkosh store, where I buy her brightly colored polo shirts to wear under blue denim overalls. With fair skin, pink cheeks, bright blue eyes, and the curliest of blonde hair, she is a picture waiting to be taken. And boy, do I take pictures! She's a bit bashful when she first meets new people, but she quickly warms up to them. She performs her many funny faces, and the "frog" sound she makes from deep in her throat amuses us all. I believe Emilee is exceptional. She made all her milestones early, cutting her first tooth at four months, taking her first steps at eight months, and reciting *The Night Before Christmas* in its entirety, from memory, at just two years old. Everyone wants to take Emilee for the day, to spoil and enjoy her. Our daughter does not lack for attention or love. It surrounds her.

Linda and I believe that children are a blessing, a gift from God—never a certainty. We are thrilled when we learn that she is pregnant again. We tell Emilee a baby is growing inside Mommy, just like she did, and we explain, again and again, that no baby could ever take her place. Because she is our Emilee, and God gave her to us first, and that's extra special. Emilee is excited to be a big sister. She rubs Linda's belly gently and talks to the baby inside. Up to this point, Emilee's Curious George doll has been her "baby". She talks to George like a mother, and I listen outside her bedroom door: "Now go to sleep, George-O," she says. "It's late."

Linda's morning sickness subsides in June of 1983, and suddenly she's full of energy. We decide it's time to paint our one-story ranch home. We can do it ourselves: I can easily reach the high points using an extension ladder. And Linda, supervising from ground level, paints the middle and lower shingles. Emilee is, of course, eager to help, too, so we give her an empty Cool Whip bowl filled with water and a 4-inch brush, so she can "paint" the very bottom of our cedar shake house.

As Emilee grows, she continues to be a great assistant. She loves helping me wash and wax our station wagon. After I wash the car with a soapy sponge, she holds the hose with both hands and sprays the soap off the sides of the car. Emilee happily helps her mother in the kitchen, too, baking oatmeal-chocolate chip bar cookies—my favorite. She calls them "push cookies"—a term that perfectly describes the method she employs. Concentrating hard, and using both little hands, she pushes the dough up against the edges and into the corners of the pan.

After our second child is born, I bring Emilee to the hospital to meet her new brother. I'm given scrubs to wear, and the nurse fits Emilee with her own set of miniature scrubs decorated with cartoon characters on them. Hand in hand, the two of us walk into Linda's room to meet Matthew. We let Emilee hold him on her lap while she sits in a chair, and we are struck by the tender way she embraces him and kisses his cheeks.

That Christmas, Santa brings Emilee a doll so lifelike people think it's a real baby. Emilee names her Tiffany, and she goes to great lengths to shower Tiffany and George-O with equal amounts of love and affection. One Sunday, Emilee asks if she can bring Tiffany to church and, taking cues from her mother, she swaddles her doll-baby in buntings and blankets. At church, as Linda unbundles Matthew, Emilee copies her every move with Tiffany. People remark she is a natural nurturer, just like her mother.

Linda, John, and *Emilee* Mazur

CHAPTER FOUR • LEARNING AS WE GO

LINDA

When I was pregnant with Matthew, other mothers made a point of telling me that two children are much more difficult to handle than one—implying having a toddler and a baby would be a lot more work. Jack and I just smiled. We believed we had this "parenting thing" down.

Of course, those experienced moms were right. Struggling to get two children bundled up in winter, strapped into car seats, and out the door for grocery shopping and doctor's appointments feels like a major accomplishment. But Emilee is a wonderful helper. While I change and dress the baby Emilee stands on a red stool, amusing her brother by singing songs, reciting nursery rhymes, and acting just plain silly. If I'm busy with Matthew and the phone rings, Emilee rushes to answer it. I love it when my curly-haired, rosy-cheeked little girl holds the phone next to her ear and asks, "Who you are?"

Seven months after Matthew's birth, we decide to enroll Emilee in a pre-school summer session of "Fit by Five", a popular program offering two hours of supervised play a few mornings each week for pre-school-aged children. Emilee spends so much time at home, and Jack and I agree the socialization will be good for her and a great segue into pre-school. We explain the program to her, and Emilee is excited to go. On the first day, she holds my hand as we enter the building. Her eyes light up when she sees the other children; however, when it's time for the parents to leave, the corners of her little mouth turn downward. Standing there with her thumb in her mouth and George-O tucked under her arm, she begins to sob. Unable to console her, I pick her up and hold her close.

"If you go quickly she'll be just fine," the teacher promises, but I worry about Emilee the whole morning. When I arrive to pick her up, the teacher reports that Emilee continued to cry after I left. "It was her first day," she says reassuringly and with authority. "Give it time."

In light of Emilee's tears, I'm surprised two days later when Emilee begs to go back to Fit by Five for the next session. She packs her special tote bag and picks out the clothes she wants to wear. Everything is fine until it's time for me to leave. Again, Emilee falls apart.

The teachers assure me separation anxiety isn't at all unusual for a three-year-old, especially the first week or two. They tell me I should give her more time to adjust. However, at the end of the second week, I'm politely asked not to bring her back. Apparently, during group tours of the facility, Emilee's crying was unsettling to prospective parents and their children.

I'm assured I can enroll her again later in the year. It breaks my heart to see Emilee so upset.

"Oh, well," I joke to Jack. "Our daughter was expelled from "Fit by Five.""

"There are worse things," Jack says with a smile.

We speak with Emilee's pediatrician, and he tells us not to worry. We value his professional opinion, and we trust him. He reminds us that Emilee is extremely bright, doing fine developmentally, and that she is well adjusted. He explains, "It makes sense. She's just very attached to you, due to the fact you work from home. She's used to having you nearby. She's a lucky little girl."

In September, the four of us attend a nursery school's open house just up the road from our home. In no time Emilee is playing with Laura, a little girl with an infectious giggle and big brown eyes. The girls act like old friends, standing side-by-side, running their hands through a large wooden box filled with hundreds of buttons of every color and size. The girls delight in scooping up the buttons and pouring them in different sized containers. They dump the buttons out, laugh, and repeat the process over and over. We're glad to see Emilee so happy. The room is filled with families, laughter, and the anticipation of a wonderful pre-school experience.

Emilee thrives at nursery school, adapting quickly to the routine and structure of the program. Though she is shy at first, this time there are no tears. "I'm a big girl now," she exclaims.

Emilee and Laura, fast friends from the open house, become close, and Laura's parents become good friends: Doctor V., Laura's father becomes our physician, and Madaline, his wife, becomes my client. As the years go by, our friendships evolve and deepen.

Emilee transitions to elementary school easily, though I'm shocked at how quickly time passes. One spring afternoon, when the yellow daffodils in our yard are blooming and the sweet smell of lilacs fills the air, I walk down the driveway and wait for Emilee's kindergarten bus to arrive. I'm always eager to hear about her day at school, and either Jack or I wait in the driveway to greet her and to see that she crosses the road safely. Emilee's bus driver is a retired older gentleman with a white beard. He's very fond of Emilee, and the feeling is mutual. As the bus rounds the corner, I see the driver's signature cowboy hat through the oversized windshield, and directly behind him I see Emilee's blonde curls. When the bus doors part she skips down the wide steps, her pink backpack harnessed around each small shoulder.

"Mom!" she calls, hurrying to the center of the driveway. "I got invited to a sleepover!" She unzips her bag and sifts through her papers, searching for the invitation with all the details.

I'm excited for her, but privately I worry that Emilee isn't ready to sleep away from home. She's only in kindergarten. I know she's mature in some ways, but immature in others. She's shy in new surroundings. I wonder what the rush is all about—I never went to a slumber party until I was in fifth or sixth grade.

Jack and I discuss whether we should allow Emilee to attend. "She has trouble going to sleep here," I say, but Jack is optimistic about the matter.

"Clark Road is just a few minutes away," he insists. "She'll have all her friends with her."

I speak with Emilee's classmate's mother and let her know Emilee might have trouble sleeping. She assures me she will pay close attention and call me if there are any issues.

The week before the party Emilee and I have many talks about how much fun it will be, and how I will come and get her if she feels uncomfortable or has trouble sleeping. I suggest she bring George-O and she agrees. Emilee is sure she will be staying all night.

On the night of the party, Emilee says goodbye to her father and Matthew and jumps into the car. When we arrive at her friend's house Em insists on carrying everything herself, but the pink pillow and George-O are all she can manage. I carry her Strawberry Shortcake sleeping bag and matching overnight case. We ring the doorbell and, once inside, Emilee runs off with her friends. I stay a little while, just to be sure. All is well.

Jack and I enjoy a quiet dinner at home with Matthew. We assume things are going fine for Em and turn in on the early side.

It's strange not having Emilee in the house when we're going to bed. Lying on my back in our full-size bed, I look around our modest room and think about how often our bed is filled with the four of us, cuddling in the morning, or Jack and I comforting a sick child, or sometimes easing the fears left after a nightmare. It's a cozy room, with small-flowered wallpaper covering the walls and matching bedside tables on either side of the dark pine headboard. Jack's side table holds a shiny silver lamp and the digital alarm clock; I have the matching lamp and the telephone. Just as I start to fall asleep the phone rings, startling me.

I hear a soft, familiar voice. "Mom," Emilee whispers. "I can't sleep. Will you come get me?"

I knew it. I think. *I knew she wasn't ready.*

Jack and I exchange looks as I hurriedly throw some clothes on over my pajamas.

"Well," Jack says sleepily, "she tried."

Within a few short minutes, I arrive at the gray house on Clark Road and knock gently on the front door. The door opens, and Emilee is standing in the foyer next to her friend's mother. George-O is tucked under her arm. I notice her cheeks are rosy and her hair is flat on one side. Her long flannel nightgown hangs beneath her coat. Her chin seems to be resting on her chest. I can't quite decipher her mood.

"She's fine," the other mother assures me. "She just misses you."

Emilee holds my hand as we walk down the driveway. "Thanks for getting me," she says. "I had fun." Emilee is quiet on the short ride home. Jack and I tuck her into bed, where she falls fast asleep.

That kindergarten sleepover is the first of many overnights attempted, but not completed. Jack and I choose not to make a big deal about it. We understand Emilee prefers to stay close to home and, truth be told, we rather like that, too.

It's evident to us that even if things don't turn out exactly the way Emilee wants, she keeps trying. She always does things to the best of her ability, and in her own time. She knows she always has our support. Her resilience amazes us.

When Emilee is in second grade, we give her a small allowance for chores she completes at home. She saves her money, and in December she begins talking about buying holiday gifts for everyone. One cold afternoon, Emilee and I go shopping at a local shopping plaza where she easily decides on a toy for her brother and a coffee mug for her father. When we pass by a lovely little gift shop, where we've purchased greeting cards in the past, Emilee stops and tugs on my sleeve.

"I want to buy you a present," she says.

I look at her, dressed in her pink winter coat with her blonde curls peeking out of her white knit hat. "You don't have to buy me anything," I say.

"Yes, I do!" Emilee says adamantly. "I want to go in, and I want to go in alone."

"Honey, you can't go in by yourself. . . " I protest, but Emilee interrupts.

"I can do it by myself," she assures me. I know that look of determination on her face.

I think about it a minute and look inside the large storefront window. I can see straight through to the back of the store. There are only two shoppers inside, and I can tell this is important to Emilee, to show me she is capable. She wants to shop independently, like a grown-up, and she doesn't want me to see my Christmas present. I admire her spirit.

"Okay," I say. "But if you're not out in a few minutes, I'm coming in."

Emilee marches into the store while I keep watch from outside. In just a couple of minutes she's at the cash register, pulling dollar bills out of her tiny purse. The clerk steps around to the front of the counter to help her. I see Emilee point toward the entry door and the storefront window. The clerk glances in my direction and nods. She smiles at Emilee and hands my daughter a small white bag.

On Christmas morning, Emilee can hardly wait for us to open our gifts from her. When it's my turn, there's no hiding her excitement as I remove the Christmas wrap and bow and open the little white box. Nestled inside is a small, white porcelain figurine— an angel, playing the violin.

"I love it!" I squeal, grabbing Emilee's hand. "She looks just like you!"

Linda, John, and *Emilee* Mazur

CHAPTER FIVE • FAMILY

JACK

Growing up in the small upstate city of Oswego, New York, I was close to both of my parents. I never felt bad about not having siblings; I never even thought about it. There were lots of kids in my neighborhood, so I never lacked playmates. My mother always said I was the perfect child. I was an A student, and I didn't cause any trouble. I did my homework, practiced my coronet, and completed all my chores before going outside to play baseball, kickball, and touch football with friends. But I wasn't perfect. I just did my best, and I didn't want to disappoint my parents.

My father didn't show much outward affection, but there was no question how much he loved me. He worried about my safety and scolded me if I wasn't home before the streetlights came on. He bought me a football helmet because my friends and I used a concrete sidewalk that cut across the field as the 50-yard line. I painted the letters NY on the helmet for the Giants, my father's favorite football team. He bought me model car kits, and when I finished gluing them together and painting them we raced them down our driveway. When I was fourteen and wanted a pair of Converse brand sneakers my dad balked at the seven-dollar price tag, but he bought them for me anyway. The next day he spoke to me about the value of earning my own money and helped me get me a job cutting a neighbor's grass.

As I grew older he tried to teach me the plumbing and electrical knowledge he'd acquired, but I wasn't interested. I wish I'd listened. He told me I'd regret my decision one day when I owned my own home, and he was right. A pipefitter at the local textile mill, he worked hard to provide for us but he wasn't paid very well. If he arrived home from work before my mother got home from her secretarial job, he would start dinner for us. This set an example for me to help out. No matter who made it, our meal always consisted of meat, potato, vegetable, and a small salad. At 5:30 each night, the three of us sat down at the small kitchen table and talked about our day, and afterward it was my job to dry the dishes and put them away. Life was predictable and orderly, and I liked it that way.

While I was away at college, my father became chronically ill and was hospitalized frequently. Having served in the military as an aviation mechanic in Italy and North Africa during World War II, he was hospitalized at a VA hospital in Syracuse, a one-hour drive from their home. After working all day, my mother would then travel to visit him at night. She did this day after day, during each hospitalization, and during this time I returned home as much as I could. Unfortunately my father passed away at age sixty, the year before Emilee was born. I miss him terribly. He would have been a wonderful grandfather.

My mother is a great mother and an outstanding grandmother. Grandma Grace is the kind of grandmother who gets down on the floor to play with the kids, and Emilee and Matthew are her only grandchildren. Thoughtful and generous, she takes a great deal of time in choosing just the right gift for her loved ones and friends. Because my mother never had a daughter, she especially enjoys buying things for Emilee. When we visit her in Oswego, she brings all of my old toys down from the attic for Emilee and Matthew to play with.

When Grandma Grace comes to visit, she stays with us for a few days at a time. Energetic and fun to be around, she is not shy when it comes to offering her opinions about things in general, and most especially around childrearing. Linda and I understand she means well, but sometimes the visit is a bit stressful, especially for Linda. Emilee and Matthew are good kids, who get along well but, upon occasion, they argue with each other. It's difficult for them, like any pair of siblings, to be on their best behavior for days at a time.

Following one of my mother's longer visits, I remember the four of us standing on the front porch watching her back her brown Honda Accord out of our driveway.

"Grandma Dot and Grandpa Carmen think we're perfect," Emilee says as she waves. "But Grandma Grace knows we're not."

Upon hearing Emilee's comprehensive assessment of her grandparents, I remember being amused at the way my daughter processes the undercurrents of conversations and comments, and I'm impressed she speaks her truth. *Her mind is always working,* I think to myself, confident that this is a positive attribute. An indication of Emilee's intellect and curiosity.

"I don't know anyone who's perfect," I say. "I don't think we're supposed to be perfect."

Emilee shrugs and runs into the house.

I feel everything is going along fine for both of our children. They play together in the backyard on the swing set I assembled, and in the playhouse I built for them. They swim together in our pool and enjoy our family vacations. As a boy, growing up in a lower-middle-class family, my father insisted on taking us on a family vacation every summer. Like my father, I enjoy taking time off from work to share adventures with my family. With the children buckled in the backseat of our station wagon, we sing silly songs by Raffi—a singer known for his children's music, listen to the music from the Broadway Musical "Annie" and, of course, we're always on the lookout for license plates from other states.

The four of us visit Santa's Workshop in North Pole, New York during a vacation in the Adirondacks. Four-year-old Emilee takes charge, holding her little brother's hand as she leads him to the smallest reindeer and tells him there's nothing to be afraid of. She holds her kibble-filled hand under the reindeer's nose. "See, Matthew," she says. "This is how you do it."

For many years, Emilee is the recipient of much individual attention. Although she loves her brother, when he starts kindergarten Emilee resents the fact that Linda's and my attention is now divided between herself and her brother. Two children running up the driveway, eager to empty their backpacks and show us their papers, have to learn to take turns. Sharing that attention with her brother is an adjustment for Emilee, and sometimes she pouts when it's Matthew's turn to go first.

Linda, the oldest of three children, is used to sharing parental attention and takes this all in stride. As an only child, I never had to compete for my parents' attention, so I read books about sibling rivalry and jealousy and make an effort to spend more time with Emilee. I always try to give equal amounts of attention to our children, but suddenly I begin to sense that Emilee needs a little extra attention. In the winter months when Matt goes bowling, I take Emilee sledding, and when the weather grows warmer I take her to the driving range. I show her how to hold her golf club, so we can hit balls together.

LINDA

Though Jack and I grew up in different small towns, we had parents who worked hard, led simple lives, and were well-liked by everyone. However, the household in which I grew up wasn't quiet and structured like Jack's. It was lively and had an energy of its own, fueled by three very different children who weren't perfect. There were times we argued with each other, brought home a less than desirable grade on report cards, and forgot to clean our rooms. Mom and Dad told us to do our best, and when we missed the mark they got us back on track. My parents had some financial hard times, and that made our family grateful for what we had and especially grateful for each other.

Staying close is important to my family, and I'm thrilled when my sister Ellen moves to Rochester after our children are born. Emilee and Matthew love their Aunt Ellen, and she often comes to our house for dinner directly after work. Emilee is impressed with Ellen's professional attire, especially her high-heeled shoes and polished fingernails. Ellen sometimes brings the children trinkets from her office—leftover business cards and stationery from people who've left their jobs—which Emilee and Matthew use to play school or office. In these vignettes Emilee is always the teacher or boss, and Matthew her pupil or employee. Emilee takes pride in being studious and smart, and she loves to be in charge. Matthew never seems to mind.

After dinner, Emilee and her Aunt Ellen cozy up on the couch together. "You are my first niece and the first baby I helped care for," Ellen says. "I fell in love with you. You're the reason I want to have children of my own."

During this time, when our kids are small, my brother Mark, eight years my junior, attends college in Rochester. He regularly babysits for Emilee and Matthew when Jack and I need to work late. The children really look forward to Wednesdays with Uncle Mark. Conservative by nature, Mark is playful with his niece and nephew. They love it when he pretends to be a chef, wearing my apron and a multicolored wig retrieved from a bin in the hall closet. Though I always offer to pay him for his time, there are days he refuses payment. "I can't take it," he says. "I had too much fun."

My sister and brother are very important to me and always have been. I'm thrilled they live close by, and I'm grateful we've remained close. Over time, our extended family grows with the addition of their respective spouses, Al and Trish, who mesh seamlessly into our lives and bring their own brand of love and humor. Their children—my five nieces and nephews—are a delight to me, and when they are young I make a point to steal them away from time to time. We go to the movies, or out to lunch, and sometimes I bring them home with me, and together we make homemade pizza or pasta.

The entire Christmas season is a highly ritualized experience in our family, and it's something everyone looks forward to each year as we celebrate the birth of Jesus. We gather together and express gratitude for loved ones and friends. Every year, immediately after Thanksgiving, Jack and I bundle the kids and drive to Wilbert's Christmas Tree Farm, located just a few miles from our home, to cut down just the right tree. This task takes forever, and by the time we leave our arms and legs are as cold and stiff as the tree limbs. After we bring home the tree and have dinner, we listen to carols while decorating the tree. And later, after the kids and I go to bed, Jack stays up to rearrange the ornaments because he likes our tree to be balanced and symmetrical. Christmas Eve and Christmas Day always include grandparents, aunts, uncles, and cousins.

When the kids are small, on Christmas Eve I tuck Emilee and Matthew into bed while Jack strategically sprinkles a little kibble in the backyard to resemble reindeer droppings, draws sleigh tracks in the snow with a yardstick, and then, before coming inside, he shakes sleigh bells so the kids will hear their jingle and think Santa's close by. Before going to bed we spread gifts under the tree, Jack eats the cookies and drinks the milk the kids put out for Santa, and he scribbles **THANK YOU** on a napkin for Emilee and Matthew to find in the morning. On Christmas Day Emilee and Matthew wake early, eager to see if Santa has come.

Jack and I share our children's anticipation and enjoy watching them under the tree, tearing the wrapping paper off their gifts. After breakfast we all go to church and return home to host Christmas Day festivities, which includes more shared time with our extended family. This is the way things continue for many years, and I love the predictability of our holiday rituals and the feeling of stability these traditions provide.

One November day, things change. I'm in the kitchen, stirring spaghetti sauce while Emilee shapes the ground beef mixture into meatballs. We're talking about her school day and what movies she wants to see, when Em suddenly looks pensive.

"I have a question, and I want you to tell me the truth," Emilee says. Her blue eyes meet mine. I feel this is going to be an important question. "Is Santa Claus real?" she asks. Our practical Emilee!

Up until this point, Emilee hasn't inquired much about Santa. The previous year I overhear her telling her brother, "There has to be a Santa because Mom and Dad could never afford to buy all the things Santa brings for us," she'd reasoned.

But now that she is in fourth grade, Emilee is full of questions.

"I believe in Santa..." I say, sliding the tray of meatballs into the oven to brown, stalling for time.

"Mom," Emilee pleads. "You have to tell me the truth. I need to know if I have to buy gifts for my kids someday."

I'd been hoping for one more Christmas with Emilee believing in Old St. Nick, but now I realize I'm pushing it. After telling her the truth, I ask Emilee to promise not to share the secret with her brother. She nods her head and seems satisfied with my explanation, and I think she is pleased to be part of the grown-up world. At nine years old, Emilee is already thinking ahead—way ahead. *She'll be a wonderful mother someday,* I think to myself.

Linda, John, and *Emilee* Mazur

CHAPTER SIX • PERSONALITY

JACK

Throughout elementary school, Emilee excels in her studies and makes new friends effortlessly. Achieving high grades in academic studies is easy for Emilee—as it was for me. In our home, she's relaxed and enjoys listening to music and doing arts and crafts projects. Emilee continues to model herself after her mother, which is not uncommon for a young girl, especially when she has such a great example. Family and friends often comment that Emilee is a 'Little Linda', and Em doesn't seem to mind this comparison.

In March of 1991, two weeks before Emilee's tenth birthday, Rochester and the surrounding areas are caught off guard by a huge ice storm. Over the course of a single Sunday afternoon, the unseasonably warm temperature dramatically plummets by nearly forty degrees. An all-day rain continues into the evening, and when the sun goes down everything freezes.

In the middle of the night, I wake up to what sounds like gunfire. There's a shooting range just a few miles away, and our family is accustomed to the pop-pop-popping sounds during the daytime hours, but no one would be there at this hour. Slipping out of bed, I raise the blinds and look out in the darkness. I can't see much of anything, but as the noise continues I hurry down the hall to the front door. Outside, large branches from our maple tree have broken off and are blocking the porch and sidewalk.

One of the things Linda and I love most about our backyard is an enormous seventy-five-foot silver maple tree, which provides valuable shade for our deck. But as the years pass and the tree grows larger, I worry about the tree's proximity to Emilee and Matthew's bedrooms. I'm afraid a large branch might break off and crash through the roof. On the night of the ice storm I share my concerns with Linda, and we gather our sleepy children and nestle them into our bed. Unable to sleep, I get up and pace the floor. Loud sounds, like gunshots, continue as I watch in disbelief as the ice-covered trees in our yard drop their limbs, one after another. Suddenly the lights flicker, and the house goes dark. There isn't much I can do, but I feel it's my job to keep my family safe, to protect them. Without power I know the house will soon be cold, so I pull extra blankets out of the closet and lay them over my sleeping family before starting a fire in our woodstove to stave off the impending chill.

The next morning, bright sunlight makes the ice-coated tree branches sparkle. It looks like a winter wonderland. Yet I'm stunned by the destruction right outside my front door. Many huge limbs have fallen; one especially foreboding one lies across our driveway. Our street, strewn with hundreds of enormous branches, is blocked in both directions. I see the telephone pole in front of our house has snapped in half and is lying in the road, with electrical wires still attached. Linda and I feel extremely fortunate that we're all safe. Miraculously, our home has no broken windows or structural damage.

For ten days our neighborhood is without power and, in an era before cell phones, we are one of the only houses with a working landline. Fortunately, we have a wood stove to keep warm. Somehow, Linda uses it to create simple and delicious meals: grilled cheese, soup, and chili.

Several weeks before the storm, we'd made plans to host a party to celebrate Emilee's upcoming tenth birthday. Without power I wonder if it is a good idea to have guests, but Emilee and Linda insist it will be great fun. Emilee tells her friends to bring flashlights, sleeping bags, and pillows. We have the party as planned. The girls stay up late and play board games by candlelight, eventually spreading out their sleeping bags on the floor in the family room to be near the stove's warmth. The following morning Emilee and the girls watch, amazed, as Linda prepares eggs and fried dough on top of the wood stove. The party is a success! Emilee and her friends tell us how much fun they've had. "We'll never forget this birthday party," they tell us, and we agree. I'm proud my wife is so creative, and I'm impressed by my daughter's adaptability.

The power company finally restores service for most families on our street, but we learn the snapped telephone pole in front of our house won't be an easy fix. We remain in the dark for days, and everyone starts to go a bit stir crazy. We're especially grateful when our neighbors, Jean and Ozzie, invite us to play cards by candlelight. Their children are grown, and they live in a well-decorated, split-level home next to ours. After we return home, Emilee says, "Their house is perfect! Everything is so neat. I want our house to always look neat like theirs."

"Our house is usually neat," Linda says. "But with four of us living here with no power for over a week, it's more lived-in than ever."

Shortly after the ice storm, Emilee decides to vacuum her bedroom—and the entire house—twice a week. Family and friends who see her in action put in requests to "borrow her" to clean their homes. I don't think much of it because Emilee's propensity towards cleanliness isn't obsessive. I like things neat, too, especially when it comes to keeping our cars clean and waxed. Looking back, I sense the lack of normalcy in our lives during the ice storm may have precipitated some kind of need for control in Emilee. She seems to be developing some definite perfectionistic tendencies.

Initially Linda discourages Emilee from being so involved with the cleaning, but eventually she decides not to make a big deal of it. "I've been thinking," Linda says one night. "So many people tell Emilee how much she resembles and acts like me. I'm sure she wants her own identity, and I can see she takes pride in doing some things better than I do. If rearranging things and vacuuming makes her happy, I'm okay with it. It's probably just a phase."

"You're probably right," I say. "As long as it doesn't become excessive."

* * *

Linda and I visit quietly with Jean and Ozzie, and tell them confidentially that we're thinking about getting a dog. My father believed that taking care of a pet taught responsibility, and "Skippy", our blond Cocker Spaniel, was a special companion to me. "A house doesn't feel like a home without a dog," I say. Ozzie nods and mentions someone whose dog recently had a litter of puppies, a Beagle and Lhasa Apso mix. Linda and I exchange looks.

"Don't go looking at the puppies unless you're sure," Ozzie smiles. "You won't leave without one."

A few days later, I speak with the pups' owner and make arrangements to visit. Linda and I want to surprise the kids, so we tell them we're delivering firewood to a couple in need. I put some logs in the back of the minivan, and the four of us drive a short distance from our home to theirs.

"Come in," a woman says, opening her front door a little wider.

We see the puppies immediately, curled up inside a crate next to their mother. Some are shy, and others actively play with each other. One puppy keeps trying to jump out of the crate.

"Would you like to pick out a dog to take home?" I ask Em. "As a birthday present?"

Emilee's eyes widen, and she looks up at me incredulously.

"Really?" she asks, looking excitedly at Linda then back at the puppies. Without a moment's hesitation, Emilee points to the wild one. "That's the one I want," she says.

"Are you sure?" I ask.

"I'm positive!" Emilee declares confidently.

We take the puppy home, and the kids promptly name him Max. Max is high strung and, as a result, he's quite a handful. When people come to visit he jumps on them, and it's sometimes embarrassing, especially when someone is not a dog lover. He's headstrong on his walks, but Emilee seems to like the challenge. Mature and responsible, Emilee makes sure Max has food and water every day. She is patient with him, walking and training him to sit and stay. Always rewarding his obedience with treats. Though we all love Max, it is clear he and Emilee have a special bond. He is Emilee's dog, first.

It's Super Bowl Sunday, 1992, and the Washington Redskins are playing the Buffalo Bills—the local favorites—and just as we're about to watch the kickoff we realize Max has somehow managed to escape our fully enclosed backyard. We're all upset. The four of us put on our coats and boots and search the neighborhood for Max, loudly calling his name. We look everywhere. Linda and I try to calm the kids and assure them Max will be fine, that he'll come back. I decide to get the van and drive around the neighborhood and see if I can spot him. When I open the garage, who do I see? It's Max, walking up the driveway towards our house.

"Max is back!" I yell.

Emilee runs out of the house and sweeps her wet and muddy friend into her arms. Instantly the two are a soggy mess, and Linda and I are surprised to see our normally neat and clean daughter quickly become as dirty as the dog. She doesn't seem to mind.

After the memorable Super Bowl incident Emilee keeps a more watchful eye on Max, and I have a new, more secure fence installed around the perimeter of our back yard.

Linda, John, and *Emilee* Mazur

CHAPTER SEVEN • DISAPPOINTMENT & REWARDS

LINDA

Emilee comes home from school and excitedly tells me about Project Challenge, an enrichment program at school designed for students identified as "gifted and talented". Project Challenge participants, some of whom are Emilee's friends, have the opportunity to advance academically and practice abstract thinking skills. Emilee is sure she belongs in that group.

When she isn't selected I speak with her teacher, who tells me that, although Emilee is very bright, there are children who have standardized test scores that are higher than hers. Her teacher shares the test score numbers with me and apologizes. There's a limit to the number of students he can choose, he explains. Each fifth-grade teacher has been instructed to use the same selection criteria, the biggest influence being standardized test results. I don't push it any further, but I feel sad for Emilee. She loves school, learning, and being challenged, and I know she'll be upset.

When I explain the situation to her, Emilee expresses confidence and frustration. "I know I could do it," she says. "I'm just as smart as they are... I know I am."

I sit down on the couch and gently pull Emilee onto my lap. "I know you're disappointed," I say, running my hand through her hair. "Just keep doing your best. There are a lot of great students who didn't make it either. You'll do just fine."

Emilee doesn't dwell on the fact she didn't make it into Project Challenge, and after that day she doesn't mention it again. However, I believe that, deep down, this early rejection hurt her. Suddenly she has something to prove, and she begins working even harder to achieve academically.

It's hard for me to believe another summer is almost over, and we're nearing the time for Emilee to transition from elementary to middle school. Emilee is nervous, as are her friends. She knows she'll have to change classes, work with a team of new teachers, remember locker combinations, and merge with hundreds of other students from three elementary schools. As summer dwindles Emilee checks the mailbox each day, anxiously anticipating her sixth-grade schedule. When the envelope finally arrives, she phones all of her friends to see if they'll be in the same classes. A few days before school begins, parents are allowed to visit the school with their child and walk their schedule with them. We help Emilee locate her locker and watch from a distance as she practices her combination, several times, to be sure she can open it on the first day of school.

During middle school, Emilee's social group grows. She has a lot of friends, and her teachers recognize her promise, intellect, and drive. She's placed on the Honors track. We're happy for her, and she is pleased with herself. She joins a variety of clubs and activities, including chorus and orchestra.

I recall a special memory: when Emilee was four, her teenage babysitters, who are sisters, brought their string instruments over one day and staged a private concert for her. Emilee was enthralled. After the girls left Emilee sat at the kitchen table, holding two pretzel rods. She tucked one under her chin and, using the other as a bow, pretended to play the violin. Soon afterward Jack and I rented a small violin for her, and she began taking Suzuki lessons at school. On the day of the first school concert, Emilee wore a navy blue jumper and a white blouse, white leotards, and black patent leather shoes. She stood tall and played beautifully. At the completion of the final song she smiled and took a deep bow. Jack and I realized that Emilee had a natural aptitude for music, and we could see how much she enjoyed playing. A short time later, we enrolled her in private lessons. Her passion for the violin continues, and in middle school, Emilee helps younger students by becoming a violin practice partner. She is pleased to be chosen by the music teacher and enjoys helping the younger students.

Around this time Emilee begins to babysit, and she quickly becomes a favorite sitter. True to her nature, she enjoys the challenge of taking care of active children that other sitters have had trouble dealing with. Emilee finds creative ways to keep the children engaged. She tirelessly plays games and is not opposed to running around the yard with them, playing catch, or kicking around the soccer ball. Emilee appreciates being looked up to, loves the children, and likes earning money. When I think about it now, I understand Emilee was always up for a challenge.

Emilee is sensitive to the needs of others, especially her friends. I pick her up from school one afternoon, and as I'm driving her to a violin lesson she tells me about a situation with a grammar school friend and soccer teammate.

"Some of the kids aren't very nice to Karen," she tells me. "She's been sitting all by herself in the cafeteria, so I started to eat lunch with her a few days ago."

"That's nice of you," I say, smiling at my daughter. "I'm sure she appreciates that."

"I don't understand why people act the way they sometimes do," Emilee responds.

It makes me feel good to know Emilee follows her heart, is compassionate, and tries to do the right thing. I know that the smallest gesture can make a big difference to someone who is hurting.

At the end of the eighth grade, a letter from Bay Trail Middle School arrives in the mail addressed to Jack and me. Inside the envelope is an invitation to an awards ceremony. The letter indicates that Emilee has been chosen to receive an award and that we should plan to attend the ceremony with her.

Emilee is excited when we share the letter with her. On the night of the event Jack, Matthew, and I are ready to go. We find ourselves waiting for Emilee, who is usually the first one ready to leave the house. After a while, I grow impatient. "Em!" I call. "We're going to be late!" When Emilee finally emerges from her bedroom, she's wearing a peach dress with small white polka dots, belted at the waist.

It takes me a moment to realize that Emilee is wearing one of my dresses. She's never worn my clothes before, and I'm a little put out she hasn't asked my permission. "Honey, that's my dress," I say.

"What do you think?" she asks, smiling brightly and twirling around.

I look at my daughter. Her hair is styled neatly, and she's even put on a little make-up. My dress is a touch big on her, but it looks okay with the belt cinched tight at the waist. The peach color accentuates her skin and bright blue eyes. What can I say? She's beaming. I glance at my watch and promptly decide to let the matter drop. I think: *We're late and it's not that big a deal.* "You look beautiful!" I say.

We sit in the audience and hear Emilee's name called numerous times for multiple awards, and we're proud to see her walk up on the stage and receive the accolades. Near the end of the evening a well-respected social studies teacher stands behind the podium, reading off the qualities of the student who has been chosen for The Citizenship Award. "This award is given to a student who shows by their words and actions leadership skills, positive attitude towards classmates, community service, responsibility, and dependability." We are thrilled when Emilee's name is announced, and we can tell Emilee is surprised. At the close of the ceremony, my friend Sue, mother of Emilee's classmate, congratulates Jack and me on Emilee's success. "Emilee won so many awards, and she looked like a little Linda, walking across the stage."

Smiling, I think to myself, *of course she does. She's wearing my dress.* I think it's a little odd that Emilee has chosen to wear my dress. However, putting myself in her place, I assume she was anxious about having to walk across the stage in front of a packed auditorium. I understand it's important for her to appear self-assured and mature, and maybe tonight the dress did that for her.

At home after the ceremony, Emilee tells us the Citizenship Award is the achievement she's most proud of. Jack and I tell her we're impressed with her accomplishments and hard work, but mostly we're proud of the person she is, and that's what the reward reflects.

In the months that follow, Emilee seems quite self-assured and becomes somewhat critical of many of the things I choose to wear. She teases me for wearing 'mom jeans'. I smile and think, *I doubt she'll be raiding my closet again.*

JACK

In the fall of 1995, Emilee starts her freshman year of high school. The transition to high school is an easy one; she enjoys her accelerated classes and likes her teachers. Emilee tries out and makes the freshman soccer team. Her passion for music continues, and she is chosen to be a member of The Hochstein Youth Orchestra. She attends practice on Saturday mornings with her best friend Kelly, at the prestigious performance hall at Hochstein in downtown Rochester. The Penfield High School Orchestra has the opportunity to play at Carnegie Hall, and in the spring Linda, Matt and I travel by train to New York City to see her play at the world-famous venue. After the concert we take advantage of some of the sights and experiences New York City has to offer, doing all kinds of touristy things. One of the kid's favorite things is to visit FAO Schwarz, where Emilee and Matthew stomp on an oversized piano keyboard like Tom Hanks did in the movie *Big*. Our children are amazed by the numerous street vendors—their suitcases filled with faux-designer purses, jewelry, watches, and sunglasses—all selling for prices that are too good to be true. "If it sounds too good to be true, it probably is," I tell them. "You have to be careful." So far, our children have made good choices, and I hope going forward they continue to trust their instincts.

In the spring of her freshman year, Emilee adds running track to her resume. I make a concerted effort to rearrange my schedule so I can attend as many of Emilee and Matt's sporting and musical events as possible, and occasionally I can make it to practice. On one particularly cool day, the north wind blows just strong enough to make it feel cooler than it is. Walking across the parking lot I see Emilee running on the track, wearing the team uniform— red sleeveless shirt and black shorts. Her skin looks pale, almost white. After running laps, she trots over to me. I'm chilled just standing there, even with a sweater on, and I can see she has goose bumps on her arms.

"Aren't you freezing?" I ask.

"I'm fine," Emilee says.

I shake my head. Emilee doesn't like to appear fragile or needy in any way.

"I didn't know you were coming today," Emilee says.

"I can bring you home after practice," I say.

Emilee shakes her head. "After practice, a bunch of us are going to the hospital to visit Jennifer. She's the girl I told you about who's been sick. Remember?"

When I don't remember, Emilee reminds me how her friend Jennifer had stopped eating lunch at school months earlier and that she had told the guidance counselor she was concerned about her friend. "She's so thin, and she looks sleepy all the time," Em reports. "I don't know for sure, but I think she has anorexia."

At the time, I know very little about eating disorders, but I know enough to understand being hospitalized is significant. "That's too bad,' I say, shaking my head. "It's good she's getting the help she needs."

As Emilee's teen years progress, there are so many changes happening. And now she worries about the health of her friend, soccer teammate, and fellow orchestra member. She has the demands of school and sports, and her social circle now consists of young women and young men. She tells Linda and me that she is especially fond of one particular boy, Randy, in her group.

One evening at the dinner table, Linda asks Emilee if she thinks she and Randy might go out on a date.

"I wish," Emilee says. "He only has eyes for one girl on the track team. He told me he likes tall girls and what "great legs" Jessica has. He and I are just friends."

We empathize with Emilee and assure her there will be many dates in her future. If she's upset by this early romantic disappointment, she certainly doesn't show it. Yet I will look back and wonder if Randy's innocent comment changed the way she viewed herself.

Throughout the year, Emilee continues to work hard and improves her soccer skills. She makes the JV soccer team in the fall of her sophomore year and is proud to wear the team jacket. Well-liked and respected by her peers and coaches, she doesn't always play, but she's thrilled to be part of the team and pleased to have her face and name in the team photo. Linda and I are delighted for Emilee and admire her dogged determination to try new things, and keep trying until she improves and succeeds. She does things to the best of her ability, and that is all we ever ask from her.

In addition to maintaining excellent grades, Emilee takes on some additional responsibilities. She now works at Shadow Lake and Shadow Pines Golf Courses, getting the carts ready in the early morning. She also assists at charity events, selling raffle tickets and driving the beverage cart around the course. When I happen to be at the courses, people tell me what a great employee she is. They think the world of her. Emilee is responsible and enjoys working hard. It makes me feel good to know she is respected, adaptable, and well-liked. I think, *These attributes will serve her well in the coming years.*

Linda, John, and *Emilee* Mazur

.

CHAPTER EIGHT • FRAGILITY

JACK

One beautiful, sunny fall day, not long into Emilee's junior year, Linda calls me at work. Her voice is high and tight, the way it gets when she's upset.

"Something terrible happened up the road," she says, her voice trembling. "At the Johnsons'..."

Though I don't know the Johnsons well, I recall Emilee has often been their family's babysitter.

"They were cutting down a big tree, and after it was completely down, somehow the tree snapped back upright. Sara was playing in the dirt where the tree had been. She was trapped underneath."

I try to imagine the freak accident that Linda has described. It seems crazy. Impossible. Suddenly, my mind switches gears, and I picture Sara and her sisters riding their bikes in their driveway, and walking their dog.

"They tried to save her," Linda weeps. "But they couldn't, Jack. They couldn't save her."

I'm so shocked, I can hardly speak. I can't imagine losing a child. I think about Emilee and Matthew, and my heart drops into my stomach. Standing there, frozen in the pharmacy, I think about the Johnson family. How their lives will never be the same. *How will they go on?* I wonder.

When I arrive home that night, I hug Emilee and Matthew a little tighter. I want them to feel safe. Emilee is inconsolable.

"She was only six," Emilee weeps, wiping the tears from her face.

I pull my daughter close. I want to say something to make her feel better, but I have no words. I think to myself, *No child should lose a sibling, and no parent should have to bury a child.*

Linda prepares a meal for the Johnsons, and Emilee bakes push cookies and adds them to Linda's basket.

The calling hours are heartbreaking. We tell the Johnsons to let us know if there is anything they need and ask them to call us if we can help in any way. I think to myself, *I couldn't get through it if something were to happen to one of my children.*

* * *

Later that same year, Linda and I notice that Emilee starts spending more time away from home. She stops confiding in Linda as much, and she comes to me more often to ask permission to attend dances or go to friends' houses for parties. Now that she's playing Varsity soccer, she's socializing with a different group of kids—honors athletes, male and female. To me they seem like nice young people from good families, and they welcome her into their circle.

But Linda worries about the change. "I don't know, Jack," she says. "Emilee seems different. Something doesn't feel right."

Becoming part of a new circle of friends brings with it a different kind of peer pressure. Emilee starts to compare her new friends and their families to ours. Some of those families live in bigger houses, drive fancier cars, and their kids have more freedom. I have provided my family with a good home and a well-balanced life. Emilee and I have always gotten along well, but now, on occasion, we argue, and I sometimes feel disrespected by my daughter.

Despite Linda's concerns and the changes I see, I support Emilee. "She hasn't given us any reason not to trust her. Did you hang out with your parents at this age?" I ask Linda, chalking it all up to normal teenage behavior.

"I just think we need to pay more attention going forward," she says. "Read between the lines."

I think Linda is overprotective. "Emilee has good judgment," I insist. "We brought her up to know right from wrong."

Linda, John, and *Emilee* Mazur

CHAPTER NINE • LESSONS LEARNED

JACK

It's Friday night, and I'm anxious to get home after a long day at work. Linda is babysitting for her brother's young children, Molly and Drew. I hope they'll still be there when I get home. Matt is helping Linda, and Emilee's at a school dance with her friends. I lock up the pharmacy and walk across the lot to my car. Spring is right around the corner, and it's reassuring to see the temperature on the dashboard registering fifty degrees at 9:00PM. Pulling into the driveway, I see Linda looking out the front picture window, holding the baby in her arms.

That's odd, I think.

Before I take a step inside, Linda meets me at the door.

"I just got a call from the high school vice-principal," she says. "Emilee and some of her friends were drinking before the dance. I have to pick her up right now." She hands the baby to me, gives me quick instructions, and leaves immediately.

While Linda is gone, I fuss over my niece and walk around the kitchen with my infant nephew asleep on my shoulder. Matthew is worried about his sister, but knows we can't say too much in front of Molly. I watch as he scoops vanilla ice cream into a small dish for his little cousin, but all I can think about is the situation that's unfolding.

I know it's not unusual for teens to experiment with alcohol. I was a teenager once, and I wasn't perfect. I had my first taste of alcohol in 1968. I was sixteen years old, and it was New Year's Eve. My friend's parents were out for the evening, and he invited three of us to come over. I was definitely surprised when he took a bottle of Seagram's 7 Crown from his parents' liquor cabinet and poured us each a glass. Though the strong taste made me shudder, we ended up drinking half the bottle. The last thing I remember about that night was watching the beginning of the eleven o'clock news on the color television. I have no idea how I got home, but my parents said, in retelling the story, that I walked in the front door of the house at midnight—covered in snow—and fell flat on my face. My mother didn't know what was wrong and was frantic. I remember hearing my father say, "He's drunk!" That's all I remember that night. The following morning, when my mother came into my room, I could feel her disappointment in the air and I could see it on her face.

"I thought you had more sense than that," my mother said, shaking her head.

After that night, I couldn't even stand the smell of whiskey.

When Linda's brother Mark and his wife Trish arrive at our house to pick up their children I briefly explain the situation to them, and they ask if there is anything they can do to help. Of course there isn't, so I help them to gather up their children and say goodbye.

Shortly after Mark and Trish leave, I hear Linda's minivan pulling into the driveway. I open the front door and see Linda helping a shaky Emilee into the house. We get her out of her clothes, into her pajamas, and put her into bed, positioning her on her side with a pillow wedged behind her back, just in case she needs to throw up.

Matthew is relieved that Emilee is home safe, and retreats to his bedroom to finish his homework. Linda puts a pot of tea on the stove, and when the teapot whistles she pours two cups and joins me on the living room couch.

"I guess your intuition was right," I say, making a mental note never to minimize my wife's feelings again.

Linda puts her teacup on the coffee table without taking a sip. "Emilee admitted to drinking before the dance," Linda explains "She was with her friends and, as you can see, she's pretty drunk. Apparently the other kids weren't visibly intoxicated, so they denied they'd been drinking."

"Where did they get the alcohol?" I ask.

Linda frowns. "I don't know where they got alcohol or where they drank it."

My head is spinning, and for the first time in my life I know what my mother must have been feeling twenty-eight years prior when I stumbled into her house drunk as a skunk.

"The other kids knew there would be consequences," Linda says, "so they lied."

The two of us look at each other in disbelief.

"This is out of character for her," I say, and Linda agrees. Less than six months ago, Emilee called and asked us to pick her up from a party where there was underage drinking. She was uncomfortable with the entire scene and asked us to pick her up at the house next door, so no one would see her leave. Linda and I had always told both Emilee and Matt that if either one of them found themselves in an uncomfortable situation, we'd pick them up any time of the day or night. No questions asked. That night I told Emilee I was glad she trusted us enough to call us, and I praised her for making a good decision.

I realize that Linda is processing things, too. She's angry with Emilee and frustrated with the way Emilee's peers abandoned her. "I don't know about these new friends…" Linda says. "Emilee seems impressed with them, but I've been concerned, and I'm even more concerned now. I'm not blaming them. I know they're just teenagers, being teenagers."

I take a deep breath and begin to script the conversation I know I'll need to have with our daughter in the morning. After a while, Linda and I check on Emilee. We open the door to her bedroom and notice the glow-in-the-dark stars on the ceiling above her bed. I put them there when she was eight years old, and they still give off their greenish glow after all this time. Emilee is fast asleep, and when we try to rouse her we can't wake her.

Because we have no idea what or how much she's had to drink, Linda and I decide to take Emilee to the hospital. We tell Matthew what's happening, and I carry Emilee out to the minivan. Linda follows behind, holding a white plastic container for Emilee to use in case she gets sick in the car. I can't help but recall a time, so many years prior, when Emilee held her water-filled Cool Whip container to help us "paint the house." I buckle Emilee into the backseat, and Linda climbs in beside her. Halfway to the hospital, Emilee vomits.

By the time we get to the emergency room, Emilee is drowsy but talkative. She is embarrassed and keeps apologizing. Our stay is short. The doctors do a blood alcohol screen, the results of which are unremarkable, and we are sent home.

Emilee's infraction requires a three-day suspension from school, and while we're glad Emilee told the truth, she's embarrassed by the negative attention she receives. And later that year, she's devastated when she fails to make National Honor Society despite her excellent grade point average. Personally, I hope she's learned a valuable lesson from this experience, just as I did when I was sixteen. And it appears she has. Over the next weeks and months, Linda and I observe our daughter working diligently to restore her reputation with her teachers and regain our trust.

***

The following summer, we take a vacation in Cape May, New Jersey. Linda and I rent bikes, and we take a leisurely family bike ride to the Cape May Lighthouse. The sun warms our backs as we pedal around America's oldest seaside resort, known for its Victorian houses and old-fashioned charm. The sounds of the ocean and seagulls calls fill the air. As we near the lighthouse, Emilee decides to speed off by herself.

"Be careful!" Linda and I shout in unison as we see Emilee stray from the bike lane into the main road. A car swerves, nearly hitting her, and I shout again. "Stop and wait right there!" I holler, and Emilee immediately complies. When we reach her, I get off my bike. "What the hell are you doing?" I scold.

"It's just you guys were riding so slow!"

"You could have been killed!" Linda hollers.

Emilee apologizes, but I'm frustrated by her inability to consider the consequences of her actions.

Later that evening, Linda and I go for a walk. "She could have been killed," Linda says, squeezing my hand.

"I think she'll be more careful now," I say. "We have to trust that she will."

The next day is warm and windy. The ocean waves are too strong for the bodyboard surfing we had planned, and we decide to have lunch at a restaurant and see a movie afterward. Emilee and Matthew want to see *Armageddon.* After we finish eating, we take some time to stand on the deck overlooking the ocean and watch the surfers riding the large waves. I hear voices behind us and turn around. An older man is pushing a blonde-haired young woman in a wheelchair, navigating the wheels up the handicapped ramp. An older woman walks alongside the man, and I assume they are a family and that the woman in the wheelchair is their daughter. As they approach, I notice the parents' gray hair and weary eyes. They appear to be in their mid-sixties. I observe the father's hands, how he grips the handles of the wheelchair, pushing his daughter up and over the bumpy wooden slats. I look again at the family and consider the logistics of bringing their daughter on vacation with them, how it must take a great deal of effort. Suddenly, tears fill my eyes. I'm overcome with gratitude for my two healthy kids, and I admire these strangers and appreciate the love they so obviously have for their child. I think the love they have for their daughter must give them the strength to push through. The family approaches, and I nod and say hello to the father. I look at the girl, her long hair blowing in the strong wind, and I smile. She's watching the surfers, transfixed. She tilts her head back and laughs.

I'm quiet, immersed in my thoughts.

"What's wrong?" Linda asks me. "Are you all right?"

This chance encounter evokes emotion in me. I can't explain it, but it feels like a significant moment in my life and I know I will remember it.

Linda, John, and *Emilee* Mazur

CHAPTER TEN • HEALTH

LINDA

Around this same time, Emilee begins to complain of heartburn. Initially, we don't think much of it. We make an appointment with the pediatrician, and he recommends an over-the-counter medication, but as the year progresses so do her symptoms.

"My chest and throat feel hot after I eat," Emilee complains. "When the food comes back up in my mouth, it burns."

I can relate to the uncomfortable feeling after eating because I experienced heartburn during both pregnancies, but it wasn't ever as severe as what Emilee is describing to me.

A few weeks later, Emilee and I take a walk after dinner, and I see firsthand her struggle with reflux. She stops, puts her hand to her chest, leans over, and spits out a mouthful of partially digested food into the grass next to the sidewalk.

I'm very concerned and tell her so. After returning home, Emilee asks me to come into her bedroom. She points to a coffee cup on the corner of her desk. "My food always seems to come up after dinner, usually when I'm doing my homework," she says. "I don't want to keep running to the bathroom. When I have to spit up, I use the cup. It's embarrassing. When I'm in public, I have to swallow it."

"Em, have you been totally honest with me—about everything? About how this started?" I ask. I know that she has a friend who battles anorexia, and I wonder for a moment if this problem could be caused by something she is doing.

"I've never made myself throw up, if that's what you're asking," Emilee says defensively. "I've been honest about the heartburn, and you just saw what happens when I have reflux."

I make an appointment with a gastroenterologist, and Jack accompanies us to the appointment. The doctor tells us it is not uncommon for runners to develop Gastro-Esophageal Reflux Disease (GERD) because running increases pressure in the stomach. Tests confirm Emilee's sphincter muscle, located at the base of the esophagus, isn't working properly. This explains why Emilee is experiencing reflux. He recommends a few dietary changes and prescribes omeprazole to help block stomach acid. However, Emilee continues to experience reflux, especially when she ingests too much liquid or when she eats a large meal. The doctor advises Emilee to eat smaller meals and supplement with easy to digest snacks during the day. Suddenly, the simple act of eating becomes something Emilee has to plan her whole life around. None of this is pleasant or easy for Emilee, who continues to see her gastroenterologist on a regular basis. He reassures us the medication Emilee is taking reduces acid in the stomach, which can help to heal damage to the stomach and the esophagus, and can help to prevent ulcers. He adds, "It may even prevent cancer of the esophagus." The doctor mentions a surgical option, but adds that he doesn't believe surgery is necessary. He tucks his hands inside his starched white lab coat. "Emilee is healthy and maintaining a normal weight. A few less invasive procedures are being tested, but we don't know if, or when, they'll be approved."

Emilee doesn't want surgery, and she's satisfied with the doctor's explanation. She continues taking her prescribed medication and makes the recommended lifestyle modifications. We trust the doctor's opinion, and the three of us hope one of the less invasive procedures will be approved soon.

* * *

Over the course of high school, Emilee keeps a rigorous schedule. She builds solid friendships and maintains a close relationship with her best friend, Kelly. She attends formal dances and has occasional dates. At the end of her junior year, she wins numerous academic awards. We're all thrilled when we learn she is the recipient of a leadership scholarship to Wells College. And in the spring of her senior year, she is finally inducted into the National Honor Society.

I believe Emilee is pushing herself even harder because she feels she has to prove something to herself and others, and I suspect the stress contributes to her stomach issues, but the doctor tells us she's healthy and maintaining a normal weight. Emilee assures us she is okay and complains less about GERD since she's been on the medication. Jack and I decide we are, perhaps, being overly concerned.

In early June, Emilee is busy studying for finals and preparing for her senior violin solo. She's become very proficient at playing her instrument and is quite excited about performing. But she is also nervous. The audience will be large, and she knows her grandparents are coming into town for her performance.

A few days before Emilee's big solo, the school nurse calls and tells us Matthew developed a high fever and asks us to pick him up as soon as possible. At home we give him alternate doses of acetaminophen and ibuprofen, but he's lethargic and shivering, and his fever spikes to 104 degrees. I call our pediatrician, explain the symptoms, and say I believe there is something very wrong. He validates my concern and suggests we take Matthew to the hospital.

Residents at the hospital order extensive blood work. Matthew's fever is controlled, and we're told it is safe to take him home. That evening our pediatrician calls and says, "We know Matthew's feeling better, but his blood tested positive for bacteria. The hospital believes the result is a mistake, but you need to take him back tonight so they can redo the blood work." The doctor assures us we will be called as soon as the results are back.

The following afternoon Matthew is resting in his bedroom, and I hear him calling out for me. He sounds panicked, and when I rush into his bedroom his face is flushed and he's scared.

"I can't move my legs!" he shouts.

I run my hand across his forehead. He's burning up. I'm terrified and reach for the phone to call the ambulance, when the phone rings. It's our pediatrician. Matthew's test results are back from the lab, and the doctor tells me he has a serious bacterial blood infection. He says it could be meningitis, and he'll need to have a spinal tap at the hospital.

"Bring him to my office," the doctor says. "We'll start him on antibiotics."

We arrive at the pediatrician's office and notice an ambulance parked outside. A staff of EMTs is waiting for us. Matthew is started on an IV antibiotic and lifted onto a gurney. An EMT fastens straps around his body, securing him for the ride. "Mom, why can't I move my legs?" Matthew asks, tears in his eyes.

I'm flooded with emotions, but mostly I'm afraid. My neck and shoulders are tight, and my stomach is queasy, but I know I need to appear calm for Matthew's sake. I'm angry with the residents who saw our son and assumed the lab results were an error. Treatment could have started yesterday. I feel powerless. Inside the ambulance, I calmly tell Matthew everything is going to be okay and ask him if he wants to pray. Prayer and connection to God is a guiding light, a grounding force, and a constant in our lives. And I feel comforted when Matthew reaches for my hand so we can pray together.

JACK

Following the ambulance, I wonder how the doctors could have released my son with a serious infection. I'm angry with the hospital. Matt is taken directly to an E.R. bay and quickly transported to another room for a spinal tap. When the results come in, the doctors tell us they expect Matthew will fully recover. That his spinal fluid is clear—with no sign of meningitis. However, because of the blood infection, Matthew will need to remain in the hospital and continue receiving the IV antibiotic. We feel some relief and hope their assessment is correct.

Once Matthew is stabilized, I realize it will be possible for one of us to attend Emilee's senior violin solo. Even though Linda has been the parent to take Emilee to her lessons year after year, and has listened to and encouraged Emilee every step of the way, I know there is no way Linda will leave the hospital when one of her children is sick. I also know how important this night is for Emilee, how long and hard she's worked and practiced to prepare for this performance.

"Give her a big hug for me," Linda says as I head toward the door. "And tell her I'm so sorry."

I can tell from the look on Linda's face that she doesn't want me to leave, but I know she understands. By splitting up, each child can have one of us there for support.

Back at home, I meet my mother and Linda's parents. Everyone is concerned about Matthew, and I reassure them he's getting the care he needs; he's improving.

"We have to keep tonight about Emilee," I say. When it's time for Emilee to play, her teacher steps up to the podium and winks at Emilee. Emilee knows Mrs. Strall well; she occasionally babysits for her young daughter. Small in stature, Mrs. Strall is an energetic and talented conductor and composer, and she is loved by all her students. Before Emilee's solo, Mrs. Strall—dressed in dark dress slacks, high heels, and an elegant, sparkling tailored jacket—turns towards the audience. "Emilee's brother is in the hospital tonight," she tells the crowd. "Emilee wishes to dedicate this performance to him."

Emilee's eyes find mine. Soon, she begins to play a complicated classical violin piece by William Kroll. The audience is still, and the sound coming from her violin is rich and full—and my heart is also full. I feel such love and pride as I watch my talented daughter performing. I remember when I played the coronet in the school band. I suffered from terrible stage fright, and eventually I quit. Frankly, I'm amazed by Emilee—the way she plays her instrument with such ease in front of a large auditorium with hundreds of eyes watching her. *She's much more confident than I ever was*, I think to myself. I feel guilty for leaving Linda and Matthew at the hospital, but I also feel grateful that my son will be okay. I'm glad I can be here for my daughter on a night that is so special it can never be recreated. When Emilee finishes, she smiles at the audience's loud applause. Her grandparents are beaming. Our friends, seated around us, smile and hug me. They understand how long and hard the seniors practice for this moment, and they can appreciate the additional stress Emilee is under tonight.

At the end of the performance I walk towards the stage, holding a dozen red roses. "I'm so proud of you," I say, handing Emilee the flowers.

"I kinda messed up," Emilee says with a shrug, and immediately asks for an update about her brother's health.

We drive back to the house. Emilee, her grandparents, and I celebrate with cake and coffee. Emilee tells me she wants to go back to the hospital with me. I tell her it's late, and I remind her that she has school the next day. I add, "Your grandparents want to spend some time with you."

"Tell Matthew I'll be there tomorrow," she says. "And tell him I love him."

Matthew is hospitalized for a week. Emilee visits her brother daily and brings him little gifts and his school assignments. Matthew enjoys her company. They play card games to pass the time and Emilee interjects her style of humor to help him laugh, sometimes at our expense, mimicking Linda and me. It's second nature for Emilee to look out for her brother. She has been there for him from his beginning, and it's comforting for us as parents to see them appreciating and supporting each other.

CHAPTER ELEVEN ● MOVING FORWARD

LINDA

Gradually life returns to some kind of normalcy. Matthew comes home from the hospital and slowly resumes his daily activities, and I'm finally able to sit down with Emilee and watch the videotaped performance of her senior solo on our television. Of course, I cry. I'm so proud of her.

"It's not that big a deal," Emilee says dismissively. "I'm just happy Matthew's okay."

When I think about it now, I realize Emilee has never been comfortable receiving too much praise. Jack and I are proud of the person she is, and to us her accomplishments are a bonus. We tell her how much we love her. We praise her, but not excessively. Because when we do, she shuns it. I wonder if we're reading her right. Maybe she needs more praise, or perhaps too much praise causes her to feel pressure. We try to find a middle road.

On a balmy June day in 1999, Emilee graduates from Penfield High School. Out of 250 students, she graduates eighth in her class. It is, by all of the teachers' accounts, an exceptional class. The graduation ceremonies are held in downtown Rochester. The beautiful Eastman Theater is an architectural gem that exudes the elegance of the 1920s: equipped with burgundy velvet seats, golden walls showcasing opulent artwork, and a gorgeous crystal chandelier suspended from the gilded ceiling. Jack and I feel blessed as we watch Emilee walk across the stage to receive her diploma. We do the things people do at graduations: we ask Emilee to pose for endless pictures, we hug and congratulate her friends and listen as they share their career aspirations—many hoping to become doctors, teachers, and attorneys. Emilee's wish is to become a veterinarian; it seems a natural choice for her, given her love of animals and her aptitude for the sciences. Though many people tell us that getting into a veterinary school is extremely competitive, and harder to get into than medical school, as there are far fewer of them. These comments don't seem to faze Emilee in the least.

The thought of Emilee going to college makes me happy and sad. I believe she will do well socially and academically, and I'm excited for her. Still, I can't help but wonder where the time has gone. Emilee and I are still close, but she's becoming more independent, and I'm aware there is a space between us.

For some weird reason, I remember standing with my mother and grandmother, on Grandma's side porch, watching as Grandma's son and daughter-in-law (my aunt and uncle) packed their car to return home after a visit at my grandmother's. After they settled their children in the backseat, everyone waved goodbye. When they were gone, the three of us talked in Grandma's cozy kitchen. Sitting at the large kitchen table, I studied the turquoise walls, Grandma Anna's favorite color, while she made a pot of tea. She filled our cups and finally sat down, too. I took a sip of my tea, (which was mostly milk and sugar) and noticed tears in my Grandma's eyes. "Just remember, Dorothy," Grandma Anna said, looking at my mother, "our children are only loaned to us." For the first time, so many years later, I understood exactly what she meant.

JACK AND LINDA

Wells College is a small Liberal Arts college for women, located in the tiny town of Aurora, New York, just an hour and a half from our home. We visit Wells the first time when Emilee is a senior in high school, and she quickly falls in love with the tree-lined campus and its regal, ivy-covered brick buildings. It's obvious that Emilee feels comfortable among the students and faculty, and she's impressed with the school's Honor Code, which all students are required to abide by. Students promise not to lie, cheat, steal, or deceive. The expectation is for them to act with integrity and hold themselves and others accountable. The Code allows students to take exams in the library, in their dorm rooms, even on the dock at the lake. Emilee is also impressed by the low student-to-professor ratio of 9:1.

"I'll get an excellent education here," she tells us, an hour into the visit.

When she learns that Wells students have the opportunity to take some of their classes at Cornell University, thirty minutes away, Emilee is excited. She frequently talks about wanting to go on to veterinary school at Cornell after completing her undergraduate degree. Though she looks at a few other schools, it's obvious Em has her heart set on Wells.

It's Move-In Day at Wells College: August 1999. We deliver our daughter to the beautiful campus overlooking Cayuga Lake. The sun is shining brightly, the sky is a brilliant blue, and the grass is a deep, rich green. The campus is buzzing. High school boys from town, hired for the weekend to unload cars and assist with moving heavier items, are all talking about a young golfer named Tiger Woods who has just won the PGA by one stroke. Emilee's room on the second floor is charming and bright, featuring hardwood floors, and large windows with a view of the lake, blue and sparkling. It's hard not to feel moved by the beauty and old-fashioned charm of the campus. Emilee takes pride in arranging her room and is delighted to meet each young woman who stops by. As Jack brings up tote after tote filled with clothes and accessories, I make up Emilee's bed and help her to unpack a few things.

Emilee's roommate is from Senegal, on Africa's west coast. We are told Koro will arrive in a few weeks. Emilee will live alone initially, but she isn't concerned and neither are we. Jack and I know she makes friends easily, and her room already seems like a gathering place.

On the way home, Jack and I reminisce about how quickly eighteen years have passed. Our baby girl has grown into such a fine young woman. We discuss the size of the school—smaller than her high school—and we hope the setting will help Emilee feel secure, being away from home for the first time. We hope it will be a good fit and trust her decision. We share stories and then we are quiet, each of us processing our own memories in our own way. As our SUV rolls down the well-traveled New York State Thruway, we suddenly feel the surface beneath us change. A section of the road has been freshly paved, and the ride is instantly quieter. Jack and I turn our heads to look at each other. When our eyes meet, I know we have the same memory. When Emilee was two years old, our town repaved our road. Driving on the newly smoothed surface, little Emilee looked out the window. "They softened our road!" she said, taking us by surprise. It's a silly memory, one that we tease Emilee about each time we drive over newly paved roads.

Suddenly, tears are trickling down our cheeks. We hope our daughter will get a good education, make good decisions, and have good friends. We hope she'll be safe, and we hope with all our hearts that her road will be smooth.

LINDA

With Emilee away at college the house is quieter, and I sometimes find Max sitting in the hallway outside her bedroom door. He misses her, too. Emilee keeps in touch via email and calls home frequently, which helps me. She tells us she's enjoying her classes, making new friends, and appreciating new experiences. On Saturday, she calls to see how everyone is doing. She is especially interested in hearing about her young cousin Tim. My sister's middle child was diagnosed with two brain tumors at just four years of age and has just begun an aggressive course of chemotherapy. While Timmy's tumors are not malignant, they are life-threatening because of their location. "The tumors are shrinking," I tell her. "They think he's going to be okay."

Emilee is quiet on the other end of the line. "Mom," she says finally. "Whenever someone is in trouble, you always step up and try to help. You taught me that when someone gets sick, it's important to show up and do whatever you can."

When I remember that awful, crazy time, my heart feels heavy. It was difficult watching my sister and her entire family suffer. Everyone they loved and who loved them was profoundly affected at every level. Our family made meals, we babysat, and we were present, but that's all we could do. I remember feeling so powerless.

"I never thought about that time being a teaching moment," I tell Emilee. "We just did what we could. If we need help someday, they'll be there for us, too."

Emilee's first year of school passes quickly, and she returns home for summer break and resumes working at the golf courses. Matthew earns his Black Belt in the Korean Martial Art of Kuk Sool Won, begins working at Wegman's, and prepares for his junior year of high school. Everything is going well.

Linda, John, and *Emilee* Mazur

CHAPTER TWELVE • SEEKING HELP

LINDA

In the fall of 2000, Emilee begins complaining that the Gastro-Esophageal Reflux Disease (GERD)—the health issue she's been dealing with for nearly four years—has gotten progressively worse. Now, regardless of how careful she is to eat small, frequent meals, Emilee reports experiencing painful daily heartburn and more regurgitation. "Sometimes even water won't stay down," she says. I make an appointment for Emilee to meet with a thoracic surgeon, who orders more testing. When the test results come back, Jack and I go with Emilee to her appointment. Dr. Waters is a handsome, highly regarded, and well-spoken surgeon. He pushes back his dark brown hair and sits down next to Emilee. She listens intently as he informs the three of us that Emilee's sphincter muscle is even weaker than when she was in high school. He tells us people with severe GERD sometimes opt for a Nissan Fundoplication. This is a surgical procedure where part of the stomach is wrapped around the weakened sphincter muscle to prevent food from traveling back up through the esophagus. "It's not a complicated procedure," he says, adding that the stomach itself is smaller after the procedure.

"What's the success rate?" Emilee asks.

"About 85% to 90%," Dr. Waters says. "I do the surgery laparoscopically and, when all goes well, my patients are able to resume normal activities after about three weeks."

"That doesn't sound so bad," Emilee says.

"It's important to know that individuals who have this surgery are no longer able to vomit," Dr. Waters says. "I mention this because Emilee is a college student, and there is an increased incidence of alcohol poisoning among that population."

Emilee sits straight up in her chair. "I'm so tired of dealing with this," she says. "I want to have the surgery."

After the appointment, Jack and I speak with Emilee and tell her she will have to be extra careful in regards to drinking. She tells us she isn't worried about alcohol poisoning; she learned her lesson during her junior year of high school. "I'm not into the party scene," she assures us, and we believe her. The surgery is scheduled for her winter break from college.

A few weeks before the surgery, Emilee confides in me. "I'm a little worried about what life will be like after the procedure," she says. "I'm used to eating more food because I know some of what I eat will come right back up. But after surgery, my stomach will be smaller. I'm not sure I remember how to eat normally. I might need some counseling."

I feel Emilee is trying to tell me something, but I don't know what it is. I ask, "Em, is there something you want to tell me?"

"I just have concerns about not being able to eat like a regular person."

Jack and I have had many conversations about Emilee's reflux, and we agree she's been open and has never tried to hide her condition. In my mind, I review the facts I know to be true. When her reflux began in high school, and since then, when she's living here she doesn't spend time in the bathroom after meals; the amount of food that comes back up is not excessive. She eats the same food we do; she is strong and at a normal weight—and always has been. We have no reason not to believe her. I'm happy she's shared her concerns with me. I make a few phone calls and get Emilee an appointment with a psychologist following the surgery.

During the surgery Jack and I sit in the hospital waiting room, leafing through magazines and anxiously watching the clock. Two and a half hours later, we see Dr. Waters walking towards us. "How is she?" we ask in unison.

"Everything went as planned," he says reassuringly.

In the hospital Emilee is a model patient, and she does even better when she gets home. I make the recommended meals, in small portions, and she tolerates them well, with no heartburn or regurgitation. Emilee is thrilled that the surgery is successful and that it's behind her. I'm relieved, too, and happy we can share quiet time together as she heals. Family and friends stop by to visit and bring her gifts and flowers.

Three weeks after the surgery Emilee is feeling great, and she begins seeing the psychologist to whom she's been referred. On the day of her first appointment, I have the opportunity to meet the psychologist before their session begins. Blonde and middle-aged, Dr. Brown seems kind, and she speaks in a calm, soft manner. In the months that follow, Emilee shares that she enjoys working with Dr. Brown, but she doesn't go into too much detail with me other than to say she looks forward to their sessions. They meet regularly for several months, and at the end of their last session I'm invited to join them. Dr. Brown sits behind a wooden desk, and I settle into a green chair that matches the one Emilee is sitting in. The atmosphere feels calm and relaxed. Emilee looks wonderful, her skin glows and her eyes sparkle. Emilee says she's glad she decided to opt for surgery, adding, "I just wish I'd done it sooner."

When Emilee says this, I feel sorry we didn't pursue the surgical option sooner. This is territory we've never navigated before, and both Jack and I trusted the gastroenterologist. Now I wonder if maybe we should have gotten another opinion sooner. *But Emilee wasn't willing to consider the surgery before*, I think to myself. *And what if I'd pushed her into having surgery, and it wasn't successful?* On this day, I refuse to keep rethinking something I can't change. I'm relieved Em is feeling better, and I respect the fact that she is now an adult who can make her own decisions about her body.

When it's time for Emilee to return to college for the completion of her sophomore year, she's anxious to see her friends and resume her routine. We visit her on campus a few weeks later, take her out for dinner, and all is well. She tells us, "It feels wonderful to be able to eat like a normal person."

Linda, John, and *Emilee* Mazur

CHAPTER THIRTEEN • FOREVER CHANGED

LINDA

Two weeks after Emilee returns to college to begin her junior year, everything changes. Jack is at work, and I'm with a client in the salon when the phone rings. "Turn on the television," Jack says. It's Tuesday, September 11th, and I, along with millions of other horrified people, watch two airplanes crash into New York City's World Trade Center. Telephones ring in every home and business as people turn on their televisions and watch in shock and disbelief, as video footage of the crashes replays over and over again. Soon after, a third plane flies into the Pentagon. Everyone wonders what's coming next. The world witnesses the World Trade Center's North and South Towers crumble and collapse, and another plane crashing into a field in Somerset County, Pennsylvania. These horrific images are seared into our collective consciousness. Soon, we hear about a group called 'Al Qaeda' and that several individuals from this group have hijacked the planes and that they are jihadists on a suicide mission. When people realize the United States is being attacked, that the attacks were carefully executed and orchestrated, everyone worries there will be more casualties. Telephone lines are jammed. The country is in a panic and in disbelief at what it is witnessing, and everyone is trying to make sure their loved ones are okay.

Jack and I reach Emilee at Wells that afternoon. I'm relieved when she answers because I'd not been able to reach her earlier. Texting hasn't been invented yet, and we aren't in the habit of keeping our cell phones turned on all the time.

"I'm fine," Emilee says. "No one can believe what's happened! Everyone's upset, but we're okay. We're like a family here. I'm just so glad you're all right."

Though we rest a bit easier after talking with her, we wish Emilee was at home with us. But we rationalize she is in a safe place, if there is such a place, on such a terrible day. We pray for all the victims and their families, and thank God our family and friends are safe.

That night Jack and I toss and turn, feeling a new and overwhelming sense of vulnerability. We realize how fragile life is from one moment to the next, and are forced to accept there is simply no way to ensure the ones we love will always be protected.

The world, as we know it, is forever changed.

CHAPTER FOURTEEN • BRANCHING OUT

LINDA

At the completion of Emilee's junior year at college, one of her professors asks her to live in Ithaca for the summer to help with a research project she is working on at Cornell University, and Emilee welcomes the opportunity. Though she loves Wells' peaceful, serene atmosphere, she's excited to have the chance to experience a larger school environment. Participating in a research project will enhance her chances of being accepted into Cornell's College of Veterinary Medicine. Although we'll miss having her home we understand what an honor it is to be chosen, and believe it will be a great experience for her. Jack and I are happy Emilee is branching out.

A few weeks before she leaves for Ithaca, Emilee, Jack, and I proudly watch Matthew as he walks across the stage at the Eastman Theater to receive his high school diploma, just as Emilee had three years earlier. We are proud of him and excited for his college experience in the fall, at Alfred University.

I know it will be a summer that passes quickly, but I plan to savor it. And I do.

The following fall I am thrilled to have the opportunity to see Em perform a violin solo at Wells, especially since I wasn't able to attend her senior solo in high school. Seeing her cross the stage, her long black skirt swirling around her ankles, I feel a rush of adrenaline and excitement. As she stands in front of the room, I watch my daughter's fingers fly across the strings of her shiny wooden violin. With her light blonde hair softly twisted back off her face, I no longer see a girl. I see a beautiful, talented young woman who carries herself with poise and confidence. Her performance is flawless, and it is a moment that will be forever frozen in time for me. I feel I am seeing her come into her own. That night, for some reason, when we are saying good-bye I feel the need to tell her again, to remind her what I have said all along. "I hope you know we love you, unconditionally, simply because you are ours. We couldn't love you more—your accomplishments are a bonus. "

Emilee hugs me then smiles at me quizzically, with one side of her mouth turning up a little more than the other, the same way Jack's sometimes does. "But Mom," she says, puzzled, "my accomplishments are a big part of who I am."

CHAPTER FIFTEEN • LOVE AND REJECTION

JACK

Emilee works hard and completes her undergraduate work in three and a half years. Returning home at Christmastime, a semester before her official graduation, Emilee obtains a job with the grocery store chain I work for, in the pharmacy department. Like all the jobs and endeavors Emilee has taken on previously, she quickly becomes one of the best employees and a favorite of the customers. One day Emilee comes home from work and announces she's met someone, a pharmacist named Adam. "He's tall with light brown hair," she says. "And he has a great sense of humor." From that day on, we notice our daughter takes more time getting ready for work. She buys new clothes and fusses over her makeup. For their first date, Emilee and Adam attend Saturday evening mass and then go out for a cup of coffee. During the course of the conversation, Adam tells her he's moved to the Rochester area from Arizona after ending a long-term relationship.

Over the next few months, Emilee and Adam spend more and more time together. One day she defies my advice and drives to his home, over an hour away, in a snowstorm. Linda calls me at work, telling me Emilee has had an accident on her way to Adam's. I'm relieved to hear she's not injured, but I'm angry that she didn't listen to me. Emilee is normally cautious and rational, and I'm surprised by her impulsive decision-making. Adam picks her up and brings her to his home, and she spends a few hours there, waiting for the car to be towed out of the ditch and for the weather to break. When she finally makes it home several hours later, Emilee greets me sheepishly. "I'm sorry, Dad," she says. "You were right."

"I just want you to be safe," I say, hoping she'll be a little more cautious. "Your mom and I love you so damn much! We want you to be around forever."

Later that evening I overhear Emilee on the phone with Adam, talking and laughing, and it occurs to me that her decision to rush out in inclement weather was based on the fact that she wanted to be with her boyfriend. I understand that kind of passion, and there is no doubt she is in love.

Emilee has applied to Cornell's Veterinary College and is anxiously awaiting correspondence to let her know whether or not she has been accepted to the program. A few weeks after the accident, Emilee puts on her winter coat and walks out to check the mailbox. Linda has finished working and is folding laundry in the family room, and I'm sitting on the couch brushing Max. We hear the front door close, and a moment later Emilee stands before us with an envelope in her hand.

"It's from Cornell," she says.

We watch her quietly as she opens the letter, her eyes darting back and forth across the paper. Slowly, a cloud of disappointment washes over her face. She pauses a moment, lowering the letter. Her eyes meet Linda's, and then she looks at me.

"I didn't get in," she says as a tear rolls down her cheek.

The letter provides more information: out of one thousand applicants, fewer than forty have been accepted. Despite the fact that her grades are high enough, and despite the fact that she's completed specialized internships and accompanied a local veterinarian to nearby horse farms to assist with several visits, it still isn't enough. She needs more large animal experience. While my heart breaks for my daughter, I'm frustrated, too. Though I encouraged her to apply to several veterinary schools Emilee put all her eggs in one basket, insisting she wants to attend Cornell and only Cornell.

The letter goes on to applaud Emilee's hard work and encourages her to apply again.

"Honey," I say. "We know you'll be a great vet."

"You can get more large animal experience and re-apply," Linda adds.

Emilee nods. She is disappointed, but she doesn't seem devastated. Still, Linda and I can tell she's more upset than she wants us to know. She continues working at the pharmacy and looks forward to her graduation in May. We assume she will re-apply to Cornell's Veterinary Program at some point in the future.

Unbeknownst to us, however, Emilee has also applied to Albany College of Pharmacy's accelerated Doctorate of Pharmacy Program, my alma mater—a highly competitive, thirty-six-month course of study—as a back-up plan. And just a few short weeks after she receives the disappointing news from Cornell, Emilee informs us that not only has she been accepted, but she's decided to attend pharmacy school. To say the least, Linda and I are surprised to hear this news. We can't believe she's letting go of her dream to become a veterinarian.

* * *

Shortly after Emilee's acceptance into pharmacy school, Adam informs her that he needs to go to Arizona for a while to tie up loose ends. Emilee tells us she feels uneasy because his former girlfriend is still there, and the situation makes her feel their relationship isn't as solid as she thought.

Adam is in Arizona when Emilee walks across the stage and graduates cum laude from Wells College. We have a large family celebration at a favorite local Italian restaurant with my mother, Linda's parents, Emilee's aunts, uncles, and cousins, all there to celebrate with her. The smell of fresh-baked bread and homemade sauce permeates the air, and enormous, ornate paintings of Venice and the Adriatic Sea hang from walls gilded in gold. Emilee sits in between Linda and me at a long table, and the night seems to be going beautifully. At some point, I overhear her tell Linda she's sad Adam isn't there to celebrate her accomplishment. Though I try to perk her up, I can't fix the situation. I feel sorry for Emilee, and I'm a little disappointed in Adam.

Shortly after graduation, Emilee's spirits are lifted when Adam invites her to spend a week with him in Arizona before pharmacy school begins. He assures Emilee his relationship with his former girlfriend is over; he'll be selling his condominium and returning to Rochester shortly. Emilee makes the travel arrangements, and we drive her to the airport for an early evening departure. The trip turns into a wonderful vacation for the two of them. Emilee tells us that she and Adam reconnected easily and that she's enjoying the warm climate, the desert scenery, and the wonderful ambiance of the Southwest.

CHAPTER SIXTEEN • A NEW PATH

JACK

A few short weeks after returning from Arizona, Emilee begins pharmacy school. With four years of curriculum condensed into three, the program is intense. Emilee knows this going in, and it appears she easily adjusts. By the fall of 2003, Adam is back in Rochester—four hours away from Emilee in Albany—and The New York State Thruway becomes the beaten path linking them together. Most weekends, Emilee winds up being the one doing the traveling and, while Linda and I understand they want to be together, we feel Emilee is over-extending herself. And we're concerned about her driving so much, especially in the winter.

"We miss each other and want to spend whatever time we can together," she says, adding that the drive helps her to unwind.

From Linda's and my vantage point, Emilee's first two years in pharmacy school appear to go smoothly. She and Adam maintain their long-distance relationship and, in her final year, Emilee returns to Rochester to gain real-life pharmaceutical experience in retail and hospital settings. During this period, Emilee sees Adam regularly. In the evenings they spend time in our guest room, watching movies, and making plans for their future. When the weather is rough Adam stays in our guest room, and Emilee asks us to allow her to sleep with him there, but we are old-fashioned and tell her we aren't comfortable with that. We'd feel differently if they were engaged. Emilee respects our feelings.

Linda, John, and *Emilee* Mazur

CHAPTER SEVENTEEN • GOODBYE MAX

JACK

While Emilee is on rotation in Rochester our beloved dog, Max, begins to fail. At fourteen he is blind, deaf, diabetic, and incontinent. We have contemplated putting him to sleep, but we have previously canceled two such appointments. However, when he becomes disoriented, it's evident his quality of life has diminished so much. We feel we are selfish, keeping him alive. The entire family meets at the vet's office, and a veterinary technician meets us at the front desk. She pets Max and walks us down the hall into an examination room. Our veterinarian comes in, explains the procedure to us, and steps out to gives us a few minutes alone with Max. Emilee is familiar with animal euthanasia, as she has worked in veterinary offices.

After the four of us say all the things we need to say to Max, our tears flow freely. He is a family member, a wonderful companion, and a friend to us all. I'm having second thoughts, but I know it's best for him. Emilee knows it, too, as hard as it is for her. The vet returns to the room and asks, "Are you ready?"

"As ready as we can be," I answer.

Emilee places Max on the stainless steel exam table, and as she bends over to give him one last kiss I stroke his fur. After the injection is given Max lowers his head slowly, and within seconds he appears to be sleeping peacefully.

"Is that it?" I ask.

The veterinarian nods and quietly leaves the room.

When the door closes, we sob. After a short time alone with Max a technician leads us out of the office, through a back door. On the ride home Matthew is quiet, while Linda, Emilee and I are tearful—each of us processing our grief. It's strange to come home and not have Max there to greet us. And even though the house feels empty without him we feel confident about the decision we made to put him down, and find comfort in the knowledge that we provided him with the best life we possibly could.

CHAPTER EIGHTEEN • ANOTHER GRADUATION

LINDA

After Emilee's internship in Rochester ends, the remainder of her rotations are in the Albany area. During this time our cousins, Donna and Michael, invite Emilee to live with them. Emilee is grateful for her 'second family', and the arrangement works out beautifully, but she continues to drive back to Rochester many weekends to be with Adam. The tightrope Emilee is walking, between her intense school load and her personal life, starts to take a toll on her health. At one point, we notice Emilee's beautiful blonde hair is thinning. "I know," Emilee says, self-consciously covering her forehead with her hand. "I wonder if I could have an iron deficiency or something." A dermatologist does a scalp biopsy and sets up blood tests, all of which come back normal. No one can come up with a medical reason for her hair loss, but I believe the pressure of school and rotations, and long-distance travel, is adding to Emilee's anxiety.

Eventually, Emilee finally confesses she's been pulling out her hair for months and has a condition called trichotillomania, which is considered an impulse-control disorder frequently caused by stress. Emilee says it feels like an itch or a tingle on her scalp, and the only way she could stop the feeling was to pull out her hair, one strand at a time. It becomes an irresistible urge; her way of self-soothing and coping with stress. I suggest we go wig shopping because we can see patches on her scalp with no hair. Emilee enjoys trying on different colors and styles and ends up choosing a lovely, straight blonde wig. She's never liked her curly blonde hair, and when she sees her reflection in the mirror she's pleased with her new look. We are hopeful that this is a temporary adaptation, that when pharmacy school is over she will have less stress in her life.

***

Emilee graduates from Albany Pharmacy College in May 2006. The Hooding Ceremony is impressive, and there's a bounce in her step as she walks up the aisle to receive her diploma. At twenty-five years old she is the first person in our family to receive her doctorate, and we are proud of all the effort she's put into achieving her degree.

One week later Matthew graduates from Alfred University with a Bachelor's Degree in Business and Marketing, and Matthew and Emilee share a joint graduation celebration at one of our favorite restaurants. The entire family is there, including Adam, and we enjoy wonderful food, celebrating our children's academic achievements. Smiles, toasts, excitement, and promise fill the room. Jack and I have much to be grateful for. Our children are on their way! Both are healthy and happy, both are compassionate, bright adults, and both are individuals— very different from each other, yet they are each other's touchstone. It's been said 'children are the true measure of time' and it's true. For a long time now, it seems in each new year there are far fewer days than in the year before, and Emilee and Matthew's high school and college years seem to have passed in the blink of an eye. I think to myself, *We've done our best as parents. There have been a few bumps in the road, and we have a few gray hairs, but we've loved them every step of the way. In turn, they've taught us more than we could have ever imagined, and given us joy beyond measure.*

CHAPTER NINETEEN • IMPORTANT NEXT STEPS

JACK

After graduation, Emilee lands a position at the same pharmacy where she'd met Adam four years earlier. She confides she's nervous about the responsibilities of being a pharmacist. However, her confidence grows quickly, and she is professional in carrying out her duties at work. Emilee gains the respect of her peers, colleagues, and patrons alike. Her natural compassion for others makes it easy for people to trust her and feel comfortable. When Emilee and Adam aren't working, they spend all their free time together: going out with friends, to dinner and the movies, playing golf, and obtaining autographs for Adam's collection.

Linda and I sense Adam is going to "pop the big question" soon, and it isn't long before he calls to see if he can set up a time to come to speak with us.

"We knew he'd be asking soon," Linda says. "They've been together for four years."

I nod my head in agreement, but I'm not without my concerns. As a father, I want my daughter to be happy. I want her to find her soul-mate, just as I did when I married Linda. Marriage is a huge commitment, one that needs to be worked at consistently for it to last. *I'm not sure he's the right man for Emilee,* I think to myself. I know Emilee tries to appear strong, and she is in many ways, but she is sensitive and feels things deeply. I want Adam to understand this about her. And, if I'm being honest, I definitely have concerns because Adam's family background is vastly different from Emilee's. His parents divorced when he was young, and he didn't see the necessary day-to-day compromises that are part of married life. *But all couples come from different backgrounds,* I rationalize. *He has a good relationship with both of his parents and sisters. And he loves Emilee.*

The next day Adam arrives with a shy grin on his face. We shake hands, and he gives Linda a big hug. He follows us into our living room and sits down on one of the two matching loveseats. Linda and I sit directly across from him. Outside our picture window the sky is blue, and the sun is bright.

"I love Emilee very much," Adam says. "I want to ask her to marry me, and... I'd like your blessing."

As I listen to Adam I decide not to voice my concerns, despite the fact that I have many. *Who am I to keep them apart?* I think to myself. Taking a breath, I hope for the best. "Please just promise me you'll love and take care of Emilee for the rest of her life," I say. "I want you to have a great life together."

"I want that, too," Adam assures us. "I promise."

He seems sincere.

I stand up, offer my hand to Adam, and he extends his. When we shake hands I squeeze his shoulder, hoping he understands that my gesture conveys that, along with our blessing, he is accepted into our family.

To celebrate, I select a special California cabernet off the wine rack and pour three glasses. Linda makes a toast. "May Emilee and Adam be forever lovers, and forever best friends."

The next night, Adam takes Emilee to one of the finest restaurants in Rochester. He's spoken with the maître d' in advance, and we know he's taken the time to select the right champagne, the right spot in the dining room, and the right shade of roses to be set on the table where he'll propose to our daughter. We're excited when they come over after dinner to celebrate the engagement with us and show us Emilee's ring. It is a beautiful diamond, and Emilee is thrilled to have it on her finger. She looks so lovely. Her skin is tan, and she's dressed to the nines, but what stands out the most is her brilliant smile and her excitement. She can hardly sit still, jumping up to help Linda bring in coffee, looking out the window, and offering Adam more snacks.

I can't help but smile. Emilee's eyes sparkle and her smile lingers, as does Adam's. The two of them exchange loving glances and subtle touches. They don't stay long, and we don't expect them to. We're just happy they stopped by. I want Emilee to have the wedding she's always envisioned, and I am hopeful that she'll have a happy life with all the things she tells us she dreams about: a loving husband, children, a nice home and, of course, a dog.

LINDA

In the fall, Jack and I take a trip with Adam and Emilee to Niagara-on-the-Lake in Ontario, Canada. On the way, we learn Adam and Jack favor the same favorite doughnut (white cream filled with chocolate frosting), the same favorite movie (Memento), and share the same middle name (Thomas). We enjoy delicious meals, visit several wineries, a butterfly museum, gift shops, and we laugh. A lot. Adam can't believe Jack and I have never been here. Emilee and I are always happy to have the opportunity to spend quality time together, and this trip is special to us. And it's a bonus to see Jack and our future son-in-law having an equally great time together.

Soon after our trip the weather gets colder, the leaves change color and begin to fall from the trees, and each day there is less sunlight than the day before. Emilee and Adam rent an apartment and move in together.

Shortly after moving in with Adam, Emilee begins to experience agitation and insomnia, and her primary care doctor, Dr. Shay, refers to her a psychiatrist.

"How did it go?" I ask.

"He says I have Generalized Anxiety Disorder."

"What does that mean?"

"It means I worry about everything."

"Is that true?" I ask.

"Lately… yes," she says. "And people who have it often have trouble sleeping."

"You've always had trouble sleeping," I say, remembering the radio playing softly next to her crib.

"The psychiatrist says Generalized Anxiety Disorder is common. He's prescribed paroxetine—an SSRI—but I don't want to be on anything."

"Well, if anxiety's impacting your life this much, maybe you should consider it. And perhaps therapy could help," I say. "It's your decision."

Emilee talks to Jack and Adam, and the three of them discuss the pros and cons of the medication prescribed. Both Adam and Jack respect Emilee's pharmacological knowledge, and she respects theirs. They understand that she doesn't want to be on the medication. However, they can see her anxiety has increased, and they agree she should try the medication and therapy. Emilee reluctantly decides to try the SSRI and says she'll think about therapy.

CHAPTER TWENTY• CONCERNS

LINDA

Weeks pass and Emilee, Adam, Jack, and I visit prospective venues for the wedding reception. We enter Midvale Country Club, and we all pause. Emilee's face lights up, and Adam nods his head. The dining room overlooks a luscious green golf course, dark wood floors add a grounding warmth to the space, and the rich, warm colors and elegant moldings hug the large windows and ceilings. We set a date to return, sample the food, and choose a menu for the wedding reception. Emilee and Adam leave before Jack and I, and we notice how happy they look, holding hands, talking, and smiling.

A short time later, I sense an uncomfortable tension and anxiety in Emilee that is especially evident whenever we discuss plans and preparations for the wedding. She's easily exasperated and short-tempered with me, which surprises me. In my mind, the preparation and planning is part of the fun, but then I take a step back and consider all the things Emilee is adjusting to: living with Adam, preparing for the wedding, as well as handling her job responsibilities. By November the holidays are fast approaching, and I make a date with Emilee to meet for coffee.

"Do you think the medication is helping?" I ask her over our lattes.

Emilee shrugs. "I guess I need to give it more time."

"I'd like to take some of the stress off of you," I tell her. "Traditionally, the bride and her family plan the wedding, while the groom and his family plan the rehearsal dinner, but times are changing. You decide what things you want to do yourselves, and we'll do the rest." I watch Emilee pry the plastic lid off of her latte. I notice how crowded the coffee shop is and how close together the tables are. "Maybe the two of you can take charge of the DJ, the photographer, and the florist. This is your wedding, and we don't need to be part of all the decisions. Most importantly, we want you to be happy together and enjoy the day. It upsets me to see you stressed. Do you want to talk about it?"

"There's just a lot going on in my head right now," Emilee says. "Adam wants a say in a lot of things! I'm not used to it." She leans back and takes a deep breath as her shoulder blades touch the back of the chair. "I'd like to shop for my wedding dress with you in January. I'll feel better when that's done. When are you free?"

"Pick a day," I say, feeling a little better.

Less than six weeks later, the entire extended family gathers around the breakfast bar in my kitchen. It's Christmas Day, and Emilee and Adam walk through the front door with bags of presents. When Emilee takes off her puffy winter coat, I see just how thin she is. "Are you okay?" I ask.

"I'm fine," she says, but I wonder if she really is as fine as she says she is.

While everyone is eating hors d'oeuvres, Emilee helps me to set up the buffet. I hear her sigh loudly, several times.

"You have way too much food!" she says. "Why did you make so much?!"

It seems as if she is scolding me. "Better to have extra than not enough," I say, trying to make light of the comment.

After dinner, while everyone is engrossed in conversation, I lead Emilee down the hallway into our bedroom and close the door. Emilee sits on the bed, and I sit next to her.

"I know something's bothering you," I say, as I rub her back. It's impossible to ignore the bones protruding beneath her sweater. "Is there something you want to tell me?"

"Adam and I have been arguing a lot," she says. The sparkle in her eyes is missing, and I'm worried. I want her to open up and tell me what's going on. We have a close relationship, and it's always been that way. We can talk about almost everything, but when I think about it, not so much lately.

"Are you having second thoughts?" I question.

Watching my daughter twist a strand of her synthetic blonde hair around her finger, I feel strangely afraid.

"We want to be married," Emilee says. She stops twisting her hair and starts twisting her engagement ring around her finger. "It's just been crazy with working and planning."

I think back through the years, to all the worries and fears I'd been able to diffuse and soothe away for our children—many on the very bed upon which Emilee and I are now sitting—as they would run into our room after a nightmare, or with a stomach bug, or sometimes because they were concerned about something and just couldn't sleep. Then, no matter the hour, my words came naturally, in a calm manner, and they flowed from my mouth. But now I am struggling to find exactly the right words, in the proper order, in just the right tone because I sense there are things she isn't telling me. Emilee is no longer a child, and I don't know if I can assuage her discomfort this time. I'm not sure she'll confide in me, or if my words might close a door, but I begin to speak anyway. I have to try. "Just because you love someone doesn't mean they're the right person for you," I tell her. "Sometimes, fine people are just not a good fit to be life partners." Emilee is still, so I continue, "You've lost weight and pulled out your hair; these are signs something's wrong. Maybe he's not the right person for you. Or is it something else?"

Emilee straightens up and looks me in the eye, "I thought you said you love Adam."

"I do," I say. "But you're my daughter. My love for you is immeasurable, unconditional, and protective. I want you to have a great life. You deserve that." I reach over and place my hand on hers. "What's going on?"

"Adam can be difficult and so can I," Emilee says, sliding off the bed. "We'll work it out."

It's evident the conversation is over. Emilee straightens her shoulders, tilts her head, and smiles back at me. When I stand up, she reaches out her arms and hugs me. We stand there, embracing, neither of us moving for what seems a long time. I feel our energy connecting, and I know she can feel my love.

That night after everyone leaves, I crawl into our bed. Jack is already sleeping. I should be exhausted, but sleep won't come. I toss and turn, and stare at the nightstand next to our bed, at the digital clock that sits on top of it. I watch as the clock's numbers keep changing, over and over again. All I can think about is how thin Emilee is, and how tense she seemed when she helped me with the meal. How she'd opened up, a little, about things with her and Adam. *If everything is fine, why do I feel so unsettled?*

* * *

One frigid day in January, Emilee and I go shopping for her wedding gown. Inside the bridal shop dressing room I look at my daughter as she stands in front of the full-length mirror, wearing just her bra and panties. Her arms and legs are thin. Too thin. I question Emilee about her weight loss, but she denies anything is wrong. She says she's lost weight because she had the flu. I remind her how thin she looked at Christmas, even before she got sick.

"You need to go to the doctor if you've lost that much weight. Something is definitely wrong," I say, but Emilee refuses to see her doctor. She says she's stressed about the wedding and work.

"I'm an adult, and I can take care of myself," she snaps. "I'll be fine."

While I'm concerned about Emilee and Adam as a couple, I'm even more concerned about Emilee's health. *Could the two things be connected?* I wonder.

JACK

As the trees bud and sprout leaves, Emilee and Adam's relationship is increasingly strained. When Linda and I are with them the tension between them is evident in the way they interact, rolling their eyes and uttering sarcastic remarks towards each other.

We have not seen this behavior before, and it makes us feel unsettled. To us, it doesn't seem like they are behaving as if they're only a few months away from what's supposed to be the happiest day of their lives. We try speaking with them. They minimize our concerns. We give them space and hope we aren't adding to their stress.

With the wedding just four months away, Emilee and Adam start calling Linda to vent about each other. One evening, after another long and exhausting phone conversation, Linda walks into the family room, sits down next to me, and leans her head against the pillow at the back of the couch. She lets out a long, deep sigh.

"This isn't right," I say. "Every time I turn around, one of them is calling you."

I know Linda is a great listener, so I can understand why they both feel comfortable talking to her. Everyone does, but I can tell she's upset.

"You can't keep doing this," I say. "What exactly are they telling you?"

"They told me some things in confidence," Linda says. "But I can tell you Emilee doesn't think Adam pays enough attention to her. She says he's critical of her."

"And?"

"He's having trouble dealing with Emilee's anxiety."

"What else?" I ask, hoping she'll share more, but I know my wife won't betray a confidence.

"I told them I need to be there for Emilee—as her mother—and that I can't be in the middle of their problems. I suggested they see a counselor and they're going this week."

Linda tells me she has made an appointment to see a counselor herself, a woman named Kathe, who comes highly recommended. "I feel like I'm in the middle of a triangle and it's taking a toll on me," she says. "I hope you'll come with me."

I nod my head in agreement.

Linda and I begin to have serious doubts about the wedding and wonder if it should be postponed. We think back to our courtship and engagement and talk about what an exciting time it was. We can't remember it feeling like work.

About a month before the wedding, I walk in the house after a long day at work and immediately notice how good the house smells. Linda has made pasta and meatballs, and I'm starving. She's set the dining room table and has poured each of us a glass of Chianti.

Halfway through dinner, I notice I've been doing all the talking.

"Everything okay?" I ask, reaching for the bread.

"Emilee said their counselor recommended that she and Adam not go through with the wedding," Linda says. "They're both upset, but they're both adamant about getting married."

"Maybe we should pull the plug on the wedding," I suggest.

"I'm afraid if we cancel the wedding, we'll risk losing our relationship with our daughter," Linda says. "After all, they don't need our blessing to get married."

"You know I want the best for Emilee," I say. "This just doesn't feel right."

LINDA

Caught between a rock and a hard place, Jack and I continue to swallow our concerns and plow ahead with the wedding plans. Emilee's friend, Kelly, and her mother, Carol, host a bridal shower for Emilee. My daughter and I are the first to arrive at Carol's house. Em is excited and a little nervous about being the center of attention. She paces around the house, admiring the tableful of appetizers, banners, and multicolored balloons hanging from the doorways and ceilings. "I'm feeling anxious," she admits. "I can't believe everyone I invited is coming!"

"You're fortunate to have so many people who love you," I say as I walk towards the dining room table. There's a large crystal punch bowl filled with sangria, and after filling a glass for myself I fill another for Emilee. "Here," I say. "Have some punch and relax. There's nothing to be nervous about."

Once the guests begin to arrive and the conversations begin to flow, Emilee settles down. Watching her open the gifts with gratitude and excitement, I'm reminded of the way she used to open her gifts as a child on Christmas morning. She has the same twinkle in her eyes and wears the same expression of awe on her face. We all laugh and play silly, but fun, shower games. My mother wins the prize for modeling the best "wedding gown", constructed from many rolls of white toilet tissue. Emilee laughs at the sight of her sweet and proper Grandma Dot, covered with toilet paper from head to toe. The two stand arm in arm for pictures, laughing until tears roll down their cheeks. It's a very good day.

Linda, John, and *Emilee* Mazur

CHAPTER TWENTY-ONE ● WEDDING

LINDA

On the morning of the wedding Jack and I wake up early and take a little time for ourselves, sipping coffee on the deck just outside Emilee's bedroom window. Emilee wanted things to be traditional and asked to stay in her old bedroom the night before the wedding. We're more than happy to have our daughter for one last night.

The air is balmy, the sky a soft blue with clouds that resemble bunches of cotton balls scattered here and there. Blue jays, cardinals, and chickadees hover around the birdfeeder, heads slowly bobbing up and down. I close my eyes and breathe in the tranquility of the moment, knowing the day will take on an energy of its own. The screen door slides open and we greet Emilee, bright-eyed and rosy-cheeked, coffee in hand, coming out to join us. She is excited, talking a mile a minute. Jack and I listen happily as she rambles on. She brings so much energy and sunshine to our lives.

A few hours later I apply Emilee's makeup, style her synthetic hair, and attach her headpiece with bobby pins. I know what she likes, and she trusts me. Emilee beams when she sees her reflection in the mirror. Together we look out the double window in her bedroom and take in the beauty of the outdoors, admiring the pink, purple, and white petunias cascading over planters that adorn the deck. The large maple tree, which caused us so much concern during the ice storm years before, stands strong and tall, its large green leaves shading part of the deck.

Emilee squeezes my hand. "Do you remember when I was little and had so many earaches?" she asks.

"I do!" I say with a smile. "I remember running a washcloth under warm water, sealing it inside a baggie, and holding it on your ear."

"You'd lie down next to me," Emilee says, tilting her head. "Even when I was at college and worried about things, you always had time to listen. Just hearing your voice makes me feel better."

"You give me too much credit," I say. "You're a joy, and always have been. I've loved taking care of you." I smile at my daughter, hoping one day she will have children so she might understand the depth of love a mother feels for her child. "I have every card and letter you've given to me," I tell my daughter. "You're an inspiration to me. You're stronger than you know, Emilee, and you've accomplished things I've never dreamed of."

"You give me too much credit," Emilee says playfully.

"Your father and I make each other better, and we wish that for you and Adam."

A short time later Emilee walks into the living room wearing a white silk wedding gown featuring tiny pink flowers, elegant beading, and delicate embroidery. She looks radiant, but I can't help but notice how very thin she is.

I hope my concerns are an overreaction, but something tells me they aren't.

JACK

As Linda and I approach the church entrance, I remember thirty years earlier, on my own wedding day, looking outside that morning and seeing the rain, and later walking up the wet concrete stairs into St. Francis Church in Geneva, New York. An old church with traditionally styled architecture, the red brick facade and tall steeple immediately draw my attention. Standing here today, in a classic black tuxedo, vest, and tie, Linda tells me how handsome I look. "Aren't you glad the ruffled, baby blue shirts from thirty years ago are no longer in style?" I say.

I realize I was not nearly as nervous on my own wedding day as I am today, the day I am giving away my daughter to another man. When I married Linda in 1977, I knew in my heart the woman I was about to marry would be my wife as long as we both lived. Our relationship blossomed naturally and has grown even deeper over time.

But on this day, I'm an observer. Linda and I have stated our concerns to Emilee and Adam. We've done everything we can do, short of canceling the wedding and, whatever happens, we will be there for Emilee. But, damn it, I want this marriage to work.

The church we belong to—Church of the Assumption—is a newer church. Its modern architectural design showcases wood and tan-colored brick, as well as an open tower rising above the entrance housing two large black bells. As we walk up the steps and enter the church, I see many of the same friends and relatives who were there for Linda's and my wedding now gathering for Emilee's big day. Linda and I mingle with the early arriving relatives for a short time, until the wedding coordinator calls us for last-minute instructions and leads me into a room in the back of the church.

Alone with my thoughts, the realization hits me hard. I am giving my beloved daughter away in marriage. Tears well up in my eyes. When Emilee walks into the room I see how beautiful she looks, how much she looks like Linda. I give her a hug and a kiss, tell her I'm happy for her and Adam, and express how lucky he'll be to have her as his wife. I remind her that I'll be there for her, anytime she needs me.

"Dad," she says, "I'm nervous."

"It's natural to be nervous, honey," I reassure her. "Just remember to walk slowly and smile. I'll be right here with you. Just follow my lead."

Adam waits for us at the altar. As we move towards him my hope is that he has a lasting, deep love and devotion for Emilee, as I did for Linda as I watched her walk down the aisle on her father's arm thirty years earlier. Taking our final steps together, I squeeze Emilee's hand, and I hope she can feel how much I love her and understand how wonderful, yet how difficult, this is for me, closing this chapter of my life. I kiss Em on the cheek, shake Adam's hand, and watch as he reaches for her hand. Taking my seat next to Linda, I watch the ceremony and listen as they exchange their vows. They certainly seem to be in love.

After the wedding, the bridesmaids and groomsmen travel around Rochester in a shiny, white limo-bus posing for pictures, eventually finishing up on the historic lift bridge over the Erie Canal on Main Street in Fairport. When they arrive at Midvale Country Club, they pile into a couple of golf carts to pose for more photographs on the course.

When Linda and I arrive at the venue Matthew is smiling, looking sharp in his tux, and he tells us the photographer is finishing up with a few extra shots of the bride and groom on the golf course. After the newlyweds arrive and appetizers are served, it's time for me to welcome the guests and recite my father-of-the-bride speech, prepared over the last few weeks. I try to keep it to a minimum, but it's not possible. I want to let everyone know how special Emilee is to Linda and me. I end with a toast to the newlyweds, expressing my wish that they be blessed with as wonderful a marriage as Linda and I have shared.

Matthew is excited to share his contributions to the wedding. He's created a compilation CD of Emilee and Adam's favorite songs, featuring a photograph of the bride and groom on the cover. In turn, he surprises them with a slide show containing dozens of photographs of each of them from birth through their engagement, set to popular music with sentimental lyrics. Emilee and Adam are genuinely surprised and pleased as the video plays on the large screen. After Matthew's tribute Linda warmly welcomes everyone, thanks the staff at Midvale, and officially welcomes Adam into the family. She says a heartfelt grace just before the delicious dinner is served. The evening is unfolding as we had hoped and expected, and it feels wonderful having so many special people gathered around us for this happy occasion.

When the DJ calls my name, I know it's time for the father-daughter dance. As I approach Emilee, I can tell something is wrong. "What's the matter?" I ask as we walk onto the dance floor. "I want you to tell me what's going on," I say, "but right now we have to start dancing." Emilee forces a smile. As we move across the floor I can tell how upset she is, and despite the fact that there are two hundred people watching us it seems Emilee and I are alone in the room.

"Adam has been with his groomsmen most of the day," she says. "He isn't paying much attention to me. It's our wedding day."

Emilee's body is shaking with tension as she attempts to hold back her tears. "I'll take care of it," I assure her, and at the end of the dance I kiss my daughter and escort her to the edge of the dance floor. Then, I turn and walk over to Adam, standing by the head table chatting with his best man. Feeling angry and disappointed in Adam, I unapologetically lean into their conversation. "Hey guys, this isn't the bachelor party." I look at Adam and give him a strong directive. "And you need to be with your wife," I add, and walk away.

From that point on Adam and Emilee are together, moving from table to table, conversing with guests, dancing, and cutting their wedding cake. I can't help but wonder if anyone noticed how upset Emilee was during the father-daughter dance. Linda and I don't mention to others what was so obvious to us.

CHAPTER TWENTY-TWO • NOT WHAT WE IMAGINED

LINDA

For as long as I can remember my parents have hosted Thanksgiving, and the entire family makes the hour drive to attend. Emilee and Adam promise they're coming, and we're a little worried because they're late. The family is packed tightly around the kitchen table, enjoying the aroma of turkey and stuffing cooking in the oven, sipping wine and nibbling appetizers. Eventually, Emilee and Adam walk into the kitchen, looking stylish in their winter dress coats, yet I notice their faces look tired, and I feel the brisk, cold air follow them into the room. My punctual father pipes in a bit sarcastically, "Better late than never."

I don't hear what Adam says to my dad, but the words are sharp and not respectful. Adam turns on his heel and walks briskly into the family room. Emilee's face drains of color, and the rest of us sit dumbfounded. My father has obviously hit a nerve. I look at Emilee. She shifts her gaze shift to the kitchen floor as if she can't look at us. My mother gets up to baste the turkey. After a few minutes I go to the family room to speak with Adam, feeling sure I can calm him down. I want us to get on with the day. He is not receptive and doesn't want to talk about it. His shoulders sag, and he appears to be genuinely hurt. It seems almost as if he is pouting. I feel bad for everyone, especially for Emilee. I take my father aside. Together we go into the living room, away from everyone. "Dad, can you please apologize to Adam?"

"I didn't do anything wrong," he says, shaking his head.

"I know. But Adam's sensitive, and Emilee's upset." I sit on the couch and gesture for him to join me. "It's Thanksgiving," I remind him. "Can you apologize to him? For Emilee?"

My father does apologize, and we move forward. But it's obvious Adam is hurt.

A month later Jack and I host the family on Christmas Day, as is our tradition. It's a lovely day, nothing remarkable happens, but we sense the tension between Emilee and Adam. It seems almost as if they are going through the motions. After the holidays are over Emilee and I talk over the phone frequently, but we don't see much of the two of them. I miss having them around, but I understand they are still adjusting to living together as a married couple. I don't want to interfere, but I feel the need for some quality time with both of them in a relaxed atmosphere. A month after the holidays I invite Emilee and Adam over, just the four of us.

One Sunday afternoon Emilee, Adam, and Jack are talking about work when I set a pork tenderloin roast, mashed potatoes, gravy, and green beans on the dining room table. The food captures their attention, and we begin to fill our plates. Outside, the snow is beginning to accumulate on the trees and the ground. I think how beautiful and how peaceful this day is. During the meal I notice that Emilee is not eating much, but she is fussing over Adam a great deal, encouraging him to eat more. "Have more potatoes," she says, passing him the serving dish. "Do you want more meat?"

I've always loved to cook, and it's a pleasure to have Adam as a dinner guest, especially since he is always very complimentary of my culinary efforts. Emilee is an excellent cook, too, and I assume Adam is just as complimentary of her cooking. After glancing at Emilee's plate again, I look at Adam beside her and wonder if he notices how little Emilee has eaten. They are polite towards each other—a little too polite—and they don't look at each other in the same way, or joke around the way they did when they were dating.

After dinner Emilee and I slip past Jack and Adam, still drinking coffee at the dining room table, and walk down the hall to the master bedroom at the other end of the house. It is in this space that Emilee feels safe and open, and it is at this moment that Emilee finally lets down her guard and confesses to everything.

She tells me Adam has been criticizing her for years.

That he's critical of our entire family.

That she feels she can't do anything right.

She tells me that she has been restricting her calories for a long time.

And then she tells me one more thing.

"I've been using laxatives," she says.

I had a feeling this day was coming, but I'd hoped I was wrong. I've been worried about Emilee ever since the day we went shopping for her wedding gown. In the year leading up to the wedding I suspected Em has a problem, and Jack and I have read many books about eating disorders. We learn anorexia can lead to serious health conditions, and that the disease has the highest mortality rate of any mental illness, and that individuals with anorexia are much more likely to commit suicide.

"When did you start with laxatives?" I ask.

"My last year of pharmacy school," Emilee confesses.

She explains when she began the accelerated pharmacy program, and her relationship with Adam became a serious, long-distance one, she pushed herself to do it all. The more she tried to do, the more she had to juggle, the less she shared her feelings with me—or anyone.

I feel sick. I watched this happening, watched her isolating herself emotionally and disconnecting from her true self. I tried to keep our connection strong, but now I realize she had simply told me what she thought I wanted to hear.

"Does Adam know?" I ask.

Emilee nods. "He wants me to get help, and he means well, but he doesn't understand the pressure I feel from him. He's a perfectionist about everything little thing. I'm neat and organized about things, but he's over the top. Way over. I try so hard, but it seems I can't do anything right enough for him."

"I'm so glad you told me," I say in a calm voice. "You know I've been worried about you since the day we went shopping for your wedding gown."

Emilee nods her head.

"You're going to need professional help with the eating disorder. Adam, Jack, Matthew and I will need help too. We need to learn how best to support you," I say as I reach over and rub her back. "And you would both benefit from couples counseling."

A few minutes later we slip off the bed, and as I stand across from my daughter I notice her usually bright eyes have no sparkle. She looks so sad. Reaching my arms around her, I whisper in her ear, "It's going to be okay. I'm here for you. Your father and I are here for you. Let us help you."

JACK

In April of 2008, Emilee leaves Adam and comes home to sort things out. She moves into the guest room in our finished basement, the same room Adam stayed in while visiting. The room has two large windows, a double bed, bookshelves, television, and an adjacent powder room. Emilee adds her own touches and is pleased to have more space and privacy than her small bedroom would allow. Linda and I understand how hard it is for our fiercely independent daughter to ask for and accept help, and we do everything we can to help her feel a sense of control in her new space.

The three of us quickly fall into a routine. Emilee goes to work each day, comes home, and eats dinner with us. Later in the evening she goes downstairs to write, watch television, or talk on the phone. One afternoon, Emilee complains of severe stomach pain that won't subside. She's doubled over when we take her to the hospital emergency department. A nurse brings out a wheelchair for Emilee to sit in while we wait. Once there, Emilee asks us to call Adam and tell him she's at the hospital. I make the call, and a short time later Adam walks into the crowded emergency room. He spots us right away, and as he approaches we can see the concern in his eyes.

We wait for over an hour before Emilee is evaluated, and during that time her pain decreases. To help pass the time, I ask permission to change the television channel to the U.S. Open Golf Tournament. Tiger Woods is in contention. The four of us talk, and when there's a lull in the conversation Adam and I watch golf. When Emilee is eventually taken into an examination room Adam shares more of his concerns for Emilee with us, telling us he's frustrated with her reluctance to get treatment. "There were times when she felt she'd eaten too much, and she'd take an excessive amount of Senna," he says. "Then she'd spend half the night in the bathroom."

When we are allowed to join Emilee, we plead with her to tell the doctor that she has an eating disorder and ask for help. Emilee refuses, so the three of us tell the doctor. Emilee doesn't make eye contact with us as we share our concerns for her health with the physician.

"She's an adult," the doctor says with a shrug. "For better or for worse she has the right to make her own decisions, and there's nothing we can do without her approval." Turning his attention back to Emilee, he explains that her pain may be from gastroparesis and that people with anorexia often have problems with delayed gastric emptying.

Emilee promises the ER doctor that she'll follow up with Dr. Shay. We take her home with us, and Adam returns to his home. We're relieved Emilee is feeling better, yet we're frustrated with her unwillingness to seek help.

LINDA

In late June, Emilee and I sit by the pool under a large royal blue umbrella. The air is warm, and the sparkling blue water reflects the bright sunshine so much that we need sunglasses to protect our eyes. Matthew and Jack bring out a tray of drinks and snacks and set it on the table.

"I've been thinking," Emilee says, pouring iced tea into her glass. "Adam and I have been talking every day. I feel like I need to go back and try to work things out..."

"What?" Jack asks. "Are you sure?"

Matt shakes his head.

"We love each other," she insists. "And I've been doing better with my eating since I've been here." Emilee dips a chip into the salsa and puts it in her mouth to emphasize the point.

Matthew, Jack, and I look at each other. We don't know what to say, or what to think. Emilee is determined to make her marriage work, and by the end of June she's moved out of the guest room and back in with Adam.

CHAPTER TWENTY-THREE • THE FAMILY REUNION

JACK

Linda and I begin making plans to attend the 23rd Annual Family Reunion. In 1986 Linda's father, Carmen, and his siblings, began the reunion in an effort to keep the family connected after their father's passing. The reunion is held in different cities each year, on or around Independence Day. For one glorious weekend the entire family gathers to eat, drink, play games, and share memories. From the time Emilee and Matthew were young they've always looked forward to playing games, swimming, singing karaoke, and reconnecting with relatives from near and far, especially their cousins.

In 2008, the reunion is set to take place in Alfred, New York, a short drive from Rochester. Alfred is located in a peaceful area in Western New York, replete with sprawling farms and beautiful old homes. We are well acquainted with the area. Linda's Aunt Mary Lou and Uncle Tom met in Alfred during college and never left. Our children adore their Alfred cousins, and I think it will be good for Emilee to reconnect with them. Unfortunately, Emilee lets us know that she and Adam have to work late on Friday, meaning they will only be able to attend the reunion on Saturday. Linda and I are looking forward to seeing them, and we hope they can relax and enjoy the festivities.

"Whenever we drive to Alfred, I feel the stress of life melting away," Linda says on the way to the reunion, and I have to agree.

As per usual, on Friday night, after lots of hugs, we join the family at long tables centered around the traditional Friday night meal: salad, pizza, chicken wings, and a plethora of Italian cookies and desserts.

Shortly after noon on Saturday, someone announces Emilee and Adam have arrived. There is a commotion in the crowded kitchen as everyone waits to greet them. From across the room I see Adam, wearing a bright blue golf shirt, as he follows behind Emilee, stopping to greet people along the way. As they get closer to us I notice Emilee's smile seems forced, and Adam's manner appears guarded. The family knows Emilee had come home to live with us for a time and that she and Adam are now back together, trying to work things out. I imagine this makes them both a little uncomfortable.

After hugging us, Emilee pulls Linda and me aside. "It wasn't a good morning," she says in a whisper. She goes on to explain that she wanted to leave early that morning, but Adam had elected to sleep in. "I got a speeding ticket on the way here."

"Don't worry about the ticket," I say. "We're just glad you're here!"

A short while later we pose for a family picture, enjoy picnic food—hot dogs, hamburgers, salads, and refreshments—and participate in lots of relay races and games. Later that afternoon I realize I haven't seen Linda in a while, so I start looking for her. Finally, I spot her across the street, among a line of parked cars. I assume she's gone to retrieve something from our minivan, but as I approach I see she is talking with Emilee and Adam. They look uncomfortable. Adam's face is red, and the closer I get I can see tears in Emilee's eyes. The ground is sloped, and I feel like I'm standing in a hole as I look up at Adam.

"What's going on?" I ask, trying to find a more level spot to stand on.

Emilee turns to Adam and shouts, "You knew I wanted to leave early so I could spend time with everyone and enjoy the whole day! It's obvious you don't want to be here, and you're taking it out on me." She turns, begins to walk away, but comes right back. "I can't keep doing this! I'm walking on eggshells all the time!"

Adam is staring at the grass, shaking his head. Suddenly, he turns to me. "What did you do to your daughter?" he shouts. "Just get her help and bring her back to me when she's better."

Adam's words strike a nerve. I've always felt somewhat responsible for Emilee's eating disorder getting so out of control. Angrily, I step closer to him. "What have I done to her? You're her husband. You need to..."

Linda steps in between Adam and me. "Calm down!" she says firmly. "Both of you! Calm down!"

Instinctively she wraps one arm around Emilee's waist, pulling her close she adds, "Emilee has a disease and she needs support from all of us."

Turning on his heel Adam walks across the street, and Emilee follows. They pass a few family members who have been watching us from afar. Most of the family has no idea what has transpired, and that's the way it should stay. Later, after the big dinner, Emilee and Adam prepare to head home as planned. There are handshakes, hugs, and smiles from all the relatives, but it's not the day I had envisioned. Linda warmly embraces Emilee and Adam before they leave, but I can't bring myself to shake hands with Adam. There is an ever-present, uneasy feeling in my stomach when I kiss Emilee goodbye. "We are always here for you," I whisper into her ear.

On our way home after the reunion I think about what happened with Adam, if lashing out at me was his way of venting his own frustrations about the situation. I know he must feel powerless, too. It's terrible to see someone you love slowly starving themselves, and it's hard to understand. It sounds simple enough— just get the person to eat more. Problem solved. But anorexia and bulimia are diseases that illuminate the inability of an individual to deal with stress, anxiety, emotions, and life's transitions appropriately. Restricting calories calms the person, and helps them feel in control. Like any disease, anorexia is best treated best when caught early. Unfortunately, the longer the disease remains untreated, the more difficult it is for individuals to recover.

During a conversation after the reunion, Emilee tells us she thinks having a puppy might be good for her relationship with Adam. Linda and I have just adopted Abbie, a gentle, even-tempered Havanese, with whom Emilee's fallen in love. Based on her research Emilee decides a Havanese would also be a good fit for her and Adam, and hopes raising a puppy will bring them closer. She finds a breeder seeking homes for a litter of new pups. Emilee and Adam decide on Duncan, the smallest of the litter. Duncan has a soft, snow-white coat and one black spot on the tip of his right ear, his one distinguishing mark. Although Adam and Em both adore the puppy, "Dunc" develops an intense bond with Emilee. After a long day at work he meets Emilee at the door, wagging his tail furiously, barking and squealing with joy.

"Who's my best boy?" Emilee asks, scooping him up into her arms as he licks her face. Although Duncan is a love, he can be a little bit of a challenge; his temperament is different from Abbie's. He's protective of Emilee, and sometimes he's aggressive toward strangers.

As adorable as Duncan is, he isn't enough to keep Emilee and Adam together. Less than a year after their wedding, Emilee leaves Adam for the second time and comes back home to live with us. This time, she comes with Duncan in tow.

CHAPTER TWENTY-FOUR • A NEW PLACE WITH HER

PUPPY

JACK

On a warm September day, about a month after separating from Adam, Linda, Emilee and I walk the dogs on the Erie Canal path in Fairport. A few canoes and kayaks slowly drift along the still water. The path is bustling with cyclists, dogs, and their owners. Linda and I are happy to have Emilee home with us. She seems to enjoy being with us and likes spending more time with her brother. She looks healthier, too, having put on a little weight. She seems calmer and, frankly, Linda and I are appreciating the lack of drama in our lives.

"I've been thinking," Emilee says, glancing at us then out at the boats on the canal. "I think it's time for me to get my own place."

Linda and I are surprised she wants to get her own place so soon. It seems too fast.

"Are you sure?" I ask.

But Emilee's already decided.

A few weeks later, Emilee moves into a one-bedroom apartment in the same complex she and Adam lived in, twenty minutes from our home. On the day her furniture is delivered I bring my toolbox and serve as a handyman, setting up Duncan's crate in the laundry room, hooking up Emilee's television, and hanging her pictures and mirrors while she and Linda clean and place dishes in the cupboards.

For the first time in a long time, everything runs smoothly. Emilee likes her job, having her own place, and seems to be putting the past behind her. Linda and I adjust our schedules so one of us can drive over and let Duncan out and take him for a walk when Emilee works long days.

Linda and I have been attending counseling sessions with Kathe for a while now, and we encourage Emilee to meet with her, too. Kathe is highly regarded as a mental health counselor, and she's familiar with eating disorders. Emilee tells us she likes Kathe's warm personality, and she agrees to see her regularly while she continues to work with her primary care physician and her psychiatrist.

In October, Emilee decorates her apartment for Halloween and decides she wants to have a costume party. *The Wizard of Oz* has always been one of Emilee's favorite movies, and when we arrive she answers the door wearing a brown wig styled in pigtails, a blue and white gingham dress, ankle socks, and patent leather shoes. In her hand, she holds a basket with little Duncan inside. She looks just like Dorothy, and Duncan makes an adorable, albeit, white Toto. Emilee is a good host. She has prepared appetizers, orders pizza, and offers wine, beer, and soda to her guests. We have a fun night, and it's so good to see Emilee laughing and enjoying herself.

The winter holidays come and seem to set Emilee back a bit. She tells me she's lonely and shares that she's having trouble accepting the end of her marriage and managing her eating disorder. She asks if she can come home again.

"You can always come home," I tell her.

"I'm so sorry about all this. You knew it wouldn't work out, didn't you?"

"You have nothing to be sorry for," I tell her. "Adam just wasn't the right person for you."

Linda, John, and *Emilee* Mazur

CHAPTER TWENTY-FIVE • HONESTY AND GRATITUDE

LINDA

After the New Year Emilee hires movers, rents a storage unit for her furniture, and moves back home. She continues to meet with her doctor and her counselors and do what she needs to do to get well. I'm sure it's hard for her to admit she needed to come home again, but we're happy she's here, and that our grand-dog, Duncan, is here, too. At twenty-five years old, Matthew is working two jobs, living with us, and diligently saving money to get his own place. Once again, Jack's and my nest is full.

One wintery afternoon, Em and I chat non-stop as we prepare gnocchi for dinner. I knead the dough, roll it into long ropes, and Emilee deftly cuts the ropes into squares that resemble tiny pillows. Standing side by side, we still find comfort in the ritual of cooking together. I glance up from the flour-laden kitchen counter, look out the dining room window, and see snow coming down so hard it looks as if someone has shaken a snow globe. It's beautiful, but a little oppressive. *Spring can't arrive soon enough*, I think to myself.

"If you could go anywhere on vacation, where would you want to go?" Emilee asks out of the blue.

I smile at her as we place the gnocchi on cookie sheets. "I was just thinking about how cold it's been," I say. "I've heard Sanibel Island is a beautiful, peaceful place. I'd like to go there someday."

Emilee looks at me. Her eyes brighten.

"You and Dad have been so supportive and understanding," she says, rubbing the excess flour off her hands. "I want to do something nice for both of you, as a thank you."

"That's not necessary," I say. "We're happy to help. We love you."

Emilee shakes her head. "I already know what I'm going to do for Dad, and I want to take YOU to Sanibel!"

Four short weeks later Emilee and I are in Florida, zipping along the highway in a rented blue hatchback. I marvel as she calmly navigates her way through heavy traffic, on the expressways en route to Sanibel Island. The breeze from the open window blows on her face and through her hair, and she looks relaxed and free. She's wearing tortoiseshell sunglasses and a new outfit; her broken heart and her body are healing. The bright light from the sun helps me to see her through a different lens. Em made all the arrangements—flight, car, and hotel. We discuss the things we want to do once we arrive at our destination. I take a deep breath and let it out slowly. I hadn't realized how much stress I'd been carrying with me, and I'm so looking forward to this vacation with my daughter. Just the two of us.

Our hotel overlooks a picturesque bridge connecting us to Sanibel Island. Driving up the entrance to check-in we appreciate the beauty of lush greenery, palm trees, and bright tropical flowers. We admire expansive outdoor pools, artfully arranged teakwood tables, and the plethora of inviting lounge chairs beckoning us.

"I can't believe we're here!" I say to Emilee as we check-in.

Emilee is adamant about paying for nearly everything. Despite the fact she has a good-paying job and has always been a saver it's difficult for me to let her pay my way, but I sense it's important to her. I tell her how grateful I am, and insist that she allow me to handle the meals and all the extras. "That's my contribution—and that's final!" I laugh.

Together we book facials at the spa, swim, kayak, and enjoy fabulous meals. We're in awe as we drive around Sanibel. So much of the island is still in its natural state, home to many species of birds, wildlife, and unspoiled beaches. The island evokes serenity and beauty and lacks the commercialism of so many popular beach destinations.

After kayaking we walk along the beach, collecting seashells. At one point, I turn around and notice the temporary imprints our feet leave in the wet sand. I'm so relaxed, and I can tell Emilee is, too. We share stories with each other we've never shared before, and I feel our relationship and our lives are melding on a different, more adult level. I hope this wonderful feeling of connectedness won't be as fleeting as the footprints we leave behind.

One morning before a Sanibel biking excursion, Emilee realizes she's left her camera in the hotel room and heads back to retrieve it. I watch the elevator doors close. With only a few free minutes, I realize this will be the only opportunity I'll have to get her something from the gift shop. I want to buy Emilee something nice, something that will remind her of our time here. I want to surprise her with it, either at the end of the vacation or when we get home. I make a beeline into the gift shop and pick out a soft, pink, lightweight jacket that zips in the front. The word 'Sanibel' is embroidered on the front in red thread, and it looks like something Emilee would pick out for herself. I pull the money out of my purse, decline the clerk's offer of a bag, and fold the jacket as small as I can, stuffing it inside my purse. Immediately after leaving the gift shop, I see Emilee exiting the elevator.

At the bike shop, Em and I and pick out bikes with storage baskets hanging from the handlebars—perfect for beach-going tourists. I put our purses into my basket and Emilee fills hers with her camera, towels, snacks, and water. The weather was supposed to be warm, but within an hour clouds cover the sun, the temperature drops, breezes pick up, and it begins to rain softly. Emilee pedals her bike to the side of the path, and I follow. "I should have brought a jacket," she says, shivering.

I'm wearing a light sweater and am about to give it to her when I remember the jacket in my purse. "I have something for you," I tell her, reaching into the basket. "I wanted to surprise you with this, but you need it now." Emilee's eyes widen with surprise as I unfold the jacket and hand it to her.

"Oh, Mom!" Emilee beams, smiling and putting the jacket on. "It's perfect! You always know just what I need."

JACK

After Linda and Emilee return from Sanibel Island, Emilee surprises me with two tickets she bought for us to see an upcoming Eagles concert in Cleveland. She knows how much I like the Eagles and they're one of her favorite groups, too. She tells me it's her way of saying "thank you" for my love, my understanding, and my support.

The five-hour car ride to Cleveland flies by, and there are no lulls in the conversation as Emilee and I discuss the history of the band—from their beginning in the early '70s, to their break up in 1980, and their reunion 14 years later in 1994. As classic Eagles songs play we talk about the pharmacies we work in, the different types of people we see each day, and we laugh at how eerily similar our stories are.

After checking into our hotel, we go to a nearby restaurant for dinner. We peruse the menu over a glass of wine. Emilee orders salmon, and I order a burger. During our meal, Emilee tells me she hopes to travel to Hawaii to visit a friend from college. After her marriage is officially over, she mentions she's thinking about buying a house. "And I'm considering dating, too," she says with a smile.

"One step at a time," I tell her, placing my hand over hers.

We leave the restaurant, and walk briskly along city streets toward the arena. It's unseasonably warm for Cleveland in April, but we aren't complaining. Inside the stadium throngs of fans mill about buying souvenirs, and I buy commemorative t-shirts for both of us. We navigate to our seats, but we never use them. Once the concert begins, Emilee and I stand the entire time—singing, applauding, and cheering—until the end of the final song.

"What a fantastic concert!" I say, hoping for one more encore.

"I'm glad you liked it," Emilee says. "I loved it, too."

Back at the hotel, we're exhausted. It's been a long, wonderful day. As I lie down to go to sleep, I reflect on the day with my daughter. The smile on Emilee's face lit up the arena. I believe my daughter is back, and for that I am thankful.

Linda, John, and *Emilee* Mazur

CHAPTER TWENTY-SIX • A NEW BEGINNING

LINDA

There isn't a dull moment with four adults and two dogs living under the same roof. We all have different schedules, but somehow we manage to eat dinner together most evenings.

Meal planning is tricky, and I tread lightly. I purchase healthy foods and snacks, and tailor dinners around Emilee's tastes. We concentrate on her getting healthier and strong, and don't focus on a number. I hide our scales and remove the batteries, just in case. Sometimes Emilee and I take leisurely walks together after dinner, which I've learned may help diffuse post-meal anxiety for people with eating disorders. I can see Emilee is becoming more settled.

Emilee has casually mentioned wanting to buy a house of her own, and one rainy afternoon we stop by a small housing development being built near our house. We stop at the builder's office and ask for a guided tour of the model home. Emilee tells me she can visualize herself living in one of these homes—she's especially fond of the open layout of the ranch and the huge master bedroom.

Three days later, Emilee picks out a lot and puts down a deposit. It will be a few weeks before they dig the foundation and a few months before the house will be completed. There is so much to do it's a little overwhelming to me, but Emilee seems to enjoy picking out fixtures, lighting, flooring, and furniture. She is excited, and we're happy for her.

Throughout the difficult times Emilee and her friend Kelly remain close, and though Kelly is a busy mom they still find time to go out for dinner and go shopping now and then. Emilee makes a point of stopping by Kelly's home to spend some time with her young daughter, Caiden. Through a friend at work, Emilee meets and begins seeing a man named Jeff. "He's a nice person," she says. "You'll like him."

And we do.

Jeff has dark hair, a great smile, and an easy-going personality. We think his calm demeanor will be good for Emilee.

During this time, Emilee meets many new people who are also in transition; some are rebuilding their lives after divorces. We are encouraged by Emilee's resilience and her willingness to put herself out there socially.

JACK

In August 2009, Emilee's house is finished. A beautiful three-bedroom ranch, the house is light yellow with bright white trim and features large windows, allowing plenty of natural light inside. A door just off the kitchen leads to a stamped concrete patio surrounded by privacy panels, which creates a lovely outdoor space to relax or entertain. Emilee's is the only ranch-style home in a new thirteen-house cul-de-sac development on Nolan Circle, and she takes great pains decorating the house inside and out, planting holly bushes under the front window and flowers that bloom into the fall.

Linda and I could never have predicted that our daughter would build her house on the farmland just down the road from our home. The same location we drove past twenty-eight years earlier when we brought her home for the very first time. We share Emilee's excitement, and we're glad she's nearby.

***

My mother's health begins to deteriorate, and Linda and I decide to move her from her apartment, an hour-and-a-half away, to an independent living complex near our home. Grandma Grace helps Emilee a great deal after her break-up with Adam, offering her advice and words of wisdom. Grandma Grace is bold, but also kind and compassionate, especially when it comes to her only granddaughter. Though they share some of their conversations with me there are many I'm not privy to, and I sense Emilee's relationship with my mother is closer than it's ever been. Emilee appreciates her grandmother's encouragement and support, and the relationship provides my mother with a deep sense of purpose as well as an opportunity to share more of her own story with her granddaughter.

In October 2009, Linda calls me at work to tell me my mother has passed away. I had just spoken with her an hour before, on my drive to work. I feel a sadness I've never felt before, realizing both my parents are now gone. I arrive at my mother's apartment, and I'm comforted that Emilee and Matthew are already there with Linda. My mother's body is lying on her bed. The four of us stand beside her, the room is quiet, and we are still. I tell my mother I love her and gently kiss her on the cheek. Linda suggests we say some prayers, so we do. Suddenly, without reason or warning, several of my mother's perfume bottles topple over on her dresser. Emilee has always commented on her grandmother's perfume, noting that Grandma Grace always smells good, and the four of us agree—it's Grandma Grace sending us a message. If there is anyone my mother would have wanted to reach from the other side, it would be Emilee. We agree Emilee is supposed to take the bottles home with her. Em promises to keep them on her own dresser and use the contents sparingly. "They'll help me feel close to Grandma," she says through her tears.

I'm the last one to leave the apartment, and the air feels heavy as I say my last good-bye. Holding onto my mother's hand, I tell her I love her. Then I lean over and whisper in her ear, "We're going to need your help with Emilee."

* * *

JACK

Winter 2010 is especially cold, and the snowfall in Rochester measures 150 inches. I frequently shovel at our home, and also at Emilee's because her patio accumulates drifts that pile three to four feet high, leaving her no way to let Duncan out in the back yard. I shovel her front walkway as well. Early one morning I put on my red parka and walk the short distance to Emilee's house, cold snow crunching beneath my heavy boots. I clear a huge drift of snow away from her sliding door and shovel an area for Duncan. Emilee peeks her head outside and says, "It's okay, Dad. I can do it," but we both know it's too much for her, and I'm more than happy to help her.

A classmate from pharmacy school invites Emilee to come for a visit in Hawaii, and Emilee is thrilled to leave the snow and bitter cold behind to visit her friend. Linda and I are encouraged when we see Emilee reconnecting and branching out socially, but she isn't gaining weight and we're concerned. Though she's getting help from medical professionals and functioning well, we understand this disease is deeply ingrained in her and has been for years. With education and our own counseling, we realize recovery won't be a straight line. Realistically, we're looking at a long and rocky road.

Occasionally Emilee shares some aspects of her treatment with us, but overall she's adamant that we are not to be involved. She reminds us she's an adult and a medical professional herself, and she needs to handle things on her own. As hard as it is, Linda and I try to honor her wishes.

One spring day, as I'm cleaning up the front yard, I see Emilee and Duncan walking up our front sidewalk. I follow her inside, and the three of us settle in the family room. Emilee curls up on the loveseat with Duncan, and Linda sits next to me on the couch. After some small talk Emilee comments that her psychiatrist has prescribed diazepam, and says she's been taking it for the past few months to help quell her anxiety and help her sleep. She mentions the prescribed dose. Personally, I'm not comfortable with the long-term use of diazepam. Though it's widely used, I believe it's over-prescribed. I discuss this with Emilee, reminding her that she has the same knowledge that I do.

"It isn't helping anyway," Emilee says, pulling Duncan closer. "It makes me feel like I'm living in a fog, and I want to wean myself off of it."

I know from experience that coming off this particular class of drugs can be difficult. "You'll need to wean yourself slowly," I say. "And your psychiatrist needs to be involved."

"I know." Emilee nods. "I'll let him know, and I'll be careful," she promises.

***

Linda and I look forward to our monthly counseling appointments with Kathe. And while she cannot convey anything about her sessions with Emilee, she listens with compassion as we voice our concerns. Kathe encourages Emilee to meet with a women's group. She tells Emilee the participants have varied issues, that they share their struggles and successes, and support each other. Emilee participates in the group a few times, but she doesn't think it's helpful. "A lot of the women are older than I am," she says. "And none of them have an eating disorder. I'm not going to keep going."

We're disappointed, but there are no red flags to indicate Emilee is any worse than she's been. In fact, she seems to be doing well with her daily routine. Each workday morning, she drops Duncan off at our house. We're happy to help out with whatever she needs, but we don't hover. Whenever she's upset or has a problem, Emilee calls Linda or she comes to our house to talk. We listen, offer our support and encouragement, and are reassured that Emilee is receiving professional help.

LINDA

One night, I crawl into bed with a terrible migraine headache. I don't get them often, but when I do they wipe me out. I'm in bed early the following morning and hear the front door open and close. I know it's Emilee, dropping off Duncan on her way to work. Most mornings I'm usually roaming around the kitchen, making coffee and feeding the dog when Emilee arrives. Today, our bedroom curtains are still shut. I need a little extra time. I glance at the clock and notice a full glass of ginger ale Jack must have set on the nightstand during the night. Duncan barks briefly and I hear Emilee shush him, continuing to talk with her father in hushed tones. After a few minutes I hear Emilee's footsteps approaching from down the hallway, and a moment later the bedroom door opens.

"Mom?" Emilee whispers. "Are you okay?"

"I'm feeling better," I say, slowly sitting up in bed.

Emilee sits down next to me on the bed, the same bed in which I've comforted her so many times, and she comforts me this time and offers advice. She tells me I need to slow down, and says she's worried about me. Suddenly, Emilee springs off the bed and rushes to the window. "Look," she says, pushing the curtains aside. "The sun is shining!"

Emilee's energy always lifts my spirits, but this morning the bright sun hurts my eyes. I don't say anything. I look at my daughter with the sun on her face, and think how special she is to me. As I study her a bit closer, I notice her cheeks are flushed. I can't pinpoint anything specific, but I feel something isn't right. When I ask her if she is okay, she glances at her watch.

"Mom, promise you'll call if you need me to pick up something for you on my way home." She hugs me and dashes out the door.

A few minutes later Jack leaves for work, too. It isn't a workday for me, so I take my time getting into my morning routine, and I treat myself to a long, hot shower. While I'm drying my hair, the phone rings. The person on the other end of the line identifies herself as Emilee's supervisor.

"Emilee fell in the pharmacy and hit her head," she says. "We're waiting for an ambulance now."

Immediately I throw on my clothes, fly out the door, and call Jack on the way to the hospital. My heart races as worst-case scenarios rush through my mind. Dashing through the crowded emergency room, I find a security guard seated outside the unit. "My daughter was just brought in by ambulance," I say breathlessly. He hands me a nametag and a pink ticket, and I rush around the nurses' station until I find the right bay. I hesitate to pull back the curtain and think how ironic it is. I'd rushed to get to the hospital and now I stand frozen, afraid to open the curtain, not knowing the severity of Emilee's head injury or what caused her to fall. Somehow, I manage to move the curtain.

And then I see her: my daughter, lying in a hospital bed, her head wrapped in a blood-stained bandage. An IV bag is connected to her arm with a long plastic tube.

A doctor comes into the bay to ask questions, and Emilee groggily answers. She tells the doctor she's been weaning herself off of the diazepam she's been prescribed and asks for something for her throbbing head.

"It sounds like you had a seizure," the doctor says, examining Emilee's eyes with a lighted scope. "It may have been caused by coming off the diazepam too quickly. We're going to run some tests."

"Did Emilee tell you she struggles with anorexia?" I ask.

But Emilee hadn't mentioned it, and she shoots me an exasperated look. The doctor's calm demeanor helps Emilee feel comfortable to open up and share more details, and I stay out of the conversation. After finishing Emilee's exam, the doctor types her notes into the computer and tells us she's ordering a CT scan along with some other tests.

Emilee starts to say something to me but stops abruptly in mid-sentence. Suddenly there's a blank look on her face and, in an instant, her body tenses and her eyes roll back into her head. I watch helplessly as Emilee's whole body begins to shake violently. A weird foamy saliva bubbles out of her mouth. I jump out of my seat. "Do something!" I shout at the doctor. It's terrifying to watch my daughter's body convulsing so violently, and I feel utterly powerless.

The doctor responds calmly. Too calmly, it seems to me. "She's having a tonic-clonic seizure—what they used to call a Grand-mal seizure," she says. The doctor places her hand on Emilee's head. "It looks like she bit her tongue, too." While the doctor times the seizure, I stand next to the bed with my hand on Em's shoulder. The odd, arrhythmic pulsations of her body make my hand jump erratically.

Her seizure lasts nearly three minutes, which feels like an eternity to me. I wonder about the side-effects of seizures, how people survive them, and wonder if she'll ever be the same.

JACK

Test results reveal Emilee has a mild concussion. She's admitted to the hospital for a few days, and prescribed anticonvulsant medication. Emilee is told she won't be able to drive until it's determined the seizures are not due to epilepsy. After her discharge, Linda and I chauffeur Emilee everywhere she needs to go: the grocery store, physicians, and counseling appointments. She follows up with a neurologist, who determines she does not have epilepsy. It's determined the seizures were the result of coming off her medication too quickly.

When she's given the all-clear Emilee returns to work, but she feels self-conscious, thinking the staff knows too much about her personal life. "Everyone saw me have that seizure," she tells me. "I feel like I'm in a fishbowl all day long." She continues working but conducts a job search, and in April 2010 she accepts a position as Pharmacy Manager at Target, where she believes there will be more opportunity for growth.

Emilee enjoys working in her new environment and is quickly respected by her peers. She appreciates the fact that Target closes the pharmacy for thirty minutes so employees can enjoy lunch—an unusual practice. Unfortunately, most pharmacies remain open all day long without any scheduled breaks, and pharmacists must eat while they work. Emilee cares about her customers and takes pride in helping manage their medications. "I have more time to counsel people," she says. "And it's a more relaxed atmosphere. It's good for me."

From outward appearances, it seems Emilee is working towards recovery. When she isn't working, she spends time cultivating her flowers and cultivating new friendships, too. She hosts a few parties and even dates a little.

One October morning, Emilee calls and asks if she can attend church with us. Linda and I are, of course, thrilled. We believe Emilee is moving forward, and take her request to join us as another sign of progress. On the way home, we stop at a local diner for breakfast. The aroma of strong coffee and crisp bacon surrounds us. After the waitress takes our orders and pours coffee into our mugs, Emilee clears her throat. "I need more help with the eating disorder than is available in the Rochester area," she says.

Linda and I have always liked to believe that we know Emilee better than anyone. We know she loves puppies, well-organized kitchen cupboards, and lots of Heinz Ketchup on her hamburgers. We know she hates winter, rude people, dirty cars, and clutter. So we are completely blown away when Emilee tells us she's been keeping secrets and that she's been showing us only the parts of herself that she wants us to see.

"I've lost more weight, and I'm tired all the time," she says, taking slow sips of her coffee between sentences. "I've decided to go to Utah, to a facility where they have multiple levels of care for people with eating disorders."

Our eyes are fixed on our daughter sitting tall in the tan booth across from us. We listen to her firm and resolute tone of voice and her carefully chosen words. She tells us she's arranged to take a medical leave from work, and says she's excited about the philosophy of the center and the favorable reviews posted by patients. She goes on to say she's impressed with their community service program, in which eating disorder residents are allowed to assist children with disabilities as they learn to connect with horses and experience therapeutic riding. "I'll receive nutritional counseling, individualized therapy, group therapy, and art therapy," she says.

Linda reaches across the table for Emilee's hand. "It sounds like a great program."

"I need to do this," Emilee says with conviction. "I'm afraid of what's happening to me."

Finally, I think to myself.

Emilee

TOMORROW

(Fourth Grade Poetry Booklet)

Will tomorrow be the same?
What if you weren't there anymore?
What if I couldn't talk to you?
What if we couldn't share special secrets together, like sisters?
Could I live without you?
Does tomorrow have to happen?
I am happy with today and want to stay in the present.
I don't want to know what lies beyond the doors of tomorrow.

Emilee

PUZZLES

(After Emilee's Wells Graduation)

2003

As a child, I loved puzzles. I worked on them vehemently until the picture was complete, and my accomplishment was visible. The pieces always fit together perfectly; no matter how small the pieces or challenging the puzzle, there was always a solution.

The enigmatic part of our lives is that we do not know how all the pieces fit together. We may think we have every moment of every day planned so we can construct our future the way we want it. Yet, our lives are more challenging than any puzzle, as we try to fill the vacant spaces without the benefit of being able to see the image on the box.

Emilee
THE MARRIAGE

I insisted on getting married despite the reservations of those closest to me. I am not yet a parent, but I cannot imagine the difficulty in supporting something that sends up so many red flags, but supporting your child because you love them so much and want to let them live out their own adult life.

My father proudly walked me down the aisle on my wedding day. It didn't matter what happened next; he knew he'd be there to pick up the pieces if it all fell apart. My mother was radiant; she guided me and tried to do everything to make me happy. She asked me several times if this marriage was what I really wanted. My answer was always the same. The day was beautiful, the guests all so happy for me. From afar, it looked like the perfect wedding day: the sunshine, the gorgeous pictures, dresses, and flowers. The only problem was all the bride was hiding. The doubts chimed loudly in my head like a church bell echoing throughout the room.

Emilee
MOVING ON

I don't know what day I realized the dream was over. I loved Adam deeply and put years of love into our relationship. Adam loved me the best he could, but he didn't know how to let his guard down and let love in. I felt unwanted, lonely, and rejected. I lost all perception of what I wanted from life. I lost all sense of those around me. I wanted to make everything work; I wanted the marriage to work. I wanted someone to look up to me, need me, respect me, to be my friend, my soul mate, my lover. There was nothing I ever failed at so badly before. My life shattered around me like broken shards of glass. I couldn't just sweep them away with a broom. I had to pick up the pieces, one by one, and figure out how they fit back together. Little did I know, grabbing hold of each piece and trying to put my life back together was going to hurt like hell.

I was thin, pale, bald, and empty. I'd pulled every hair from my head, as a means of self-soothing. I did not eat well, or much, and I cringed if the scale fluctuated up. My mind was a chaotic racing of thoughts that zipped back and forth like children on a playground that never allowed me to rest. I was exhausted emotionally and physically and simply couldn't live that way anymore; it was going to kill me.

For the first time in years, I have defined my needs and feelings. I feel like I am at the bottom of the earth, but I've just taken the first step in finding happiness again. I must find myself again so I can feel whole. I must give myself time, not deadlines, to orchestrate this process. I must let myself have bad days and learn to lean on those who love me. I know I've made the right decision.

I'm leaving Adam. I'm going home.

Emilee
MY RECOVERY HOME

I ran around to open the passenger door to grab Duncan, my best buddy in the world. He was just a puppy but had a heart of gold, and all the unconditional love a dog can bestow. He needed me, and I needed him. He made me feel more important than what I had left behind. Gingerly, I walked up the front steps balancing dog, suitcase, and purse. I didn't ring the doorbell, as my arrival was no surprise. Opening the door, the warmth poured out, the dogs jumped at my feet, and my parents emerged with hugs abounding. There were no questions asked. No explanations needed. I took a deep breath and sobbed, needing to let out of me what I thought I could fix, all by myself, surrendering to the fact I couldn't do it on my own. I needed help.

The recovery home is filled with imperfect people. They have internal battles and ongoing struggles; they are human. The house is not immaculate. There are crumbs on the floor and dishes to be scoured. It does not come with a maid or servants. It is a regular, charming, well-decorated home that accommodates almost all situations with ease.

Imagine a room filled with loving, caring, non-judgmental, and sincere people. Envision abounding generosity, warm spaces, the smell of chicken French, and the fluffiest mashed potatoes. Place yourself somewhere where the couches are always comfy, and the best cup of coffee is at a second's pour.

At the recovery home, dogs greet me at the door, exhilarated by my presence, as if they have been waiting all day just to see me. The dogs are not fancy dogs; they are ordinary dogs who fetch in the backyard, chase their own tails, and know how to dig a good hole if they catch the scent of something.

The first morning in the recovery house, I awake to the smell of freshly brewed coffee. For the first time in a long time, I feel peace within me. I'm surrounded by people who love me, people who believe I have the ability to get myself back on track. I tell myself I will do it, and there is no other option.

Here in the recovery home, I am surrounded by food because the people who live here eat all throughout the day. This is a new concept for me, as I don't remember eating this way since my high school days. I'm not afraid of becoming fat, but I am afraid of losing control of the only thing I have been able to control for so many years.

In the recovery home, I am beginning to face my fears and conquer parts of me that I have lost control over. Each day I grow stronger. I take pride in my appearance, and I am beginning to love my body for its womanly shape. My eating disorder behaviors have distracted me from reality.

Emilee
MY HOPELESS HOLIDAYS

I got up Christmas Eve morning and told myself I could do it. I bought and wrapped Christmas gifts that were ready to go. By 3 o'clock I was back in bed, refusing to move. I didn't want to show up. I just wanted to sleep through the holidays. I tried to sleep, but I felt too guilty. I couldn't disappoint my family.

I thought about Adam and the previous Christmas holidays we'd shared, and I felt sad. I missed the good times in my marriage, but then I remembered all the pain and the work it took to keep it afloat. There is no one else but me this year. I didn't think I mattered.

At my aunt's house, I wore a huge smile. I was still grieving but told them all I was great. I didn't want anyone to feel sorry for me. I wanted to be the life of the party; witty, loving, and talkative, like I always was. I put on a show because I thought that was the best thing to do. Inside I was crying.

Emilee
BUILDING MY OWN LIFE

Starting my life over again and building my new home have many striking parallels. Digging deep is necessary to build a strong foundation. I must pour my heart and soul into giving myself another chance as cement is poured— creating a basement. Once this is done, I set my goals and define my desires, while the wooden beams are erected on the foundation, and the house is framed. The next step is a difficult one, as I have to protect myself from the harshness of the outside world, to be able to stand in the face of a storm as the house is wrapped with insulation and covered with siding. I must also learn to let the beauty of the world in, and not isolate. Large windows and skylights are installed to let natural light inside.

Once the house is framed and protected, I must give myself channels to vent, find friends to rely on, and discover what sparks ignite my spirit. In the house, plumbing pipes are laid, and electrical wiring is connected, turning what was an empty box into a functional home. My life must be filled with the essential, too, and just as the builder must follow codes and town restrictions, I must decide what amenities I desire, what indulgences I deserve and are within my budget.

Sitting on my new patio, the weather is pristine, the air warm and dry, the blue sky filled with sunshine. I slow down enough to breathe in the beauty of a fresh breeze and listen to the birds singing. My world is so much bigger now. I no longer feel a dark tunnel surrounding me, yet an enormous void remains, setting up loneliness that I have never experienced before. I know I have to be lonely for a while. It is part of the rebuilding process, but I long for something. I am surrounded by family and friends, hugs and handshakes aplenty, but I want to be held again. I long for human touch, and I long for a lover's hand to caress my ivory skin.

Emilee
Angry Days

Sometimes I get so down on myself for what has happened that I just want to punch a hole in a wall or scream so loud the sound can be heard for miles. I hate that I let myself get so thin and that I didn't take care of myself. I hate the sun for shining and food for tasting good. I hate the "I feel bad for her look" I get from people. The angry days do not come often, but when they come, they come with a vengeance. On those days, I don't want to be touched, held, talked to, or consoled. They smother me so I can't breathe. Those are the days that suck the life and soul out of me.

Emilee

(Written before leaving for treatment in Utah)

Before coming to the recovery home, I couldn't imagine being able to think about anything without thinking about food, working out, and staying thin. This gave me something to do, something to focus on. I found it hard for food to be so rewarding, yet so stressful for me. I've deprived myself of the essential things that my body has needed for years. I did gain weight but still felt defeated once I ate. I tried to hold out as long as possible, but coffee drinks and cans of energy drinks only held me for so long. I hated having to eat. It was such a battle for me. I couldn't let go of the scale and the number. I couldn't feel my body and not look in the mirror. I was taking an excessive amount of laxatives each day. What would ever possess me to put so many chemicals into my body? Not just any chemicals, but ones that purged me of all the nutrition and water my body needed. I remember the day I threw my laxatives away. I was done. I knew I might die. I was miserable, unhappy, and thin as hell. I was at my lowest weight since sixth grade, and honestly I don't know how I functioned. I had to face reality. I needed help. It was my only chance for a second chance at life.

Emilee

HOPE

(Emilee's Fourth Grade Poetry Booklet)

I sat alone, with no one around to hear me.
I wanted to cry,
For someone to talk to.
Someone to share my problems and thoughts with.
Then HOPE opened my soul,
And talked to me with a heart of gold,
Open to all of my thought and feelings.
She knew everything to do,
She made the day brighter.
And gave me the greatest sense of me.

Funny Faces

My Little Helper

With George-O

The Night Before Christmas

Napping with Dad

First Day of School

Linda, John, and *Emilee* Mazur

First Violin Concert

Em with Grandma Grace

Em with Grandpa Carmen, Grandma Dorothy, and Matt

Cape May

Family Reunion

Family Reunion

High School Graduation Picture

Linda, John, and *Emilee* Mazur

Kelly's Wedding

Emilee's Graduation from Wells College

Local Family Support

Em with Duncan, Abbie, and Gracie

Linda, John, and *Emilee* Mazur

CHAPTER TWENTY-SEVEN • DEVASTATING

LINDA

The day before Emilee leaves for treatment, she calls and asks if I will come by and keep her company while she packs. She's in her bedroom when I arrive, perched on the edge of her bed, her half-filled suitcase beside her. Two piles of clothing are neatly stacked next to the suitcase. She's organized and prepared.

After her bag is packed Emilee shows me the bills that will need to be paid, and she hands me her checkbook. I'm amazed by how much money she's managed to save up at just twenty-nine years old, and I tell her so.

"I've saved every penny I could," Emilee says. "I had the feeling I'd need the money someday."

Em's always been cautious when it comes to spending money, but her savings and her words surprise me. I have to imagine she's been living in fear of the disease and what it might take from her, and now I wonder if her eating disorder has even more of a hold on her than we know.

I hand Emilee a journal I've purchased for her. She thumbs through a few of the pages with inspirational quotes on them and tucks the journal inside her suitcase.

"It was hard to tell everyone I have an eating disorder," she says. "And that I'm going away for treatment."

I nod. "I can't imagine how hard this is."

But in a way, I can. Because loving someone who is struggling with an eating disorder is hard, too.

JACK

Emilee calls from Utah to let us know she's arrived safely. She tells us she won't be allowed much contact with family, and there are specific times she's allowed to call. "They want us to take a break from the outside world," she says. We learn from Emilee that patients' belongings are searched for anything that could trigger or cause harm for someone with an eating disorder—fashion magazines, razors, certain books, revealing clothing, and manicure kits. These types of items are routinely taken away and returned at the end of treatment. Emilee reports she's been examined by a physician, and has been assigned a room in the in-patient unit where she'll remain until she's deemed medically stable. When she calls a few days later Emilee tells us she's meeting people, some of whom are so weak they can't walk and need to be pushed in wheelchairs. "I don't want to get to that point," she says. "It's hard to eat the amount of food they want me to eat, but I'm managing."

Later that week, Linda and I are getting ready for bed when the phone rings. It's Emilee. Her voice is shaky, and she's been crying. "My insurance company says I have to leave," she says.

I can't believe what I'm hearing. "You've only been there a few days!" I say, looking at Linda. "There must be some kind of mistake."

But it isn't a mistake.

After only six days in Utah, Emilee's insurance company determines she's well enough to return home. Emilee stays three extra days while the treatment center fights to get her insurance company to resume paying for treatment. We call the insurance company and the center, but because we are not on our adult daughter's HIPAA form, no one will talk to us.

On October 23, 2010, just ten days after her arrival, Emilee is discharged and sent back to Rochester.

LINDA

While driving Emilee home from the airport, Jack and I listen sympathetically as Emilee tearfully shares her experience with us. She sits in the middle of the backseat, her shoulders rounded forward, her purse on her lap. Jack drives and I sit in the passenger seat, my body twisted toward hers, and we hang on her every word. It's obvious she needs to vent.

"When I got there, everything was a mess! My ECG was off, my liver function, kidney function, and blood tests were all abnormal. After gaining two pounds, the insurance company decided to stop paying for treatment because my Body Mass Index had reached 75% of what is considered 'low normal'." Emilee reaches into her purse for a tissue and wipes her nose. "I guess I'm not sick enough."

"Why didn't you let us talk to them?" I ask.

"It wouldn't have helped. The medical director tried. I know how sick I am. I have good insurance, and they won't help me. Treatment costs $30,000 for a month. Who can afford that? What's the point of having insurance?" Emilee twists the tissue in her hands. "I'm so embarrassed! I'm sorry I even went!"

We can't believe what we're hearing. Before Emilee left, she told us she was open to learning healthier coping mechanisms and said she was proud of herself for making the decision to seek intensive help on her own. This was a huge step. Jack and I know those few days of treatment do not even begin to address the emotions, attitudes, and behaviors behind an eating disorder. People need to be treated before they're so sick and weak that they have to be in wheelchairs or have heart or kidney damage. And they need ongoing, comprehensive care afterward. Jack and I have learned about "re-feeding syndrome", a serious electrolyte disturbance that can occur as a result of the reinstitution of nutrition to patients who are severely malnourished or metabolically stressed due to severe illness. In other words, introducing food to someone with anorexia without adequate medical care and supervision can actually be fatal.

Though the facility in Utah recommends Emilee attend a particular outpatient program in Rochester, it turns out Emilee's insurance will not pay for that program either. We tell Emilee that we will help her with the cost, but she won't let us pay and chooses not to participate. Emilee's determination to do everything herself, combined with the HIPAA privacy laws, prevents Jack and me from being part of her treatment team. And while we continue to give Emilee love and support, we are quickly becoming disillusioned by the entire system.

JACK

After returning from Utah Emilee immediately returns to work, acting as if nothing has happened. She continues to follow up with regular doctor appointments, lab work, and counseling. However, as the winter months have passed and spring finally arrives, Linda and I notice Emilee is thinner and more anxious. Now when she stops at our house after work to pick up Duncan she stands in the doorway, refusing to come in even for a couple of minutes to talk. "I just want to get home," she says.

One cool April evening, Linda and I stand on our front porch and watch Emilee drive away in her black Jetta. "I'm worried," I say. "I don't know what's going on, but she's acting strange."

"I think work is taking all her energy, and the eating disorder is taking over everything else," Linda says, running her hands through her hair. "When I was at her house yesterday, I couldn't help but notice how little she had in her refrigerator: orange juice, Ensure, diet ginger ale, an apple, a bottle of chardonnay... and one frozen dinner."

I pause. "Do you think she eats any of the food you give her?"

"Who knows?" Linda says. "I've seen remnants of the food I've made in Duncan's dish. If she does eat it, she probably takes laxatives afterward."

I'm worried about my daughter, whose condition is rapidly deteriorating, and I'm angry, too.

Angry that her insurance company sent her home from Utah after just ten days.

Angry that her insurance company refused to cover the recommended treatment at the out-patient eating disorder center in Rochester.

I'm also angry because a diagnosis of anorexia is taken far too lightly. I have to believe there would be better treatment and more empathy for people who suffer with this disease if medical professionals, insurance companies, and the general population understood more about eating disorders. If Emilee had cancer, her insurance company would never have discontinued her treatment after just days. Yet, according to the National Eating Disorder Association, the mortality rate associated with anorexia is twelve times higher than the death rate of all other causes of death for females, ages 15-24 years old.

LINDA

As I load my carry-on bag in the back of our Highlander, I look up and see a cloudless blue sky. I smell the lilacs filling the morning air and hear the birds are singing in the trees. The temperature is forecasted to climb into the low 70s this day in May. It feels warm already; the outlook for the week is great, but we won't be in town enjoy it. During the dark days of winter, Jack and I made plans to visit some of his elderly relatives for a few days in Pensacola, Florida. The two of us haven't been away together in a long time. Jack feels confident that everything will be okay while we're away, but with the new developments with Emilee I have the foreboding feeling we shouldn't be going.

During our layover in the Atlanta airport, we receive a call from Emilee. She tells us she has taken herself out of work because she's too weak to continue. Jack and I both speak with her and encourage her to seek a higher level of care. I tell her I'll fly home, but she assures me she'll be okay. She says she has an appointment with her doctor and promises she'll reach out to local family. I hang up the phone feeling extremely unsettled, and then I notice everyone is standing around the airport televisions, watching a breaking news bulletin. We learn there's been a serious tornado in Joplin, Oklahoma. Houses have been ripped apart, cars overturned, wreckage and debris everywhere. Entire communities have been destroyed. Viewing the aftermath of the tornado my stomach is queasy, and I feel a deep sadness for the suffering people I see on the screen. I recall watching news reports over the years, depicting the devastation of natural disasters. They ravage the people as well as the land. While these images evoke empathy, compassion, and assistance, I can't help but think there are other terrible life events, like the suffering that Emilee and others like her are enduring, that is invisible and imperceptible to the outside world.

I want to go home, right this minute. *We have our own storm brewing,* I think to myself. From the moment Emilee returned from Utah, she's been putting off what she needs to do to get well. Angry and embarrassed, she refuses to talk about it and has remained adamant about not letting us participate in family counseling with her, or be privy to her medical care. Her arms and legs are rail-thin, and she is beginning to isolate herself more and more. It's almost as if she's putting up a wall, to close her in and protect her from her feelings from the outside world, and from dealing with the eating disorder. Yet the mortar that's cementing each brick together— keeping her isolated and sick—is the eating disorder itself.

The entire time we're away, I'm consumed with worry about Emilee. Jack's aunt, uncle, and cousins are gracious, and we have a nice time with them, but my heart is home and it's torture for me to stay. Emilee repeatedly assures me she's all right, and I feel encouraged that she's reached out to the family at home, her counselors, and a few friends. We talk every day, sometimes multiple times.

CHAPTER TWENTY-EIGHT • UNBELIEVABLE

LINDA

The first thing Jack and I do when we get back to Rochester is stop at Emilee's. She answers the door and is quick to embrace us, but her face is gaunt and she looks disheveled in her pajama pants, baggy gray sweatshirt, and a baseball cap. The three of us sit in her living room and talk. She complains that she's cold all the time, opens up about how exhausted she is, and says that the last few months work has been such a struggle for her. We ask her what we can do to help, and ask if she's worked out a plan with her eating disorder therapist, Hanna, and Kathe, her counselor. She assures us she'll be seeing them both, along with Dr. Shay, later in the week.

"Em, you're so small. I'm afraid," I say, knowing she won't appreciate my honesty. "Are you able to eat at all?"

"I've been drinking Ensure," she says.

"I think we should take you to the hospital," Jack says.

"I'm not going to the hospital!" Emilee says, sitting up straighter.

I fuss around in Emilee's tidy kitchen and make her an egg and toast. She picks at the food, eventually eating most of it.

Jack and I can't bring ourselves to leave, and Emilee refuses to come to our house, so I decide to sleep on the sofa adjacent to Emilee's bedroom while Jack sleeps in the twin bed in the guest room, just down the hall. Neither of us sleeps well, tossing and turning all night.

The next day Emilee is admitted to the hospital for a heart irregularity, severe dehydration, and electrolyte imbalances. There is no denying the eating disorder has taken control of her body and her life. During Emilee's hospitalization we are at her bedside every day, listening as physicians, residents, nurses, and psychiatrists evaluate and attend to her. She wants us there, but she refuses to give permission to her medical team to relay information to us on her behalf. After an evaluation, Emilee is considered competent to make her own medical decisions.

Because we aren't sure Emilee is telling the medical team the whole truth about her condition Jack and I make a point to speak with them privately, to help them get a truer picture of what is happening to our daughter. And though they can't legally speak about Emilee's case, they can listen to us. I give them her counselor and eating disorder therapists' contact information. We hope that, together, they can get Emilee stabilized and into an inpatient program, as well as getting the vital comprehensive care we know she needs.

After Emilee is discharged from the hospital her counselor, therapist, and doctor aggressively work on finding her a place to go for inpatient treatment. It takes many phone calls and a great deal of time to obtain insurance approval. Meanwhile, Emilee is going stir crazy at home without anything constructive to do. "I can't turn my mind off, and I can't sleep," she says, pacing the floor. Insomnia has been a problem for her in the past, but now it is extreme and debilitating. To make matters worse, as the days drag by Emilee no longer seems to be on board with going to inpatient treatment. I make a phone call to Kathe, and ask if the three of us can have a session with her.

Kathe's office feels more like a living room than an office. Soft music plays in the background, and a large window across from a tweed couch offers us a view of a wide array of colorful birds tapping at assorted birdfeeders. An unusual variety of green potted plants form a collection on the floor under the window. Simple shells, interesting rocks, and books add to the room's charm. Although each one of us has been here many times before, on this day Kathe's office feels especially welcoming. Emilee sits down first, in the center of the large beige couch, and Jack and I sit on either side of her. Kathe settles in a black leather chair across from us, dressed in a long flowing skirt and light brown blouse that, I think, flatters her wavy red hair. Emilee seems nervous at first but Kathe's demeanor, always peaceful and calm, helps her to settle in. Within minutes Emilee tells Kathe all about her increased anxiety, her anorexia, the ten days she spent in the hospital, and about the insomnia she's experiencing. During this meeting, Emilee also admits to drinking a few glasses of wine in the evening.

Jack and I knew Emilee had wine in her house, but we hadn't thought much about it. "At your weight and with the medications you're on, you shouldn't be drinking wine," Jack says. "And certainly no more than a glass."

"We love you, and we're afraid what might happen to you if you don't get help," I chime in.

Kathie listens to each of us and tells Emilee how pleased she is that she's come to the appointment, and that it is most beneficial we're all here together, as a family. "I, too, am concerned about what will happen to you if you don't get the help you need," Kathe says. Leaning forward, she takes one of Emilee's hands in her own. "I've found a place for you to go."

Emilee looks up at Kathe. "Where?"

"An in-patient behavioral facility in Philadelphia," she says. "If alcohol is an issue, it can begin to be addressed there, too. They're equipped to handle co-occurring disorders."

Emilee closes her eyes and takes a deep breath.

LINDA

The day Emilee is scheduled to leave for Philadelphia, Matthew drives over to accompany us to the airport. I lock the door, and Matthew and I start walking towards the driveway. When I look back I see Emilee standing still on the front porch, with her hand on the doorknob.

"I don't think I can do this," she says, shaking her head.

I'm surprised by her comment, and I'm not quite sure what to say. I try reasoning with her, but she refuses to move. The clock is ticking, and I feel intense pressure to get to the airport. Finally, I enlist Matthew's help. "Can you help me get her into the car?" I ask him as I pick up Emilee's carry-on.

Matthew is amazing. He knows just what to do, remaining calm even when Emilee is resistant. At one point, Matthew almost has to carry his sister. "You can do this, Em," he says, opening the front door on the passenger side.

Seeing the two of them interact in this way is a strange inversion. I'm reminded of all the times Emilee helped her little brother, calmly reassuring him that things would be okay, whether it was feeding the animals at the petting zoo, going on amusement park rides, or taking the school bus for the first time. Before we even leave the driveway, Emilee reiterates her reservations about treatment. Matthew and I repeatedly reassure her and, eventually, she sits back in her seat.

I drive to the airport and take note of the green lawns, colorful flowers, and leafy maple trees. "It's a beautiful day to fly," I say with a smile, trying to keep things light. On the expressway, I check the time on the dashboard clock. *We're doing fine*, I think to myself, breathing a sigh of relief. Though I'm sure we're doing the right thing to help our daughter, I wish we had in-patient treatment closer to home. It would make it so much easier.

As I drive I can't help but notice how restless Emilee is, changing radio stations and squirming in the passenger seat. At one point I assume she is readjusting her seatbelt, but a second later I hear a clicking sound and realize Emilee has unfastened her seatbelt and is reaching for the car door.

"I can't do it!" she shouts, pulling the door handle. "I'm not going!"

Suddenly the roaring sound of tires spinning beneath us is amplified, and a gust of air rushes through the car. My eyes dart back and forth from the road to Emilee, and I'm instantly aware of how fast I'm going. Emilee leans forward, towards the door. I scream, instinctively reaching my arm across her body as the car veers toward the shoulder of the road. Matthew lunges from the backseat, grabbing his sister's arm with his left hand in an effort to prevent her from jumping out of the vehicle, while two lanes traffic race past. Matthew stretches his right arm toward the door handle. Somehow, by the Grace of God, he manages to pull the door closed and I regain control of the car. Holding onto the steering wheel tightly I steer the car back onto the highway, avoiding the vehicles around us. For the remainder of the trip, Matthew keeps one arm around his sister's shoulder, restraining her.

We arrive at the airport, visibly shaken. Matthew calls his father to let him know what has happened, and I'm not surprised that Jack is leaving work immediately to meet us at the airport. Matthew and I walk on either side of Emilee as we make our way toward the airport terminal, reassuring her the whole way. Once inside, the three of us stand at the ticket counter, waiting for an attendant to check her bag.

"I need to use the bathroom," Em says suddenly, and begins walking toward the restroom.

"Wait!" I call, thinking she might run out of the airport and try to hail a taxi. "I need to use the restroom, too." I fall into step behind her, feeling sad that I can't trust her, and at the same time feeling even sadder that she is losing trust in me. My daughter hasn't been herself for a long time, and I'm trying so hard to do the right thing. Inside the bathroom I check my watch, hoping Jack will arrive soon. Emilee is in the stall for a long time, and it becomes evident she's taken an excessive amount of laxative. She makes a terrible mess and, privately, I'm thankful we're alone in the bathroom.

While standing in front of the sink washing her hands, I notice Emilee's blouse looks odd. Lumpy even. "What's in your shirt?" I ask. My daughter shoots me a look and turns away. "Come here," I command in a voice I don't recognize as my own. Moving closer, I detect the smell of alcohol on Emilee's breath. The two of us wrestle for a minute and end up against a mirrored wall. I cannot believe it has come to this. I'm not proud of this moment but it speaks to how afraid I am, how desperate I am for Emilee to get help, and how desperately Emilee needs help. With my body pressed against hers it's obvious something is there, underneath her shirt, something hard. Though she tries to pull away from my grasp I hold her in place and reach inside her top, inside her bra, and retrieve a miniature size bottle of rum. At that precise moment a woman walks into the bathroom, and I close my hand around the bottle to conceal it. I make small talk with Emilee while the woman applies lipstick and combs her hair. "I can't believe this!" I say as soon as the woman leaves. "What else do you have in there?" Emilee lowers her head and reaches into her bra, revealing three more tiny bottles of liquor and a baggie filled with laxatives. "What are you thinking?" I ask, hardly able to believe this is happening.

I'm angry with her for what she's putting us through, but I also understand why Emilee is so terrified to start treatment. Emilee has told me patients in treatment are expected to eat at least 2,500 to 3,500 calories a day, and that it is extremely difficult—emotionally and physically. I think about how different everything is compared to last fall when she chose to go to Utah and was willing to do the work. This time she's essentially being told she has to go. For someone as independent as Emilee, the lack of input seems to offend her sense of independence. She's not the same Emilee—the disease is consuming her, and she's depressed, unhappy, and ashamed. To complicate things further, she's numbing her feelings with alcohol. I think she's lost hope, and I suspect she doesn't think she's capable of enduring treatment and achieving recovery.

When we exit the ladies' room Jack and Matthew are standing together, waiting for us. "I got here as soon as I could," he says. Jack hugs Emilee and me and asks if we're okay.

I explain what happened in the ladies' room, and turn to Emilee. "You can't fly alone," I say. "I'm going with you." Emilee doesn't argue with me. In fact, I sense part of her is grateful I'll be with her. Luckily there are seats available, and I'll be sure she gets there safely.

During the flight, Emilee and I sit next to each other in the rear of the plane. I take a breath and feel relieved we're on our way. Emilee doesn't seem angry anymore, and we talk about things we'll do when she gets home. Eventually the flight attendant comes around, offering snacks and beverages. Emilee flashes me a wry smile, then looks up at the flight attendant and says, "I'll have a Bloody Mary, please."

JACK

During the next two weeks, I rest easier knowing Emilee is safe and receiving treatment. Even though Linda and I miss her terribly, the break gives us some peace. While Em is in Philadelphia Linda, Matthew, and I attend the Fourth of July Family Reunion, which is held in Virginia this time. At one point all sixty-five of us stand outside, holding hands and praying for Emilee.

But one week later, just two weeks into treatment, Emilee calls and tells us her time at the Philadelphia treatment center is being cut short. "It's happening again," she says, which is to say her insurance company has once again denied paying for further treatment. "I'll be home on Thursday," she announces matter-of-factly. She doesn't seem upset this time.

Emilee's first day back home is sunny and warm, with a subtle breeze that stirs every now and then. Emilee has agreed to stay with us for a while and, as it's the right weather for a cookout, and we extend a dinner invitation to Matthew, who has recently moved into his own apartment. Linda prepares some of the food ahead of time and is setting the table when Matthew arrives. Waiting on the deck for the gas grill to heat up my family joins me, and together we catch up on everything. Duncan curls up in Emilee's lap, and they both seem quite content.

"How did it go in Philadelphia?" I ask, though we've surmised from our phone conversations she'd found being there difficult. She tells us they had to eat six times a day, and complains, "There was no privacy. An aide watched me at all times... even when I showered."

"Why?" I ask.

"To make sure I didn't inflate my weight by swallowing a lot of water. And to make sure I didn't throw up," she says. "And when I used the toilet, I had to leave the door open while an aide stood outside to make sure I wasn't purging." Emilee moves her chair into the sunlight. She pulls Duncan close and speaks to us while looking into her dog's eyes. "It was a waste of time. It was like a prison."

While I understand Emilee's feelings about what must have felt like an uncomfortable level of surveillance, I can also see how that level of observation would be necessary for patients whose destructive behaviors have become habitual.

"Why won't you let us pay for in-patient?" I ask. "Mom and I want to help you. There's nothing more important to us than you and Matthew."

"I won't let you pay," she says, stubbornly. "My insurance should pay."

"Come on, Em!" I plead.

"And I'll tell you something else. I'm not going back to Kathe anymore either—she sent me to Philadelphia."

Linda tilts her head. I can tell she's concerned. "What about the alcohol problem?" she asks.

"I don't have an alcohol problem," Emilee insists, stroking Duncan's white coat.

There isn't a cloud in the sky, but suddenly I feel strangely cold. I see Linda's shoulders sag, and I notice Matthew shaking his head. I think to myself, *Emilee's not taking this seriously enough. I've read it takes months and sometimes years of comprehensive treatment to adequately nourish the brain of someone with an eating disorder—before they can learn new behaviors. And I don't know what to think about the alcohol issue.*

She stays at our place but only for a couple of days, insisting she'll sleep better at home. We can't force her to stay with us.

Soon after, Emilee is admitted to the hospital again via the emergency room, where she is treated for dehydration, an electrolyte imbalance, and a high blood alcohol level. Now Linda and I recognize the pattern and anticipate the outcome. This time, Emilee remains in the hospital for five days. While she is hospitalized we are there every day, pleading with the medical staff for help and comprehensive care. We are told she is an adult who has the capacity to make her own decisions. We're told nothing more can be done until she asks for help. As her father, I feel powerless and begin to have doubts about our medical system. Once again, Emilee is stabilized and discharged. When she gets home she eats almost nothing, and because she weighs so little the volume of wine she consumes increases to dangerous levels. Though we check on her many times each day, it is clear our daughter is on a path of self-destruction.

Linda and I try everything we can think of to help her snap out of this stupor, even calling 211, the mental health helpline, as Kathe advises us to do. The crisis counselor at the health line listens as Linda explains the situation. It's determined Emilee will need an evaluation with a caseworker and that she will need to be told about the appointment ahead of time. We agree to inform Emilee and set up the appointment for the first slot available.

A few days later a caseworker arrives at Emilee's house, but because Emilee is able to anticipate the visit she is sober. Her house is tidy, she is dressed well, and her bills are paid. Without anything remarkable to see, nothing comes of the visit. We know Emilee is just pretending to be well, and we're certain she won't be able to maintain the charade, but as long as she can muster up enough energy to pretend she isn't sick we're unable to get her the help she needs.

After the caseworker leaves, Emilee shouts at her mother and me. "I want you both to leave!" She feels she's been manipulated—forced by Kathe to agree for treatment she didn't want and forced by us to endure an uncomfortable level of intrusion into her personal life.

We give her space. After a few days, I stop at her house on the way home from work. Emilee is sitting up in her bed, typing on her computer keyboard. I notice she has circles under her eyes, but everything in her house is in impeccable order. "Let's go sit on your patio," I suggest. "I brought something for us to eat." She closes her computer and follows me outside, and we sit across from each other on two wicker chairs. Emilee tears off a piece of her grilled cheese sandwich and stuffs it into her mouth.

"I know you're angry, Em, but we all have your best interests at heart."

Emilee flashes me a pained look. "Kathe's your counselor. I'm not seeing her anymore."

"She's a family counselor," I say. "And she's certified in drug and alcohol treatment." I scratch my head and know what I'll say next, as Linda and I have discussed this option. "Your mother and I will stop seeing Kathe. It's more important for you. We'll find someone else."

"I'm done with Kathe. I'll keep seeing my eating disorder therapist," Emilee says. She takes a sip of iced tea and starts walking towards the house. "Thanks for the sandwich."

Sitting inside my car, I have a terrible realization. My daughter isn't going to change her mind.

In the following weeks, Emilee stops seeing her psychiatrist. She becomes reclusive, living in her bedroom with the blinds closed. Concerned about her client, Emilee's eating disorder therapist, Hanna, makes several home visits because Emilee is now intoxicated most of the time and in no condition to leave the house. Dedicated and knowledgeable about eating disorders, Hanna hopes she can make a difference, but Emilee sinks deeper into despair.

JACK

Throughout summer and fall, we try everything we can think of and have been advised to do to help Emilee. We lean on family, a few friends, and prayer. Emilee's lack of nutrition and low weight, paired with alcohol consumption, not only affects her mind, body, and spirit but ours as well. At thirty years old, the doctor's scale registers the same number it did when Emilee was eleven years old.

As the tumultuous days and weeks pass, Emilee's condition worsens. Hospital visits become the norm. Linda and I have a key to Emilee's house, and we start to use it because Emilee is drinking throughout the day and won't answer her phone or the door. We live in fear for her life and feel the need to check on her. Emilee's alcoholism is apparent now, too. We find Ensure bottles filled with wine hidden throughout her house and throw them away. When I take away her car keys so she won't be tempted to drive, she calls a cab to take her to the liquor store.

One morning, on my way to work, I see a taxi in Emilee's driveway and catch a glimpse of my daughter walking into her house carrying a brown paper bag. Turning the car around, I park my car alongside the taxi and get out of my car. The driver gets out of his cab, and we stand in the middle of the driveway.

"What the hell are you doing?" I shout. "Can't you see how sick she is?"

The driver tells me in broken English that he is worried about my daughter. "I no want her money," he says, handing me the check she's written.

I rip up the check and tell him not to come back, and he drives away. I try Emilee's front door, but it's locked. I use my key and find her in the kitchen, opening a bottle of wine. "It's 9:30 in the morning, Em!" I say. "You need help!"

"I'm fine," she says. "Go away!"

LINDA

During this time, Jack and I live in a state of constant crisis. Our phone often rings in the middle of the night, and we wake to hear Emilee's barely audible voice: "I need help," she says. I love my daughter and want to help her in any way that I can, but my efforts aren't appreciated, and they aren't making a difference. The numerous emergencies and hospitalizations have wreaked havoc with my work schedule, and I find myself having to change appointments much more often than feels professional. When I'm at work I'm exhausted, physically there, yet, mentally I'm perpetually distracted. I know Jack feels the same way, and his work has been negatively impacted as well.

Though we don't realize it at the time Jack and I are using all of our energy, navigating through the daily craziness and putting one foot in front of the other. We have no time, energy, or desire to do anything extracurricular. Emilee is all we think about. No one we know can comprehend what we're living, and regular conversations with people suddenly feel like small talk to us.

I can't blame people for not understanding. After all, even the medical community has limited knowledge about eating disorders. And there are so many myths: many believe eating disorders are a choice, that parents are to blame, that only rich white girls have eating disorders. But an eating disorder is *never* a choice. No one would torture themselves on purpose. The truth is, you can't always tell when someone has an eating disorder. Families can provide support and be the best allies in the treatment and recovery of someone with an eating disorder, but it's extremely hard on everyone. The disease affects people of all genders, ages, races, ethnicities, and all socio-economic classes.

Meanwhile, alcohol is making everything worse. I still believe Emilee wants to get better and live the life she's dreamed of, but over time the controlling eating disorder and the numbing alcohol become her two best friends. And everyone else, the enemy.

At her next hospitalization, Emilee winds up in the Intensive Care Unit. Her potassium level is so low, doctors are afraid she will have a heart attack. Over time her brain, heart, kidneys, and digestive tract become increasingly compromised. It's amazing to all of us how resilient her body is with the abuse she's putting it through. As Emilee's condition continues to deteriorate we beg the doctors, psychiatrists, and social workers for help.

"She has to reach her rock bottom and beg for help," one social worker says.

But my fear is that Emilee won't survive her rock bottom.

I try to believe the saying, "God only gives you as much as you can handle," but at a certain point, I feel like I simply can't handle much more. As Emilee's condition worsens, Jack and I realize we need more support. We decide to explore different churches, and after attending a single mass at Spiritus Christi we know we've found a community that feels like home. The homilies, the music, and the friendly, non-judgmental atmosphere show us this is where we belong. Father Jim counsels us spiritually and prays for Emilee and our family. The renewed connection we feel with God through Spiritus Christi is amazing, and helps us find the strength to endure these trying times. At one point, Father Jim goes to Emilee's home to meet with her. He is compassionate and kind, but Emilee isn't receptive. Still, we're grateful to him for trying. Ultimately, we know our daughter's fate is in God's hands.

JACK

With her body and her brain so malnourished, and alcohol making matters so much worse, Emilee is unable to think rationally, especially when it comes to nourishing herself and making good medical choices regarding her health. But when Emilee is hospitalized she is a model patient, even when it comes to eating all the food on her meal tray. She lies in the hospital bed with her tan Wells baseball cap camouflaging her nearly bald head, her heart monitor beeping, and an IV dripping, as an array of doctors and residents cluster around her bed. They ask her questions, order tests, and tell her she needs to take her drinking problem and anorexia more seriously. They tell her if she doesn't, she won't live much longer. Once stabilized, she is always deemed competent to make her own medical decisions. "Your daughter is brilliant," we are often told. *Yes,* I think, *brilliantly manipulative.* When she discovers she can leave the hospital against medical advice she exercises that privilege often, and always against our wishes. The revolving door to the emergency room continues, and the definition of the word 'insanity' has never been more evident to me since we all keep doing the same thing over and over again and expect different results.

"Something needs to be done!" I insist. The tall young doctor and I stand in the hall, outside Emilee's room. He listens to me patiently, tucking his hands inside white jacket pockets. "She's not getting the necessary nutrients to fuel her brain, so her neurotransmitters aren't firing properly. She's not thinking straight or nourishing herself, no matter how with it she seems after being here a few days."

"You know all this, yet you let her go home," I say.

The doctor puts his hand on my arm. "I'm sorry," he says, looking down at the floor then up at me. "I'll make sure psychiatry sees her."

The next day a young psychiatrist sits across from me, the corners of her pink lips turned down and in a stoic frown. I tell her, "Look at Emilee's records; the number of visits here, the frequency, and her condition, each time getting worse." The stone-faced doctor in front of me does not show a modicum of compassion. Her lack of empathy infuriates me, and I find myself rising from my chair, walking towards her, and leaning over so that my face is very close to hers. "If she were your daughter, would you let her go home?" I demand.

"I'm calling security," the psychiatrist says.

"Don't bother. I'm leaving," I say, disgusted. "This really isn't right!" On my way out, I let the door slam behind me. As I sit in the waiting room, I hope Linda's gentle demeanor might invoke some sense of compassion from this psychiatrist. I pray she'll be able to see how much we love our daughter, that we are at our wits' end, and desperately need her help. But a few minutes later Linda walks out, shoulders slumped, tears streaming down her cheeks.

Emilee is going to be discharged.

Again.

Emilee makes fifteen separate trips to the emergency room between July and November of 2011. She is admitted seven times.

In between hospital visits Linda and I continue our counseling sessions with Kathe, who is a godsend. She understands how anorexia and alcoholism change the brain, and she recognizes how sick Emilee has become. Linda and I are grateful someone understands, and we are shocked when she tells us Emilee is the sickest patient she has ever worked with.

At the end of a therapy session she reminds Linda and me, once more, of the 3 Cs.

"You didn't cause it."

"You can't control it."

"You can't cure it."

"You have to understand," she says, "It's as if the two of you are in a boat together and the boat is taking on water, and all you're doing is bailing water. There has been no time to think or do anything else." Kathe implores, almost demands us, to take care of ourselves, to go on a date, to get away, even if only for a weekend. "Be good to each other," she says. "Situations like this can destroy a marriage."

Linda and I go out for dinner from time to time, and we stay connected with family and a few close friends, but we just don't feel comfortable leaving town.

Nearing the end of our rope we are willing to try anything, and when someone asks if we have ever considered holding a family intervention on Emilee's behalf, we decide to give it a try. Linda invites Emilee to join us at our house at noon one Sunday in August, and she agrees. Unbeknownst to Emilee, her aunts, uncles, and cousins will also be there, in addition to Linda, Matt and me.

Linda takes Emilee out for breakfast and brings her back to our house afterward, to make sure she's in good form for the intervention, but Emilee tells us she needs to lie down in her own bed for a short rest. "I'll be back before noon," she assures us, and we can't stop her without her becoming suspicious.

The family arrives at noon, and we talk amongst ourselves while we anxiously await Emilee's arrival.

Emilee finally walks through the front door, thirty minutes late. "I'm here!" she calls out in a cheery tone.

Linda and I glance at each other and, from the sound of her voice, we suspect she's been drinking. We watch Emilee closely as she walks into the living room with Duncan by her side.

"What do we do now?" I ask her.

Linda shrugs. "I guess we go on as planned. Everyone's here, and she seems relatively with it. We won't be able to get everyone together again anytime soon."

From my spot on the loveseat, I look at Emilee's five younger cousins. Ranging in age from 13 to 21, they appear nervous and, in truth, so are we. Em is the oldest cousin, and they all look up to her. In addition to babysitting for all of them when they were young, Emilee tutored Molly and Paige in Biology. And Taylor, now 21, has always shared a special bond with Emilee. *And today, they are part of her intervention*, I think to myself sadly. When Linda sits down next to Emilee, I know it's time to begin.

After clearing my throat once or twice, I find my words. "Emilee, there are things we'd like to say to you." I look into my daughter's eyes and ask, "Will you listen?"

Suddenly Emilee realizes why everyone has gathered at our house. She crosses her arms and her legs and listens politely, but I can tell she is not pleased.

Each of us has written a personal letter to Emilee, telling her how much we love her and that we're afraid of losing her. Linda, Matthew, and I have done this repeatedly, but we hope today the concerns of the others will resonate with her. Everyone states their fears about what might happen if her behaviors continue, how we would be affected, and how much we want her to seek help.

Finally, it's Aunt Ellen's turn. "You know you were my first love, the first baby I fell in love with. You were so happy, so bright, and you are the reason I wanted to have children of my own. You are so precious to me and to all of us, and you always have been." Ellen's voice is cracking, and tears run down her cheeks. "We can't imagine our lives without you in it."

Everyone weeps except Emilee, who sits on the couch, emotionless.

After everyone has had a chance to speak Emilee picks up Duncan, says goodbye in a polite manner, and walks towards the door.

The Emilee we all know seems to no longer to exist.

The following day Linda tells me she is taking some food to Emilee's house and asks me to pick her up there, so we can run errands together. From outside on the driveway, I hear Emilee yelling. "Get the hell out of my house!" she hollers. "Leave me alone!"

I march into the kitchen and shout at my daughter. "How dare you speak to your mother like that after all she has done for you! She is your truest friend—your ONE friend." It is at that moment I know I need to try the 'tough love' that's been recommended. The family intervention failed to make a meaningful impression, and I'm furious at how Emilee is treating Linda.

Now, when Emilee is hospitalized, I visit less frequently, and when I go my visits are short. During one hospitalization, Emilee calls me to ask us to pick her up from the hospital.

"Are you leaving against medical advice?" I ask.

Emilee dodges my question.

"If you're leaving against medical advice, we're not coming," I say. "You can call a cab." It takes all my willpower to say no to my daughter.

"You have to come," she says. "You're my parents."

As I hang up the phone, the guilt rushes over me. Falling back in bed, I close my eyes and rub my face with both hands. I want to get my daughter and bring her home, but I convince myself that I can't go this time.

Emilee calls back. Linda answers the phone. I tell Linda to stay firm. It's hard for her, excruciatingly hard, but she refuses to give in.

"When you do the right thing, we'll be there to support you," I hear her say. "We love you. That's why we can't come to pick you up."

Emilee takes a cab home.

During counseling with Kathe, I learn new terms: codependency, enmeshment, boundaries. Though it's hard not to be there for my daughter, I don't want to enable Emilee's destructive behavior. Linda respects my decision and knows I will be there if she needs my support. Emilee has always wanted to please me, and I hope this approach will encourage her to try harder to get well.

After a few weeks, Linda tells me the 'tough love' thing isn't working for her. "I've read the codependency books. I listen to the expert's advice, and I take a lot of it," she says. "I'm open to suggestions of the experts, Jack, but they haven't walked this walk. I have to live with myself if she dies, and so do you. Do what feels right for you."

The last morning in October, I walk down to Emilee's with Linda. Yellow and orange leaves rustle beneath our feet, the air is crisp, and it smells like fall. "Look," Linda comments, "Emilee put a fall wreath on her door." I know it's important for Emilee to have things appear normal and, to most of the outside world, it probably does.

When no one answers, we use our key and find Emilee in her bed with blood all over her face. As Linda cleans the gash on her forehead, Emilee explains she fell on her way back from the bathroom. Without hesitation I call my old friend, Doctor V.—the father of Emilee's old friend, Laura, from nursery school—and he offers to come over and examine Em right away. Known for his down-to-earth manner, he determines Emilee doesn't have a serious injury. I walk Rocky to his car, where he tells it to me straight.

"I'm sorry this is happening to your family," he says as we stand face to face. "The medical community has failed you."

When he says this I feel he's speaking to me as a friend, not a doctor.

"Seems like maybe the best thing that could happen would be for Emilee to get pulled over for a DUI or something," he says. "Maybe she could get help via the legal system?"

I don't know what to say to him, so I shrug and thank my friend again for making the trip. I think about his words. *Is this what it's come to? After all the emergency room visits and hospitalizations, is it possible that Emilee might get more help if she got in trouble with the law?*

***

LINDA

Emilee's health is precarious enough with her eating disorder, but the alcoholism adds another layer of complexity to it all. When a person drinks alcohol for weeks, months, or years, they can develop both mental and physical symptoms when they stop or seriously cut back on how much they drink. Mild symptoms include headache, nausea, vomiting, agitation, anxiety, and insomnia. More serious symptoms include visual and aural hallucinations. And, if an individual experiences seizures, withdrawal can even be deadly.

Desperate to help our daughter, Emilee's primary care doctor, Dr. Shay, along with her eating disorder therapist, Hanna, use all their connections from the hospital. There now is a solid plan in place to get Emilee involuntary treatment for her eating disorder in White Plains, New York. The single caveat: she'd need to be admitted to the hospital first, be medically stabilized, and be transported via ambulance when a bed downstate becomes available. Because most hospitals will not admit people for the purpose of detoxing, and because she won't willingly go to a detox facility, the only way any of us can be assured Emilee will be admitted to the hospital is if she is in distress.

Dr. Shay tells us the easiest way to get Emilee admitted to the hospital is to see that she begins to experience alcohol withdrawal, with a plan in place once she arrives.

She's been hospitalized so frequently, and we fear we will lose her soon if something doesn't happen fast. My part of the plan is unconventional and risky, and it speaks to the lengths to which we are willing to go to save our daughter's life. On a mutually agreed upon night, I'm supposed to go over to Emilee's house with the intention of staying overnight to make sure she doesn't consume any alcohol after bedtime. While she is asleep, I am to dispose of all her wine and, when she begins to experience the first signs of alcohol withdrawal, I am to call an ambulance.

It's the third week in November, and the early morning sun shines through the window in Emilee's guestroom. Any sun in November is a bonus in Western New York, and I feel particularly grateful for the sun and hopeful this plan will work. Tiptoeing into my daughter's bedroom I see Emilee is still asleep, with Duncan at her side. When I open her blinds, Emilee begins to stir.

"Why are you here?" Emilee asks, rubbing her eyes.

"You were out of it last night," I say. "It wasn't safe for you to be here alone." Duncan rolls onto his back, waiting for me to rub his belly. "Also, I threw out your wine," I say. "And I'll be staying today."

On this morning, Emilee is so weak I actually have to feed her an egg and toast. We talk, and I do some laundry, but the longer I'm there the angrier she becomes. I knew this would happen, but I'm not going anywhere. I pray our plan will work, knowing that if it doesn't I'll lose my daughter. Tears blur my vision, and my chest feels tight. *I can't imagine my life without Emilee,* I think to myself. *This has to work.*

Opening the patio door, I call for Duncan to go outside. After hooking him on the chain, I step outside with him for a minute. The sun is warm, and the air feels refreshing as I breathe it in. I watch Duncan run past the stamped concrete patio, through the space between the white privacy panels, and out into the green grass. It's obvious he feels like a king here on his turf. Back inside, I close the door and overhear Emilee talking to someone on the phone, and minutes later, two sheriff's deputies show up at the front door. I step outside to speak with them.

I can't believe it. My daughter has called 911 on me.

"My daughter has anorexia," I tell them. "She's also an alcoholic." It's hard for me to say those words out loud, in public, to officers of the law. I'm not embarrassed that my daughter is suffering from mental illness—it could happen to anyone—but I'm still in the process of digesting all of this myself. I feel protective of her and don't want her to be judged by those who don't know her. "There've been many ambulance calls to this address for those reasons," I say.

"If she wants you to leave, you have to go," one officer says. "That's her right."

I plead with him. "There is finally a plan in place for her to be deemed incompetent and get sent to involuntary treatment for her eating disorder. I'm waiting for her to experience alcohol withdrawal symptoms, and then I'm calling the ambulance. It's taken months for this to happen. This is her only hope."

The two officers move to the other side of the front step and begin talking quietly amongst themselves. I take a deep breath and glance out into the yard, when I notice a tall man walking up the driveway. I quickly recognize him to be our neighbor, Jerry.

My eyes fill with tears. For years, Emilee babysat Jerry's sons. They were a handful when they were little, yet Emilee enjoyed them immensely. She played soccer with them, did pull-ups with them, and created crazy games for them to use up some of their energy. Jerry and his wife often told me how effortlessly Emilee handled the boys, and of the high esteem they all have for her.

While the deputies go inside to talk to Emilee I explain the situation to Jerry, who gives me a big hug. I think to myself, *Boy, did I need that.* I think how serendipitous his presence is and how his support makes me feel less alone.

When the deputies come out of the house, I offer to call Dr. Shay's office and ask them to speak to him. After a brief conversation with the doctor, the deputies inform me that I still have to leave. I'm shocked at what I am hearing. They talked to the doctor; I don't understand. I feel the hope I had quickly fading. As I walk to my car, one of the officers calls out to me. "You have a key to this house, right?"

"Yes," I answer.

"Good," he says. "We need to make sure you leave, but… y'know…" He pauses a moment then lowers his voice. "We won't be here much longer."

I drive around the block twice, then pull back into Emilee's driveway and let myself in the front door. "I forgot my purse," I call as I walk back into the house.

"Are you kidding me?" Emilee calls from the bathroom.

Peeking into my daughter's bedroom, I notice she left her cellphone on the bed and I quietly slip it into my pocket. She doesn't have a landline, so she can't call 911 on me again. When she gets back into bed, she doesn't notice her phone is gone and, surprisingly, she doesn't seem angry to see I'm back. She looks exhausted, and I offer to make her a cup of tea. After a while, Emilee begins to shiver.

"I don't feel good," she moans, crossing her arms over her chest. As a pharmacist, Emilee understands what's happening to her. She knows shaking, nausea, and agitation are symptoms of withdrawal.

Honestly, I'm relieved things are happening as quickly as they are. "I'll call the ambulance," I say.

Emilee is admitted to the hospital, and five days later Jack and I are told two doctors have deemed Emilee incompetent to make her own medical decisions, and that arrangements are being made for her to be involuntarily admitted for intensive treatment for the eating disorder at a psychiatric facility.

Later that morning, Jack and I sit next to Emilee on her bed in the psychiatric unit when a psychiatrist enters the room and, in a kind and gentle way, explains the situation to Emilee. "You are very sick, and we are sending you for intensive treatment to help you get well."

Emilee begins pacing around the room. "Do I have a choice?" she asks.

"No," the psychiatrist answers. "You'll be transferred later today."

Tears roll down Jack's cheeks. "You're going to a place that's helped lots of other people," he says. "They understand anorexia and bulimia. We'll come and visit you."

"How long will I be there?" Emilee asks me as she's being wheeled away.

"I don't know," I answer truthfully.

I sob as two attendants strap my daughter into a collapsible bed, and I keep watching as she's loaded into the back of the ambulance. It's a five-hour ride to the psychiatric hospital. I pray she'll be okay and hope we're doing the right thing. The thud of the double doors slamming shut startles me. I wonder how many times I've ridden in an ambulance with Emilee, or followed one with her inside it. I think of all the trauma we've lived through these last months, and through my tears I watch the blurry vehicle as it weaves its way down the driveway, turns onto the main road, and drives out of sight.

JACK

A few days after Emilee leaves for treatment Linda, Matthew, and I drive to Geneva for Thanksgiving, hosted by Linda's parents. It's a bittersweet holiday, as everyone hopes and prays that this time things will be different. We try our best to enjoy the day, but it's another family gathering, and Emilee is not with us.

As the weeks go by, we speak with Emilee on the phone when she's allowed to reach out to us. She sounds better each time we talk. From what she tells us, she won't be home until after New Year's, but it's impossible to imagine celebrating Christmas without Emilee, so Linda and I decide to bring Christmas to her.

We pack our silver SUV with two small suitcases and lots of Christmas presents, and head for White Plains. The long car ride is peaceful; we listen to a variety of different music and talk. As we drive up the road to the hospital, we notice the park-like setting and imagine how beautiful it must be when all the trees and flowers are in bloom. The red brick building the unit is housed in has an A-frame roofline. "Kinda looks like a building you'd see at an Ivy League school," I remark, but once inside, as we pass through heavy steel doors, it is clear we are in a psychiatric facility. I can tell Linda is surprised and unsettled by this level of security, and we are relieved when we see Emilee's unit has some charm, with its large windows trimmed in dark wood.

We are excited to see Emilee, who smiles and hugs us and seems happy we're there. She looks better, has color in her cheeks, and her eyes are brighter. She gives us a tour of the unit, shows us the activity rooms and the dining room. There are games to play and books to read, and she shows us a craft kit of the Statue of Liberty she's working on as part of art therapy. Emilee's room is small, with a twin bed, a nightstand, and a dresser. It looks a lot like a tidy dormitory room.

Linda has spent a lot of time shopping and is anxious to have Emilee open her gifts. Emilee's face lights up as she tries on a few of the clothes Linda has bought, and it's obvious she appreciates everything. She tells us how much she misses Duncan and how she can't wait to get home. We keep the conversation light and mostly listen to Emilee as she explains her routine, emphasizing that she's expected to eat six times a day—three meals and three snacks. "It's a lot of food," she says. And it is, as they try to weight restore patients as safely, and as quickly, as possible.

Emilee introduces us to some people she's met. She tells us about her counseling and therapy groups, and we play Scrabble. Later in the afternoon, we go into a large recreation room to talk.

"Do you think you're making progress?" I ask.

Emilee looks out the window. "We're all just doing what we have to do to get out of here," she answers in a smug tone. "These places are all the same."

My heart sinks.

The next day we're back at Emilee's unit, this time in a narrow conference room. Emilee's team—her physician, her counselor, and her social worker—joins us in chairs placed around a long rectangular table. Linda and I don't know what to think, and I can tell Emilee is on edge. When we have an opportunity to talk, Linda and I emphasize there has to be a plan in place when Emilee returns home, or whatever progress has been made will be lost. We also say that there needs to be accountability and counseling for Emilee, as well as family counseling. Linda pulls a sheet out of her purse with the levels of care outlined and tells the team we believe that, minimally, a plan is needed where she would attend a program five days a week for meals, counseling, therapy, and support. Emilee shifts in her chair and gives us a disapproving look.

The treatment team makes specific recommendations about what Linda and I need to change in regard to our behavior. "You have to stop enabling her," they say. Their list is not very long, but it is going to require consistency and strength from both of us. It reads:

- Do not follow the ambulance.
- Do not feed her. Sharing meals is encouraged, but she should feed herself.
- Do not check on her multiple times during the day.

Linda and I promise to be supportive as long as there is a genuine effort made on Emilee's part not to consume alcohol, stop abusing laxatives, and keep all her doctor and counseling appointments.

"Honestly, I can do this on my own," Emilee insists.

But Linda and I know otherwise, and we hope Emilee's thinking will change in the coming weeks.

On our way home, we discuss the meeting and the fact that we were told Emilee would probably remain in White Plains for several more weeks, at least into the new year. But the very next day, we receive a call. It's Emilee.

"They're sending me home," she says. "My insurance coverage is stopping again."

Once again, Linda and I are stunned.

The doctors may be the experts, but the insurance companies make the final decisions. After thirty-one days of in-patient treatment Emilee is discharged on December 22nd, with yet another follow-up plan. Upon her return home, she looks physically healthier than when she left, but to us it seems obvious she needed to stay longer to get her cognition back online. Doctor appointments and counseling sessions are set up at home, but with Christmas just three days away we know nothing is going to happen as quickly as it needs to. Emilee tells us she has every intention of following the recommended plan and has already begun making phone calls. When we pick her up from the airport, we return her car keys to her so she can make it to her appointments.

LINDA

The day after Emilee arrives home, a package addressed to her is delivered to our house since she's not had a chance to stop the forwarding of her mail. It's a package from an out of town aunt and uncle. I decide to bring it to her on my way to finish some last-minute Christmas shopping. Turning into her driveway I see Emilee in her garage, retrieving some bags from out of the backseat of her car.

Following her to her door, I stand behind her as she fumbles with her keys. I can't help but notice a tall, long-necked glass bottle poking out of one of the bags.

"You bought wine?" I ask.

Emilee empties the contents of the bags onto the kitchen counter. "I have an eating disorder," she says. "I'm not an alcoholic."

Jack and I agreed to treat our daughter as an adult and not continue to enable her. It sounded good when we agreed to it, but we thought she'd be in treatment longer. We assumed the next step would be residential care or, minimally, out-patient care. And we assumed when she did return home, there would be a plan set up for immediate comprehensive care and accountability from Emilee.

I swallow hard. "Okay, Em," I say, shaking my head.

I back out of her driveway and drive aimlessly around town. I have many things left to do, but I can't think about any of that. I'm worried about my daughter, and I feel so very sad for her. She didn't choose to have anorexia or become an alcoholic. But part of me is exhausted, and I can't help but wonder: was her inpatient treatment just wasted time?

JACK

Even though Emilee is home, she refuses to join us for Christmas Eve festivities at her aunt and uncle's house. Even though her house is just a short walk from our home, she opts out of the larger family gathering at our home on Christmas Day. We plead with her to stop by, if only for a little while. She declines, and we have to respect her decision and honor our agreement to treat her like an adult. We understand re-assimilation is difficult for people returning from in-patient treatment. Linda, Matt, and I still host Christmas Day, and we try to keep things as normal as possible for everyone else. Matthew and I do all we can to help Linda with the preparation and cleanup because we know she's struggling to keep it together, as are we. After the meal, Emilee's cousins from Alfred walk to her house and spend some time with her. When they return they tell us Em was polite, but she didn't seem herself and kept their visit short.

The day after Christmas Linda's parents insist they need to see Emilee before they return to Geneva, so they stop at her house a little before noon and are surprised to find Emilee in bed, complaining of a headache. Grandma Dorothy and Grandpa Carmen were not part of the intervention in the summer; they want to see their granddaughter and read her a letter they've written, expressing their love for her and their hope that she'll get better.

When I return home from work that night, Linda meets me at the door. Looking into her eyes, I can see she's upset.

"I feel so bad for my parents, to have to see Emilee like that," Linda says.

I put my arm around her. "What do you mean?"

"She's falling down the rabbit hole."

LINDA

It's three days after Christmas, and I have the day off. I'm putting away some of the Christmas decorations when the phone rings.

I hear Emilee's voice. "Will you come pick me up?"

"Where are you?" I ask.

"I got a DWI," Emilee says in a quiet voice.

On the way to the police station, my mind is racing. I'm angry with Emilee and scared for her, too. I wonder what has happened to our once-responsible daughter. Somewhere along the way, she's lost herself. Or perhaps the strong sense of self I believed Emilee had was just an illusion. *Did I just see what she wanted me to see?* I think. *Is it possible that, deep inside, Emilee is just an insecure little girl who feels she has to prove something to everyone by pleasing and achieving?*

Inside the police station, a petite woman with reading glasses resting on her nose looks up at me. I tell her who I am, and a few minutes later Emilee appears before me accompanied by an officer who asks me to follow them. Emilee shoots me a quick glance, then lowers her head. With one hand on her upper arm, the officer guides Emilee into a colorless room. Emilee and I sit at two small desks across from the officer.

"Your daughter ran a stoplight," the officer says. Tall and fit with broad shoulders, his hair is cut in military-style. "The Breathalyzer indicates she's been drinking," he adds.

This feels like a bad dream unfolding in slow motion, like it's happening to someone else. I turn to my daughter and notice her jacket is wet and she's shivering. I unwrap the scarf from my neck and drape it around her. "Em, what were you thinking?" I ask. I don't know what I expect her to say. There's only silence as she looks down at the floor, holding her hands in her lap.

"What do we do now?" Emilee asks the officer, her speech a bit slurred. We listen as he explains the way the system works, and points out the court date on the ticket. Emilee seems distant, far too calm, and I sense her reaction is more than just the alcohol she's consumed. I sense she is disassociating.

Outside the police station, the parking lot is filled with slushy puddles. When I put my arm around Emilee's waist to steady her I feel her pull away, and I can sense her inner struggle. I understand

196

how much she needs me and how much she doesn't want to need me.

JACK

When I learn what's happened, I grab my keys. "Another Emilee crisis," I tell a co-worker. "I have to go." I'm grateful for the car ride home, as I have a few minutes to digest the news Linda has shared and it gives me a chance to think about how I'm going to handle the situation. I understand how important it is for me to remain calm because I know how fragile Emilee is. She needs to know I'm not embarrassed by the things that have happened, and that nothing will change my love for her.

When I arrive home, Linda and Emilee are sitting on the couch in the living room. Linda is drinking a cup of tea and Emilee is staring into her cup, a sullen look on her face. As I approach her, she looks up and starts to cry. "What am I going to do?" she weeps. I'm going to lose my driver's license! How will I—"

"Slow down, Em!" I say as I put my arms around her. "This is the very thing we've been afraid of. Your mother and I have tried to prevent this from happening. "

"I'm so sorry," she says, wiping the tears from her cheeks.

"I know you're sorry, and you say the right things, yet you continue to make bad decisions." I pause, knowing I'm lecturing her retroactively but, I feel it has to be said. I tell her she is fortunate that no one else was involved, and no one was hurt. I assure Emilee that we love her and her mother and I will support her. "You have to get more help for the eating disorder *and* the alcohol," I say.

"I'll take care of it," she replies curtly.

"Em, if you could have done this on your own, you would have by now," I say in a gentle voice.

I remember how, a few months earlier, Doctor V. suggested that the legal system might be what Emilee needed since the medical system has failed her. I understand individuals convicted of a DWI are required to attend classes and participate in counseling. I wonder if Emilee getting pulled over might be a blessing in disguise.

Emilee willingly hands over her car keys and thanks us for being there for her. In the weeks that follow, Emilee's friend Kelly reaches out repeatedly and tries to help Emilee remember who she really is. And Jeff, a young man Emilee dated briefly, who remains a good friend, stops by her house frequently and tries to reason with her. Their attempts to awaken the real Emilee are unsuccessful. Linda and I are, again, counseled by all the professionals not to enable our daughter, and to let things play out.

LINDA

Emilee continues to drink excessively right up until the day she's scheduled a consultation with an attorney she's found online. I ask my sister to accompany us to the office, due to the fact that Emilee is perpetually drinking, unsteady on her feet, and sometimes verbally lashes out at me when she's in this condition. I'm not sure how things will unfold or if I'll be able to handle the situation myself. Deep down, I know I need my sister's moral support. Most days Emilee is somewhat functional in the mornings, but by afternoon she's under the influence and back in bed. Jack has already taken a great deal of time off from his job, and I'm not sure how much more he might need to ask for.

"Ellen and I have this," I assure him that morning. "Go to work."

Timothy Melcher's office is located in a beautiful brick home in a historic neighborhood off of East Avenue. We're greeted by an attractive young paralegal wearing a nicely tailored pantsuit, a white collared blouse, and a simple gold necklace. She tells us her name is Nesha, and we follow her through the opulent entryway and into a waiting area with walls of bookcases filled with legal journals.

Emilee is pale and extremely thin, and her hand shakes as she fills out the necessary paperwork. Before she finishes, she complains she's feeling nauseated and excuses herself to use the bathroom. Nesha sees Emilee is in distress and hands her a small wastepaper basket, in case she doesn't make it in time. While Emilee is gone, I explain that Emilee has been drinking and I'm privately grateful we're the only ones in the waiting area. When Em returns, Nesha hands her a box of tissues and a bottle of water.

By the time the attorney calls us into his office, Emilee is feeling better. Mr. Melcher sits behind a large wooden desk. A tall, middle-aged man with broad shoulders and thinning blond hair, he's dressed in a navy blue sweater with a starched white buttoned-down shirt underneath. The two of us sit across from him and listen as he explains the protocol, and describes what to expect in court. His manner is professional and he seems knowledgeable, as DWI's are his specialty. He tells what his fee will be.

Mr. Melcher is surprised when Emilee starts to write him a check to pay his retainer fee. "Can she afford this?" he asks.

"Emilee is an outstanding pharmacist, and she's always been a saver," I say. "She just needs to get back on track."

I'm not delusional about what's happening to my daughter. I know her life is in danger, and her mind is compromised due to lack of nutrition and alcohol abuse. I no longer hover or check on her multiple times a day, yet at the same time I have to trust what my heart tells me. I know that no one is harder on Emilee than Emilee. She needs my love more than ever. Not to enable her but to help her remember who she still is, to help her believe in herself, and to understand she is still lovable—in the hopes that she can learn to love herself again.

JACK

Before Emilee can make it to court, she is hospitalized again during another drunken incident. This time there's a gash on her forehead, surrounded by a large contusion. It's determined that she has a concussion, and her head injury requires stitches. After a full work-up we learn she is dehydrated, that she has abnormal kidney function, electrolyte imbalances and, to make matters worse, she begins experiencing alcohol withdrawal—complete with tremors, disorientation, and vomiting. Several days later Emilee is discharged from the hospital with a black eye, and her court appearance is rescheduled for the following month. The pattern continues. There are two additional hospitalizations before her next court date.

This is a dark and terrible time for Linda and me, and we feel like we're watching our precious daughter slowly killing herself. We all have concerns about Emilee making it to court, and fears about what will happen there.

LINDA

One week before Emilee's court appearance, I take her to see Dr. Shay. The large waiting room isn't crowded, and the receptionist recognizes us right away—as we're there frequently. Emilee and I leaf through magazines, and she insists I remain in the waiting room while the doctor examines her. But I insist she let me come in at the end of the appointment. When it's my turn to talk I explain our concerns to the doctor, expressing fear about what might happen if Emilee doesn't show up at court again. Dr. Shay takes a great deal of time with Emilee, explaining how she should be detoxed and have attended AA meetings before court. He's aware Emilee resumes drinking after each hospitalization and is cognizant she is presently under the influence.

Emilee keeps saying she is terrified of alcohol withdrawal, as she's experienced the severity of it a few times already. "What if I have to go to jail?" she weeps. "What if I have a seizure?"

"People die in jail all the time," Dr. Shay says. He goes on to explain that she needs to get sober and that there are places she can go to detox, but she refuses. He understands it is essential for Emilee to make it to her court appearance. Ultimately, he hands me a prescription for two doses of lorazepam which, he explains, will decrease the likelihood of Emilee having a seizure when she stops drinking.

COURT

LINDA

On the day of Emilee's court appearance the weather is unseasonably warm, with the thermometer reaching 68 degrees. It's a record high temperature for March 7th in Rochester, New York. Inside the crowded courtroom, Jack and I sit on either side of our daughter and wait. Aside from being painfully thin, Emilee looks lovely in her gray pantsuit.

All of a sudden, Emilee jumps up from her seat. "Kelly!" she loudly exclaims. "You came!" It's as if she's forgotten where she is and is behaving as one might at a high school reunion or a party.

People turn their heads. It's obvious she's still intoxicated from the night before.

"Shhh!" I say, tugging on her sleeve. "Sit down!" I whisper, embarrassed for her. Kelly hugs Emilee, Jack, and me, then sits with us as we wait for Emilee's case to be called.

Upon hearing her name announced, the color immediately drains from Emilee's face. Jack and I stand beside our daughter, each of us holding one of her arms as we slowly walk up the aisle to the front of the now overflowing courtroom. I can feel Emilee's body shaking as we stand there, waiting for what seems like forever. Jack and I exchange a long look. Emilee's attorney, Mr. Melcher, previously seated with other attorneys on the side of the courtroom, joins us, briefcase in hand. He stands with us until the judge asks him to approach the bench. We watch as the two men quietly converse for several minutes. We don't know what to think, and we're becoming more unsettled the longer they speak.

Finally, the judge looks up. He tells Emilee to take a seat. "I'd like to speak with your parents in my chambers," he says.

Emilee sinks down in one of the chairs in the front row of the courtroom. She looks sad, and I'm not certain she understands the magnitude of the moment, given her intoxicated state. Jack and I walk behind the judge, Mr. Melcher, and the District Attorney, towards the judge's chambers. I turn to give my daughter a reassuring look, and I feel her eyes follow me out of the courtroom.

The door closes quietly behind us, and we find ourselves in a room that is crowded with our presence. This is a small-town court and the chambers are modest, to say the least. A bookcase, a large desk, and a leather chair take up much of the space.

Jack and I are instructed to sit in chairs in front of the desk, and the judge takes a seat in the large leather chair behind his desk. "This is a very unusual case," he says, and we infer that Mr. Melcher has explained the details of Emilee's situation to him.

Jack and I are given an opportunity to share with everyone in chambers how concerned we are about our daughter's health and wellbeing, "We've tried everything," I say.

Tears well up in our eyes as quickly as our concerns spill out of our mouths. Everyone listens as Jack explains that Emilee has been struggling with an eating disorder for years, that she's been in treatment to address this illness three times in the last seventeen months. He tells the judge that the disorder has taken over her life since she pulled herself out of work ten months prior, adding that she's started drinking to numb herself.

The judge asks more questions: Would Emilee stay with us? Could she make bail? What would happen if she goes home?

"She can make bail," I tell him, looking down at the shredded tissue in my hands. "But she refuses to stay with us or let us stay with her for any length of time."

Jack looks at me and then turns to the judge. "If she goes home, she'll drink herself to death."

While the judge, Emilee's attorney, and the D. A. confer, Jack and I hold hands. We feel compassion from everyone in the room. They all take the situation seriously and seem to genuinely care about what's happening to Emilee, to Jack and me, and to our family.

A few minutes later, the judge leans forward. "I can get her help for both the eating disorder and the alcohol," he says.

It sounds like an answer to prayer.

He explains that with a first offense, where there is no accident or injury, a person would not normally be taken into custody, but he appreciates our predicament as parents. "The legal system can mandate treatment," he explains. "If we take Emilee into custody, she will have to go to the jail and be processed and evaluated, but then she'd be able to receive treatment for both the alcohol and the eating disorder."

Jack and I shake our heads in disbelief. There are no other options, nothing we haven't tried, except for legal guardianship. And we both fear Emilee may attempt suicide if we pursue this angle. Furthermore, our attorney has advised us that it is highly improbable that guardianship would be granted because Emilee is still paying her bills, her house is in order, and she'd show up at the trial looking presentable. The intensive in-patient treatment Emilee received in White Plains interrupted the symptoms and stabilized her, but without the follow-up care she needs it's the equivalent of pulling a drowning child out of the water, reviving the child, and returning the child to the same deserted beach. The medical community and the insurance company have failed Emilee. Our daughter is dying before our eyes—wasting away, a little more each day, unable to eat, drinking to numb the reality of what her life has become. She has lost hope and has forgotten who she is. We want to believe the real Emilee is still there, underneath the sadness and shame. We're given a moment to talk.

I look at Jack and exclaim in a whisper, "This is crazy!" suddenly feeling queasy.

Jack grabs both my hands. "It's her only hope," he says.

Pulling my hands out of his, I run my fingers through my hair— it's so hard to breathe, and I wonder, *why is this happening?* I know there are no better options. We have utilized all our resources.

***

An officer escorts Emilee down the corridor, and Jack and I trail behind. Outside, a black and white sheriff's car waits to take our daughter to jail. We're allowed to hug Emilee quickly. She feels like a rag doll in our arms. Our faces are wet with tears, and the expression on her face is a mix of fear and confusion. The officer helps her into the backseat of the patrol car, and we watch as the car drives out of sight.

Jack helps me walk across the parking lot and eases me into our SUV. I can hardly swallow. My throat feels so tight it aches.

"What have we done?" I weep.

"The judge says he can get her treatment for both," Jack says. "Honey, we had no choice."

I try to think optimistically. *She'll only be there for only a few hours,* I think. *She'll be evaluated, sent to a facility to detox, and then transferred to in-patient treatment for alcohol. Afterward, she'll go to inpatient treatment for the eating disorder.* I look at the digital clock on the dashboard. "Hurry, Jack," I say. "We have to get her medicine to the jail before she goes into withdrawal."

JACK

It's mid-afternoon when I drive across the Frederick Douglass-Susan B. Anthony Memorial Bridge and park on the street across from the jail. I've crossed this bridge and seen this building countless times from the outside, but I never thought I'd have a reason to go inside. People make mistakes, and I understand that, yet no one imagines that, one day, their child will be incarcerated. All I know is that we have to get the lorazepam to Emilee, quickly, as alcohol withdrawal symptoms can ultimately lead to seizures and even death. People much healthier than Emilee have died as a result of the effects of abrupt alcohol withdrawal.

A policeman points out the appropriate entrance. After we explain the situation to another officer behind a sliding glass window, we're directed to a barren room and made to wait on an uncomfortable wire bench. A round black clock with a white face and black hands hangs on the wall. After a few minutes, a middle-aged woman wearing a white cotton lab coat comes out and informs us, in a matter-of-fact way, that she is the nurse. "Unfortunately, Emilee won't be evaluated today," she says, sliding her dark-rimmed glasses up to the bridge of her nose. "It may take several days."

"What?!" I exclaim. "We were under the impression she'd be evaluated and admitted into an alcohol treatment program today!"

Linda begins frantically searching the contents of her purse and retrieves a tiny brown pill bottle. "You have to give her this medication," she says. "She can die without it."

"I'll have to make some phone calls," the nurse says. "This is highly irregular. If it's approved, we'll make sure she gets the medicine—assuming she needs it."

I can't believe this. I'd hoped mandated incarceration would be a bridge to Emilee's recovery, and I suddenly realize we have no experience with the legal system at all. And that, perhaps, out of desperation, we've made the wrong decision.

"We're not going anywhere!" I shout. "We're waiting here until our request is approved! Our daughter weighs 72 pounds! She may not survive a seizure."

We aren't allowed to see Emilee, due to strict visitation rules pertaining to what days and times inmates are allowed visitors. To our relief, the nurse informs us the medication has been approved, and she takes the lorazepam into her possession. Sadly, she also confirms Emilee won't be evaluated for a few days.

"I'm sorry," the nurse says. "This is the way the system works."

"We have to go back and talk to the judge!" Linda says.

The two of us rush out of the jail and drive back to court. As we walk back into a nearly empty courtroom, Linda and I are relieved that it's still in session. We wait at the back of the room. Our nerves are frayed, and we find it nearly impossible to sit still. Fortunately, we don't have to wait long. After the last case on the docket has been handled, the judge looks up and motions us to come forward. He can tell we're distressed and leads us into chambers.

"They told us it could be a few days before Emilee is evaluated!" I blurt out.

The judge shakes his head. "I never said it would be today."

Linda looks at me. "Oh my God!" she exclaims. "Did we just assume it would be today?"

The judge tells us there is nothing he can do. "She's in the system now."

Outside in the parking area, I can feel the record warmth of the day quickly fading. The hope we had a few hours earlier has turned to fear. We're afraid Emilee won't physically survive jail, and if she does survive we fear what it will do to her mentally.

It's hard for me to be positive. This has truly been the worst day of my life—of our lives. I let the dogs out the backdoor, and while I'm waiting for them to come back inside Linda says she's feeling weak and is going to lie down. I realize we've not eaten anything since early that morning and I call and order a pizza to be delivered.

Matthew stops by on his way home from work. Linda calls her parents and her siblings, to tell them what has happened.

Later that night Linda goes to take a long, hot shower, but just a few minutes later she emerges from the bathroom, wrapped in a towel. "She has so little of the medicine," Linda cries. "What if she has a seizure in jail?"

"They know how fragile she is," I say. "I'm sure they'll look out for her." But inside, I have the exact same fears.

LINDA

I can't sleep; my eyes are riveted on the phone on my nightstand. I can feel the bed move each time Jack tosses or turns. When Emilee was in the hospital we could rest, knowing she was getting medical attention and was where she needed to be. Tonight is different. Our daughter is in jail.

The next morning, my first phone call is to Emilee's lawyer. His paralegal, Nesha, assures me that she and Mr. Melcher will do whatever they can to see that Emilee's evaluation is done as soon as possible. Nesha explains that there is nothing we can do ourselves, and reiterates she understands how sick Emilee is. She promises she'll keep us informed.

Jack and I try to convince ourselves that no news is good news. In an effort to resume some sense of normalcy Jack goes into work, and I plan to make my mid-morning dental appointment, but inside I'm frantic.

As I walk back into the house, I hear the home phone ringing. A stranger identifies herself as someone from the town court. She tells me that Emilee has been taken to the hospital by ambulance.

"I shouldn't be calling you," she says, "but I'm a mother, too."

"Is she okay?" I ask, barely able to get out the words.

I can only imagine the worst.

***

Jack and I dash down the long hallway in search of Emilee's hospital room. When we find it we're stopped by a young, fit, and armed police officer sitting outside her door. After identifying ourselves as Emilee's parents, we ask if we can go in.

"Yes," the officer says in a deep voice. "But remember she's still in custody. Also, ma'am," he adds, "I'll need to check your purse." He must see the pained look in my eyes because he quickly apologizes. "I'm sorry," he says. "It's procedure."

We walk into a dark room. The curtains are drawn, and Emilee is asleep in the center of the hospital bed. Her pencil-thin arms rest on top of a white sheet. One arm is attached to an IV bag, which drips a clear fluid into her vein. Her face is pale and drawn, and there are only slight patches of wispy blonde hair covering her scalp. She is so small and broken. We wonder how much more her frail body can endure. It seems absurd that there's an armed officer outside her door—as if she's a threat to anyone.

In the far corner of the room we notice a woman seated in a chair, reading a magazine. She looks up and introduces herself. She's from the Monroe County Jail, and she tells us that there will be a female from the jail with Emilee at all times. She's friendly, and it's reassuring to us that Emilee won't be alone.

A tall doctor with dark hair and a full beard enters the room, accompanied by a young blonde nurse.

"What happened?" we ask. "Is she going to be okay?" Instead of answering our questions, the doctor takes the stethoscope out of his white coat pocket and begins to examine Emilee.

"Your daughter had a seizure," he says. "It lasted for nearly ten minutes."

I think back to the seizure I witnessed Emilee experience many months prior. That one was three minutes long, and it felt like it would never end. After a while Emilee opens her eyes and stares at us, gathered around her bed. She surveys her surroundings. "Where am I?" she whispers with a bewildered look on her face.

"You're at the hospital," the doctor says. He continues the neurological exam, checking her eyes, reflexes, and asking her questions.

The nurse says she'll be back with medication and the doctor tells us he's ordered additional blood work and more tests. "We'll know more after that," he says as he walks out the door.

Emilee begins to cry as she recounts her night in jail. "It was awful!" she says in a scratchy, barely audible voice. "I started going into withdrawal. I was nauseous and shaking. They put me in a special area. I was going through withdrawal, and I was so sick! They gave me the medication after a while, but it didn't help. I kept begging them to call the ambulance, and finally they did."

As I hold a glass of ginger ale to her lips, Emilee sips a little through the straw and almost immediately falls back to sleep. Later, when she wakes up, it becomes obvious that in addition to being very weak and traumatized, she is cognitively confused and believes she's at her home.

"Will you go into the other room and get the bills out of my desk?" she asks at one point.

During her week-long stay in the hospital, Nesha works diligently to find a treatment program for her. Unfortunately, no alcohol treatment program will accept Emilee because of the eating disorder, and no eating disorder program will accept her because of the alcohol dependency. Nevertheless, Nesha assures us she'll keep trying. Jack and I feel responsible, and if we'd known Emilee would actually have to do jail time we never would have let this happen. We were desperate, and we had to make a decision on the spot.

Emilee's condition improves as she is detoxed, hydrated, and nourished. However, after exhaustive checking, not a single alcohol or eating disorder facility will accept her, and eventually we receive a call stating Emilee is being returned to jail—where there is no care—because there is no other alternative.

***

Having to wait for days to visit Emilee after being released from the hospital is torture. It's nearly impossible for me to believe I'm here, sitting across from my daughter, in jail.

"It wasn't supposed to happen like this, Em. None of it," I say.

Emilee shakes her head. "It's horrible here," she says. "I can't do this."

I find myself apologizing profusely and pulling my chair closer to the table. "We thought you'd just be evaluated at the jail and get right into treatment."

"What's wrong with me?" Emilee asks. "Is there anyone in the family who has anxiety like I do?"

"Everyone has some," I say, trying to sound as normal as possible, although there is nothing normal about this situation. I look around the room and see several inmates visiting with their children, as well as inmates who appear to be in their late teens talking with people I assume are their parents. The inaudible buzz of voices surround us and makes each conversation more private. "Grandma Grace struggled with anxiety and had trouble sleeping," I say, being honest with Emilee. "Your father inherited some of that same anxiety, and he's wired more that way, too. But mostly he worries about us." I think about myself and my side of the family. Nothing remarkable comes to mind until, suddenly, I remember.

"My Aunt Vincenza was fun to be around, and I loved her. She was kind and beautiful, with dark hair, ivory skin, and a flawless smile. She reminded me of Snow White. She made us laugh when

209

she did impressions of people she'd meet. But even as a child I could feel her nervous energy, and I sensed she wasn't really happy."

"She wasn't happy?" Emilee asks.

"Grandpa Carmen always said her early life wasn't easy. She married and had a beautiful family of her own, but after her mother died she broke ties with most of her siblings."

"Why?" Emilee asks. She's fidgeting in her seat, and I can tell she's uncomfortable about something, but I'm not sure what.

"I don't really know the whole story. It's a bit of a mystery. Maybe it was anxiety that caused her unhappiness, maybe it was her experiences growing up. She was the oldest girl in a family of six children, and she was expected to help out with children and chores. Maybe being with her siblings was a reminder of a difficult childhood. I'm only guessing. I never really thought about her having anxiety issues until now." Looking up at the ceiling, I find myself thinking of my aunt—the masterful way she made a sandwich, the vigorous way she brushed her teeth, the enthusiasm she displayed when she cleaned the house—but I don't have any memories of her being relaxed. She didn't seem happy. "Poor Aunt Vincenza," I say. "Something wasn't quite right."

Placing her elbows on the table, Emilee holds her head in her hands. Tears stream down her face, and I can tell she's in a great deal of emotional pain.

I put my palm against the clear partition, and Emilee does the same on her side; her hand aligns with mine. "You're so precious." I smile at her and look deep into her blue eyes that look so much like mine. "Things will get better."

Emilee's face is red. "Mom, you don't understand," she says.

"You'll get the help you need," I say. "I'm here for you. Your dad and I are here for you, every step of the way." I'm babbling now, but I want my daughter to know the lengths I'm willing to go to help her recover.

Emilee leans back in her chair, and her hands fall into her lap. She shakes her head from side to side. "I'm not right, Mom," she says. "I'm really not right."

JACK

Two weeks pass, and I still haven't gone to see Emilee in jail. I worry that she blames me, and I wonder how I'll be received if I visit. Linda has continued to see Emilee at every opportunity, and she hasn't pressured me to go with her. Instead, she keeps me apprised of Emilee's mental and physical condition. Meanwhile, I continue working my regular schedule at both jobs, and at home I keep busy with spring yard cleanup. In an effort to lighten Linda's load, I take on more household chores. I try to maintain as normal a life as possible, but internally I'm haunted by Emilee's incarceration. Linda appears to be handling things better than I, and I'm ashamed for not visiting our daughter sooner. After working out some logistics, I finally make plans to visit Em at the Monroe Correctional Facility.

"I'm sorry I haven't been here until now," I say.

Emilee smiles. "It's okay, Dad," she says.

"You shouldn't be here at all," I tell her. I'm trying to remain strong and not become emotional.

Emilee talks about how much she misses Duncan. She tells me about the people she's met, about the nicknames they call her, specifically "Cracker" (a pejorative reference to being white) and "Taco" (in reference to her genitalia). However, she insists she's made friends with these same inmates by trading tater tots and desserts from her meal tray for their vegetables, carrots, and celery sticks, and she doesn't feel threatened by them.

It amazes me, as I listen to her, how resourceful she is. Here's a girl from the suburbs, bargaining with inmates—many of whom are pretty rough around the edges.

"You're going to come through this experience, get better, and inspire others," I say positively, and I honestly believe she will. "I'm so sorry you have to go through this."

After thirty minutes of conversation, Emilee yawns. There are dark circles under her eyes, and her skin is colorless. "I need to go lie down," she says, but I don't want to leave her.

We stand up, move to the side of the partition, and I give her a short hug and a kiss on the cheek. "I love you!" I say.

Em thanks me for coming, tells me she loves me, and I watch her walk through the heavy metal door separating us. As I shuffle out of the visitation room, I notice all the people— some white, some black, some Hispanic, some young, and some old. I nod at a woman who looks up at me as I walk by, and I wonder if I will ever see any of these people again.

Back outside, I look up at the sky. It's a warm day, perfect in every way, except for the fact that my daughter is locked up inside.

LINDA

In the salon I say goodbye to my last client, sweep the hair off the floor, and as I begin to wipe down the mirror I can't help but notice my reflection. I almost don't recognize myself. My hair is flat, and my eyes are puffy. The makeup I apply each morning seems to slide off in an hour's time, and it doesn't help much anyway. I'm going through the motions of daily life, painting on a "Linda face", pretending to be me, but I'm not the same. Too much has happened, and I know the way I experience life is forever changed. This is Emilee's truth, as well. I lay awake half the night, feeling guilty for resuming my life and trying to imagine what my daughter is going through. I'm grateful for the distraction of work, as it gives my mind a break from constant worry. I listen to my clients—their lives sound so normal—and when they share their concerns, I can't help but think most are trivial compared to mine. It would be difficult to get out of bed each morning if I didn't have purpose. My father often says, "Sometimes work is a prayer," and I believe he is right. My clients understand Emilee has anorexia, yet they have no idea what's going on in our family. That Emilee is so ill, that she got a DWI and is currently holed up in a correctional facility as a kind of last-ditch effort to save her life. I know people won't understand. She's a shadow of her former self—literally and figuratively—as fragile emotionally as she is physically. Most of my clients and friends don't understand anorexia, mental illness, or addiction, and

I don't want others to judge her. I've told a few trusted people, but mostly I feel this is her story to tell, someday, if she chooses, not mine. I want to go back in time and change some things and emphasize others, yet I can't. I want her to have another chance. She deserves that. I want my words to reach her and my actions to save her.

The phone rings and it interrupts my thoughts. I'm hoping it's Emilee. I look forward to the times she's given permission to call. Her calls are infrequent, and random, always coming through on the landline.

"I have some good news!" Emilee says when I answer the phone. I can't remember the last time I heard excitement in my daughter's voice. "There's an in-patient alcohol treatment center here in Rochester that's willing to take me now that I'm stable and have gained some weight." She tells me the few details she knows and asks me to meet her there the following day.

"I don't know much about it," she says. "I'm just excited to go outside."

Fifty-five days have passed since the judge told us he could get Emilee treatment for her alcohol dependency and eating disorder. For every one of those days Jack and I have questioned the decision we made in the judge's chambers, yet we both believe Emilee would not be alive on this day if she'd been allowed to go home on her own recognizance that day.

Linda, John, and *Emilee* Mazur

CHAPTER TWENTY-NINE • HOPE

JACK

Suddenly, it's May again. Flowers are beginning to bloom, and the air is filled with hope and promise for a wonderful summer. Turning in to the driveway of the two-story treatment center, we note the painted brick façade and the bright red roof. Emilee is already inside, and she's excited to see us and thrilled with the things we've brought: her own clothes, toiletries, some books, and journals. We visit her at every opportunity and quickly become familiar with the interior of the center, equipped to house over forty residents. The following week we're invited to attend an AA meeting with Emilee and the entire group. It's a proud moment for her, and us, when she receives her coin for two months of sobriety. Emilee seems to be adjusting and appears to be comfortable in her new environment.

On Mother's Day, I wake up early. It's already warm outside, and as I stand on the deck, sipping my coffee, I look at the huge silver maple tree—its tiny bright leaves attached to the larger branches—and a lilac bush dressed in purple. Linda's parents are coming to join Linda, Matthew, and me when we visit Emilee at the alcohol treatment center later in the day. At this point, Emilee has been an inpatient for two weeks. She's doing well, and that's the best Mother's Day gift Emilee could give to her mom.

It is wonderful to have our family together today, and on our way to visit Emilee we run into heavy traffic from Rochester's Lilac Festival. Named "The Flower City", Rochester has celebrated the blooming of the lilacs at Highland Park every year since 1898. Initially a one-day event, the event is now a full-blown spectacular lasting ten days. Thousands of people come to ogle the lilacs, photograph themselves in front of the trees and the enormous pansy bed, and participate in parades and races. They purchase items from local artists, enjoy delicious food truck offerings, and come to hear to singers and bands. We've enjoyed the festival as a family in years past, but today we are going to enjoy the afternoon with our daughter at the center just down the street from the park.

"I'm so glad you're all here," Emilee says when she sees us. She becomes misty-eyed, and we know she's speaking from the heart.

"Sorry we're late," I apologize. "You should see the festival traffic."

Emilee pipes up, "Remember when I ran the 5K there?"

I smile, remembering how strong Emilee was and how effortless it seemed for her to run that race. She took pride in having an athletic body and always said running helped her de-stress and stay focused. I can't recall exactly when she stopped running—maybe it was when she was in the accelerated pharmacy program, or when she graduated from pharmacy school and began working so much. Somewhere along the line Emilee began running a different kind of race, a grueling marathon to save her own life. With the impairment of an unrelenting voice in her mind, imparting all kinds of false information—anything to keep her from crossing the finish line, alive and healthy. "I remember," I tell my daughter. "It was a beautiful day. Just like today."

Outside on the lawn, we sit at a picnic table to eat lunch with Emilee. We hear a band from the festival playing in the distance. The sun warms our faces, and there is no lack of conversation. The staff watches us from afar, and we observe other patients reuniting and eating with their families. Laughter can be heard from every table.

"I'll never take being outside for granted again," Emilee tells her Grandma Dorothy and Grandpa Carmen.

As I watch her interact with family members, I must say Emilee looks healthier than she's looked in the last two years. She's not had a drink in over two months and, finally, the promised help from the legal system is kicking in. Emilee is embracing alcohol dependency counseling. She's eating. She's watched closely at mealtime and, just like at the jail and the correctional facility, her medications are dispensed so there is no opportunity for laxative abuse. I'm not sure what will happen next, or what kind of treatment she'll receive for the anorexia and bulimia. The court mandate gives Emilee no choice: she has to follow the rules, or be taken back into custody. She's angry about her eight-week incarceration, but she's also talking about the future, eager to get back to her home, and she says she hopes to go back to work eventually. On this day, Linda and I are feeling better about the decision we made.

Five days later Emilee is discharged with subsequent outpatient alcohol counseling to follow, three times a week, for two hours each session. For a short time, she's required to wear and is fitted for a court-ordered Secure Continuous Remote Alcohol Monitoring ankle bracelet (SCRAM), which monitors her blood alcohol and sends weekly reports to the court.

The following week she begins the out-patient phase of alcohol treatment, attending group and individual counseling sessions throughout the week. A man twenty years her senior helps Em navigate the program, and he looks out for her. Due to the fact her driver's license has been suspended, either Linda, Matthew, or I have to chauffeur her to and from her out-patient program, therapy sessions, doctors' appointments, grocery stores, bank trips, and more. Sometimes Emilee rides her bike to the program. On those days, I pick her up after work and put the bike in the back of the SUV. The judge mandates Emilee follow up with Dr. Shay weekly to have her weight monitored, and she's required to receive counseling for her eating disorder. Hanna graciously goes to Emilee's house for many of the sessions. During this time, Emilee sees a psychiatrist who prescribes clonazepam and monitors her anxiety. The judge further mandates Emilee to eat one meal a day with us. She is required to attend AA meetings and bring signed forms to the judge each month at her court date. Progress reports from her medical team are periodically sent to the judge.

In 2012, shortly after Labor Day, Emilee's driver's license is conditionally reinstated, as she's been compliant with all the court's demands. She's still not allowed to leave Monroe County, and can only drive to medical appointments, the grocery store, bank, and locations deemed necessary to address essential needs or business, including traveling to and from work, should that need arise. At this time, a "Smart Start" device is installed in her car, which Emilee must blow into before being allowed to start her car. If any alcohol is detected, the system locks the ignition, and the car will not start.

Emilee adjusts to her new driving adaptations, and the fall is a good one. For many months Emilee is stable and maintaining her weight, but it's far from easy. She still struggles with the eating disorder and tells us she continues to experience anxiety each time she eats. "It's impossible to turn off my mind," she tells us. "I'm bored, and I want to go back to work." She reiterates these sentiments every day, and in early February Emilee begins working full-time as a "floater" at a local pharmacy. As a floater, she sometimes is required to travel two hours from home to cover a twelve-hour shift. The court grants her permission to travel outside of Monroe County for work only, and she is also expected to be on call for emergency coverage. It's a difficult job, not meant for everyone, yet Emilee handles the rigorous demands and is there to cover any emergency situations. She says she likes the challenge and the people. We are cautiously optimistic when she achieves one year of sobriety, and we praise her accomplishment. "Managing my eating disorder is much harder than not drinking," Emilee says.

Once a month, Linda and I accompany Emilee to court. Matthew joins us when he's able, and sometimes Kelly shows up as well. The judge occasionally speaks with us in chambers, and Emilee's attorney is always present. Hanna comes to court with us on occasion, to educate the judge about the complexities of eating disorders. She explains to him that it will take time, especially with Emilee, because she has suffered from this disease for so many years.

On May 18, 2013, nearly a year and a half after being cited for DWI, Emilee stands in front of the courtroom once again. Linda and I watch the judge shuffle a stack of papers. Eventually, he tells Emilee he's pleased with her progress to date, but wants her to continue to answer to the court and continue on the road to recovery.

"Three years' probation," he says.

As her sentence is read, I see Emilee's shoulders drop. I don't think she ever thought she'd be on probation for three more years. She takes a deep breath, graciously thanks the court, and assures the judge she will be compliant with the terms of probation.

"I never want to go back to jail," she tells him.

Later that night, we take our dog for a walk and I turn to Linda and say, "Honey, I'll know we'll always question the decision we made in the judge's chambers, but our daughter is alive, no longer drinking, working on recovery from the eating disorder, and is back to work."

***

Over the course of the next few months, Emilee works sometimes up to fifty hours a week. Linda and I worry about her traveling such long distances and working so many hours. Despite her busy schedule Emilee continues to keep her medical and counseling appointments, but she refuses to let us accompany her. We only know what she tells us. We respect the fact that Emilee doesn't want us to be involved in her personal affairs, but we begin to suspect she is still abusing laxatives. Our fears are confirmed when her purse spills open on the floor, and a bottle of Senna tablets rolls out.

Linda, John, and *Emilee* Mazur

CHAPTER THIRTY ● DESCENT

JACK

After working over a year as a floater, Emilee begins to complain about the travel required for her job. She tells us she's weak and says she has no stamina. She isn't feeling well a lot of the time, and there have been a few occasions when she's been unable to complete her shift. It's apparent that Emilee's medical condition is beginning to affect her ability to do the job.

One evening in June I'm in the backyard, hooking up the pool filter, when Emilee stops by. She's talking a mile a minute, and I can tell something is wrong.

"I got a text from my supervisor," she says. "He wants to meet with me tomorrow."

We exchange worried looks.

The next morning, I drive Emilee to the meeting and wait for her in the car. I have a foreboding feeling she's going to lose her job. I try to pass the time by reading a magazine, but find myself reading the same paragraph over and over. Ten minutes later, I look up and see Emilee walking towards the car. She slides into the passenger seat, pulls the door closed, and begins sobbing. "I got fired!" she cries.

Instinctively, I extend my arms and envelop my daughter in a hug, the way I did when she was little and skinned her knee or fell off her bike. But I don't know how to make this better. On the way back to our house, I wonder how many more devastating blows can my daughter can have thrown at her, and still endure?

LINDA

I see my daughter's face, the devastation in her eyes, as soon as she walks in the door. Emilee takes so much pride in her job, and I know it's an important part of her identity, but we all agree this job, with the added stress of travel, was too much for her. We suggest Emilee use the time to focus on her recovery and do the things that feed her soul and nourish her body. As always, Jack and I talk with Emilee. We tell her we love her, we believe in her, and emphasize she's a wonderful person as well as a great pharmacist. But it's like she doesn't hear us. With the dogs at her heels, Em walks towards the front door and clips the leashes on the dogs' collars. "I need some air," she says. "We're going for a walk."

When Emilee returns, she tells us she needs to keep busy. Jack and I do our best to keep her engaged. She waters the plants on the back deck and in the front yard, and then she organizes my kitchen cupboards. The afternoon passes quickly, and soon it's time for dinner. Jack starts up the grill, and the three of us sit outside on the deck. Emilee confesses she's afraid for her future. She picks at her salad and barely eats any of her chicken and baked potato. We invite her to stay overnight at our house, but she insists she'll sleep better at home. "I'll call you in the morning," she says, walking out the door with Duncan.

That night, Jack and I fall into bed early. I'm just drifting off to sleep, when the phone rings. A woman's voice on the other end of the phone asks, "Are you Emilee Mazur's mother?"

"Yes," I answer. "Who is this?"

Jack springs up in bed, instantly awake and alert.

"Your daughter has been hit by a car."

***

Before I know it Jack and I are on the expressway, traveling fast, but it doesn't feel fast enough. We don't say a word to each other.

At the hospital, a security guard gives us each a nametag and pushes a button that unlocks and opens the doors. In the distance, at the end of a long hallway, we see an officer standing beside a gurney. As we get closer, we see the patient on the bed; it's Emilee. She's wearing a neck brace, her head is wrapped in gauze, and her face is bruised and spattered with blood. Jack tells the officer we're her parents.

Emilee opens her eyes. I wait for her to say something, but she's staring off into space. She's dazed and groggy, but conscious.

"Did you walk in front of that car intentionally?" the officer asks.

Emilee hesitates, and before she says a word we know the truth.

Our precious daughter has tried to kill herself.

Jack and I spend a long night in the emergency room. They wheel Emilee away for x-rays and CT scan. When she returns to the bay, I drag my chair close to her bed and place my hand atop her cold fingers. Jack pulls the sheet up over her shoulders, and she attempts a smile. Emilee drifts in and out of sleep, intermittently complaining of back pain, neck pain, and a headache. We observe our daughter closely while the sounds of phones ringing, patients crying, and doctors being paged flow freely into the bay. Below the curtain, we see the sneakered feet of medical personnel milling about as we impatiently await Emilee's test results. We are much too familiar with hospital time.

I can't begin to imagine the hopelessness and the mental anguish Emilee must have felt to step in front of a moving car. I worry about my husband, who has experienced every traumatic event alongside me. He believes it's his job to protect his loved ones or, minimally, to be able to get the people he loves the help they need, and I know he feels guilty. As if somehow he's failed. He's frustrated, and so am I. I strive to be a positive, calming, loving presence for my family. I'm not always successful, but I try. I want to right the ship. I want all of us to stay afloat and forge ahead regardless of the height of the waves. But Emilee's stepping in front of a car is a wave that blindsides me. While I am normally the beacon in the storm, at the moment I am not able to muster even the smallest bit of light.

Jack tells me he'll call everyone first thing in the morning to let them know what's happened, and he offers to call my clients and cancel my appointments for the next several days.

I smile and thank him. I don't want to talk to anyone.

A few hours later, a physician informs us Emilee has no broken bones and that her head injury is limited to a concussion. "She's very fortunate," the doctor says optimistically. "She should make a full recovery."

I think to myself, *a full recovery*. Those words are music to my ears—if only her mind could heal as quickly as her body.

***

A few days later, Emilee is transferred from the medical floor to the psychiatric unit for observation and evaluation. Jack and I walk to the cafeteria to get lunch and rehash everything that's happened. We feel fortunate Emilee is alive and not seriously injured, and we hope now the doctors will see how desperate she is.

Eventually, we're called into a small white room to learn the results of Emilee's mental health assessment. When a young female psychiatrist with bright lipstick enters the sterile space, we realize we are meeting with the same psychiatrist Jack confronted years before. This time, however, her brown eyes are filled with compassion. "I'm sorry for what you've all been through," she says. She tells us she understands how deeply the eating disorder has taken hold of our daughter, that eating disorder cases like Emilee's are complicated. She admits the system is overwhelmed, and says she wishes there was more she could do. "Unfortunately, hospitals are for acute care," she says. "Emilee is here because of her suicide attempt. There isn't anything I can do to help her with her eating disorder."

Jack and I shake our heads in disbelief.

"Everything that's happened to our daughter is a direct result of her eating disorder!" As I speak, I hear my voice begin to escalate. "The trichotillomania, the alcohol, the suicide attempt—all of these things happened because she isn't able to deal with her feelings or express her emotions. She's stuffing them inside, and they're killing her. Please!" I beg. "Please, help us un-stuff our daughter. She's already walked in front of a car."

Incredibly, Emilee is one again deemed competent, and two days later she is discharged from the hospital with group counseling scheduled.

Once again, Jack and I speak with our attorney about legal guardianship. Which would give us the ability to oversee Emilee's medical care and, perhaps, get her into an in-patient eating disorder program. He tells us, "As long as Emilee pays her bills, maintains her home, and shows up in court looking presentable, guardianship is very unlikely to be awarded."

All summer, Emilee complies with the court-mandated counseling and appointments, but she loses more weight and, by the end of July, with summer at its peak, Emilee's disposition is anything but sunny as she sits beside me at the dining room table. A stack of unpaid bills looms before us. "I can't afford to stay in my house anymore," she says, her lips forming a tight white line.

As much as I hate to admit it, I know she's right. Emilee's medical bills and legal fees have exhausted her savings. Unable to work, she has no source of income. Even if she applies for and receives disability, the payment wouldn't be enough to bridge the deficit she faces at the end of each month. Jack and I help her as much as we can, but we can't afford to maintain two homes, and she refuses to live with us.

Shortly thereafter, Emilee puts her house on the market. It sells in a few days, and with the proceeds from the sale she purchases a small townhouse located just a few minutes from our home. Though it's a nice townhome, she mourns having to sell her beautiful house. The weekend before the move, Emilee has a garage sale. Sitting in a chair with large sunglasses covering half of her face, she watches people rummaging through the things she can't take with her. She is understandably sad, but she doesn't talk about it.

On the day of the actual move Emilee is in the hospital again, leaving Jack and me to handle things. As we close the door of her house for the last time, a veil of sadness envelops us. It feels as if we're closing the door on a chapter of her life, which, five years earlier, was full of hope. Emilee doesn't have the strength to see the door close on her dream, and it's no coincidence she's not here. Matthew, Jack, my brother-in-law Al, and I follow the moving van to her townhome, where we unload her belongings.

A month later I stop by Emilee's townhouse, and I find her sitting on the couch with her head in her hands. "I just found out Adam is getting married next month," she tells me through her tears. She dwells on the fact her ex-husband has moved on and she hasn't, and it's obvious to all of us that she is deeply depressed.

CHAPTER THIRTY-ONE • NOTHING IS NORMAL

LINDA

In the midst of our concerns about Emilee my parents' health is failing, and they rely on me more and more. The family rallies together, helping them sell their home in Geneva and moving them into a senior living community close to our home. Around Thanksgiving I learn that my father is becoming disoriented, having accidentally ended up in someone else's apartment. By Christmas he has difficulty remembering the names of family members, and he's falling. My father's dementia is worsening, and my mother is overwhelmed with it all. In January, my father has another fall and hits his head. My brother Mark meets me at their apartment, and after the ambulance rolls out of the parking area he helps me have a difficult conversation with my mother.

"Mom, you can't take care of Dad anymore," I say softly.

She sits down on the bed with my father's half-packed bag on her lap. Mark and I sit on either side of her, and Mark explains that we're all worried about Dad, and that we are just as worried about her. I think to myself, *This is so difficult for us. I can only imagine what she's feeling.*

Our mother shakes her head. "It will be so hard not to have him here. I'm supposed to take care of him."

My father is admitted to the hospital, and it's determined he can no longer remain in independent living. He needs full-time nursing care. In late January, he is admitted to a nursing home around the corner from the senior living apartment in which my mother will continue to reside.

I think about my father's situation, his physical and mental condition, and how the medical community responds to his need. He's admitted to the hospital with an injury, he's promptly evaluated, and when it's determined he can no longer safely remain at home physicians and social workers quickly place him where he'll receive the level of care he needs to remain safe. He will be nourished and cared for.

Then I think about our daughter's situation. Emilee has developed many serious maladaptive behaviors, and it's obvious she is in denial about how sick she is. She cannot take care of herself yet, time after time, she is treated acutely at the hospital, and after only a few days she is deemed competent and sent home. She's given a plan she can't follow because the disease has rendered her too mentally ill. Emilee lives in the same county as her grandfather, goes to the same hospital, where the identical medical system prevails. Yet the very same system that ensures my father is cared for repeatedly sends my daughter home to become sicker.

JACK

For over a month, the temperature never rises above freezing. Linda's father adjusts to his new life in a nursing facility, but it's clear his wife of fifty-nine years, Dorothy, is depressed. We offer to bring her to visit Carmen each day, but sometimes she says it's too cold—other times she's not feeling up to it. Her legs begin to swell, and her breathing becomes labored as her heart condition worsens. I'm sure we are living in a frozen version of hell when one more thing is added to our plate.

One afternoon, I check my work e-mail and notice one is flagged IMPORTANT. A conference call has been scheduled for that very evening, and the e-mail explains that all pharmacists receiving the notice need to call in and participate. The pharmacy business has become less profitable over the last few years, and the company I work for has also become less profitable. I know what's coming, and I know it isn't good. I'm going to lose my job.

"There's a conference call tonight," I call out to Linda as soon as I walk in the door after work. "I don't think I'm getting a raise," I joke, trying to add some levity to what is likely going to be a long, dark night.

Linda puts her arms around me. "Whatever happens, we'll be fine," she says.

Linda always sees the positive in a negative situation, and I know she's right. The stress of this job has been awful. I've dreaded going to work for more than a year, but as the primary breadwinner I fear, at sixty-two years old, no one will hire me with only a few years left before I will want to cut back on hours or retire altogether. At the moment, however, I'm not mentally or financially ready to stop working. That night, I eat very little of my dinner.

Sitting alone in the kitchen, I dial in just before the conference call is scheduled to start. The call begins exactly on time, and after a brief greeting by the director of pharmacy the call is turned over to the Chief Financial Officer who cuts right to the chase. In an almost robotic voice, he explains to all the pharmacists listening that a difficult decision has been made: twenty-seven pharmacy departments will close by the end of the month, and the prescription files will be sold to a major chain store pharmacy.

I remember how proud my parents were when I became a pharmacist. "You'll always have a job," my mother always said. But the world is different now and, in an instant, my twenty-two years of loyal service are over just like that. I calculate how long our savings will last, based on our current spending habits, and I'm angry with myself for not taking the ominous signs more seriously.

For years I've watched small pharmacies go out of business, unable to compete with larger companies. Long ago, I predicted that three or four gigantic chains would run pharmacy services in our country, and my prediction now seems to be coming to fruition. I'd hoped to be able to ride it out. Now I'm worried about being able to get Emilee the help she needs, and I wonder what we're going to do.

It's a sleepless night, but in the morning I feel calmer as I drive to my exit interview. I have to have faith that this is happening for a reason. I feel sorry, not so much for myself but for the younger pharmacists with families, especially since the layoffs are happening at a time when the job market for our profession is saturated.

The manager's office is small and filled with an office desk,
chair, a filing cabinet, and two silver framed chairs with black plastic
seats. Several security monitors are displayed on one wall. I've been
in managers' offices before, at various stores, through my years
with the company, but this time the conversation is not of a friendly
nature. A woman from Human Resources and my pharmacy
director are in the room, waiting for me as I enter. Bill is a good guy
and a friend. This isn't his fault. He greets me, shakes my hand, and
introduces me to the HR representative who stoically tells me about
my compensation package. There is no offer of a position in another
store. There isn't even a perfunctory 'thank you for your service
these past twenty-two years.' As the meeting concludes, I look at
this woman. "How can you do this all day long?" I ask. "How does it
feel to turn people's worlds upside down?" She doesn't respond,
and I realize this is just part of her job, and maybe she doesn't like it
right now. As I walk to my car, I remember Emilee crossing this
same lot just seven months earlier, when she was fired from her
position.

At home, I call some of my colleagues to see how they're
handling the news. I want them to know I care. I remember Emilee
telling me how she wished a colleague would've called her after
finding out she'd been fired. In the following days, I reach out to all
the contacts I've made over my forty years as a pharmacist and let
them know I'm seeking employment.

As the days go on I realize that losing my job, in some ways, is a
godsend. Suddenly, I'm available to my family in a way I never have
been before. I'm able to help Linda with her caregiving
responsibilities: taking my mother-in-law for her weekly blood
work, visiting with her and my father-in-law more frequently, and
helping out more with Emilee's needs.

Around this same time, Emilee begins seeing Kathe again. As
the weeks pass, Kathe observes Emilee is losing more weight and
becoming weaker by the day. She contacts Dr. Krebs, an adolescent
medicine doctor, who specializes in eating disorders. He worked
with Emilee for a short time, and he understands how serious
Emilee's condition has become. He recommends she go to a

dedicated in-patient medical unit for severely medically ill eating disorder patients in Denver, Colorado.

The specialized unit is willing to accept Emilee, but she must agree to go. Knowing how resistant Emilee has been in the past, Kathe arranges an intervention in February 2015. This time Matthew, Linda, and I are joined by members of Emilee's support team: Linda's sister, Ellen; Emilee's friend, Kelly; Emilee's eating disorder therapist, Hanna; and Father Jim from our church. Kathe believes we will all benefit from his spiritual guidance and support.

Emilee fidgets in her seat as we express our feelings of love and concern. It's obvious, and not at all surprising to us, that Emilee does not want to go for treatment. We know she is using Zolpidem to help her sleep, and we suspect she is using too much as she often appears sedated—sometimes slurring her words. When we confront her, she tearfully admits to using more than is prescribed. "Sometimes one isn't enough," she says.

"Where are you getting more?" I demand.

"I order them online," she says.

Frustrated, I tell Emilee what she already knows: the medication she's ordering is unregulated. The dosage may be too high, or it may not contain any of the drug at all. "It could be laced with other dangerous chemicals," I say.

"I don't know what else to do!" she says.

As each person expresses love and concern for Emilee she sits very still, listening. When everyone finishes, the room is silent for a few moments. Kathe leans forward in her chair. "If you don't agree to go for treatment for your eating disorder, I'll have to tell the judge you're abusing your sleeping medication."

With this ultimatum, Emilee looks up resolutely. Kathe places a hand on our daughter's shoulder and looks into her eyes. "Emilee, this disease is going to take your life if you don't do this. Now."

Linda, John, and *Emilee* Mazur

CHAPTER THIRTY-TWO • HURTING & HEALING

LINDA

On the way to Denver, Emilee falls asleep almost immediately. With her head resting against the airplane window, her blue knit cap accentuates her pale and bloated face. She is shivering, so I ask the flight attendant for a blanket. Even with her winter jacket on and a scarf around her neck, it's obvious how thin her body is. I keep telling myself, *I can do this, we'll get there,* but I miss my husband and the emotional support he provides. Jack has been fortunate to find a part-time pharmacy position at an independent pharmacy. Though he wanted to come with us, I insisted Emilee and I would be fine. He acquiesced when my cousin, who lives in Denver, invited me to stay with him. But right now I feel alone, and Denver feels terribly far away.

It's a turbulent flight, but Emilee is unaware as she falls asleep almost immediately. I close my eyes, and my thoughts drift to all the people who came together to make this opportunity happen for Emilee. I feel my perspective shifting. Despite my frustration and anger, I understand the counselors, doctors, and social workers navigate an imperfect system to obtain help for Emilee, who has a disease and mental illness most medical professionals don't understand. Over the years, Jack and I have learned how little education on eating disorders American doctors and nurses receive during their years of medical training. I'd hoped Emilee would recover enough to help other people who suffer from eating disorders improve awareness, provide education, and advocate for better treatment, and maybe even write a book. *She's skirted death many times*, I think to myself. *There has to be a reason she's still alive.*

Closing my eyes tighter, I reflect on my life of late. I've always been able to trust my inner compass, especially in times of crisis, but it seems as if I've been living in a state of flux for a very long time. When I first realized Emilee was suffering from anorexia, I was confident in myself, my actions were instinctive, and I was sure we were all on the right path. Yet as Emilee becomes sicker and my efforts fail, I find myself questioning everything. There is no clear path for me to follow anymore. I'm improvising daily, making everything up moment to moment. In addition to my travails with Emilee, my parents' health demands increase more each week. There isn't enough of me to go around. The perpetual details and duties of life remain, and I attend to them, providing encouragement and support for my daughter, my parents, my husband, and my son. They all depend on me, and I worry about them. In spite of all my efforts, I don't know if I'm making a difference. It feels like I'm stuck, incapable of moving, as though my inner compass is perpetually spinning, unable to find my true North. I've been living in a state of fear for a very long time. I'm afraid of losing my daughter, and now, at the same time, I'm afraid of losing my parents. I know I'm not in control of anyone's destiny, and I vow to myself, *I'm going to make the most of whatever time I have left with my daughter and my parents.* I repeat the sentence over and over. My mind is quiet. Taking a deep breath, I feel my body begin to relax.

A flight attendant rolls by with the beverage cart, waking Emilee. I listen as she complains of nausea and a headache, and she tells me she understands why we want her to go to treatment and admits that she's afraid. Emilee unscrews the top off her miniature bottle of water and takes a sip. "I don't think I can do this," she says. "You don't understand how terrible I feel all the time, and how awful it is to feel so out of control."

"I can't imagine," I say, my eyes brimming with tears.

Turning her head from side to side, Emilee says, "I'm sorry for everything I've put you through. You're always here for me."

After we land, Emilee and I stand up and wait to exit the plane. I curl my arm around my daughter's tiny waist and, as we walk into the aisle, I feel a tap on my shoulder. Turning around, I see a middle-aged woman with short brown hair. A teenage girl stands beside her. It's obvious they're traveling together, and I assume they're mother and daughter. The woman smiles at me and hands me a small card. I take the card and thank her, but for the life of me I can't imagine why a stranger is handing me a business card. As we walk slowly toward the front of the plane I look at the card, which features a photograph of an adorable small white dog with tan markings, his face resting between its paws.

"Look, Em!" I exclaim, holding up the card for her to see.

"Looks just like Gracie," she says.

The dog on the card looks exactly like our second Havanese puppy. We've recently adopted Gracie into our family, and Jack has given her his mother's name. Abbie and Duncan have fallen in love with the puppy. We all have. I smile and notice that there are words printed below the picture, and I read them now for the first time. "Help me to remember, Lord, nothing is going to happen today that you and I can't handle together."

As I wheel Emilee through the airport terminal, two black women wearing blazers approach us. "May we pray over her?" one woman asks.

I look at Emilee. She smiles and nods her head. And then, right there, in the middle of the busy, noisy airport, we close our eyes and listen to the strangers' soft voices as they pray for my daughter's wellbeing.

For a minute I am speechless, overwhelmed by a sense of deep-knowing—the card, the kind women praying. It feels like divine intervention. Suddenly, I am reminded that everything is a God-incidence, that He is the reason Emilee has another chance. He is the reason we are here. I'm so grateful for the signs and for more time with my daughter. During this most difficult day I am amazed to find my faith has been rejuvenated and I know now, I haven't veered off the path. Emilee and I are exactly where we're supposed to be.

***

At the specialized unit in Denver, Emilee is immediately admitted and brought to a large modern room with hardwood floors and a huge window overlooking the city. As a nurse covers her with a warming blanket that has filtered warm air running through it, tests are ordered, blood is taken, and IV medications for pain and nausea are administered. Emilee sinks deeper into the bed, and I see her begin to relax.

Emilee's doctor is not much older than she is. Well dressed, highly regarded in the field of eating disorders, Dr. Lee sits next to Emilee on the bed. I listen to their conversation from a nearby chair. The two quickly develop an easy rapport. Dr. Lee shares some things about herself and her background. Emilee does the same, telling her about her schooling, her work as a pharmacist, and how much she's already missing her dog.

"Do you understand why you're here?" Dr. Lee asks.

Emilee lowers her head. "My life is a mess," she says.

"I'm not surprised at the maladaptive behaviors that have developed," Dr. Lee says. "I believe you can get better—but it will take everything you've got."

Emilee squirms under the covers. "I can't do it."

Dr. Lee frowns and sits a little straighter on the bed. "It's my job to get you medically stable and put you on the road to recovery," she says. "You're here because the people who love you want you to have another chance."

My eyes are fixed on Emilee. The silence is deafening.

"We'll manage your pain and nausea, and we'll work with you and listen to your concerns. You may see things very differently when you're nourished and feeling better."

"How long do I have to stay?" Emilee asks.

"That will depend on a lot of things," Dr. Lee answers honestly. "But I assure you, you're not leaving Denver anytime soon. The civil commitment laws are different here." She pushes herself off the bed and looks down at Emilee. "I hope you'll make the most of your time here," she says. "I'm looking forward to getting to know you better."

Emilee closes her eyes. I can see her resistance and defiance beginning to evaporate.

I'm allowed to see Emilee every day. Mostly I watch her sleep. I wonder how we made it here safely, traveling across the country, with Emilee so critically ill. When she's awake, we talk about the things we'll do together when she gets home. I read her e-mails and texts from loved ones and keep her company when her meals come. She's allowed to have a supplemental protein drink if she can't manage to eat all of the food that's on her tray. She's compliant and seems grateful for the care she's receiving. Emilee meets daily with a nutritionist and a psychologist, and she's told she will be receiving physical therapy to regain strength and balance. There will eventually be opportunities to meet other patients.

Like Emilee, all of the patients being cared for in the unit are seriously ill with medical complications stemming from their eating disorders. I sense a somber mood in the other visitors, which reflects my own. There isn't much conversation amongst us in the lounge or in the cafeteria. We nod and smile at one another, but choose to sit at tables by ourselves.

After five days, it's time for me to go. "I'll be just a phone call away," I say, hating to leave but knowing I must. As I walk down the hall, I try to imagine how difficult it must be for Emilee to live in a world where most people don't understand her disease or the shame and judgment she feels for having it. If she could have had an opportunity like this, with all the levels of care, years ago, before the eating disorder was so deeply ingrained, I don't believe we would be here today. I'm grateful that this time the stars have aligned. Even her insurance company is on board for the next phase of treatment.

In the lounge, Dr. Lee is waiting for me. There's no one else in the room. It's bright, and the sun shines through the large rectangular picture window and illuminates this space. We sit facing each other in comfortable leather chairs. I ask her to be honest with me about Emilee's prognosis.

"Emilee's condition was grave when she arrived," she says. "A toxicologist was consulted because Emilee has confessed to taking extreme amounts of Zolpidem to help her sleep. We're weaning her now."

"Do you think she'll get better?" I ask.

The doctor runs her fingers through her hair. "For patients like Emilee, with severe and enduring anorexia, we strive to get them to eighty percent of a normal weight. Sometimes when they reach that weight and can retain it, something shifts in their brain and things get easier."

I try to recall the last time Emilee was considered 'normal' weight. It was probably when she graduated from pharmacy school, nine years prior.

"Mrs. Mazur," Dr. Lee adds, "I'll be honest with you. If she doesn't get better this time, she's probably not going to make it."

I feel my heart drop, and suddenly I feel sick to my stomach. My ears ring and the bright room drains of color. Dr. Lee gets me a glass of water and stays with me until I tell her it's okay for her to go. After she leaves I stare out the window for a long time, unable to focus on anything. I know this is Emilee's last chance.

After three weeks in Denver, Emilee shares her progress with us. "Dr. Lee says I'm well enough to move to the next level of care," she says, telling us her medications have been changed, that she's eating her meals, her kidney function has improved, and that she's feeling better. "Tomorrow I'm being transferred to Residential Care at another center." She tells us about what she anticipates will happen at the center. "Everything revolves around meals and snacks, with therapy in between," she says. "No privileges at the beginning of treatment, no exercise, and constant supervision."

Is it really that bad?" I ask.

"It's torture to have to eat so much," she says. "People have meltdowns during meals, and there's no privacy."

"It's been years since you've been in treatment; maybe some things have changed," I say.

"These places are pretty much the same," she says. There's a moment of silence. "Being far from home makes everything harder." Emilee sighs. "I wish we had residential care in Rochester."

We hope the treatment in Denver goes well enough so that Emilee will continue with the next two steps: Partial Hospitalization where the patients go to a treatment center for therapy and meals, seven days a week, sleeping in a supervised apartment, then to Intensive Outpatient where patients live at home and go to the treatment center, much the way they would go for a job, Monday through Friday, for meals and support.

Jack and I agree Emilee needs a slow transition to practice the coping skills she's learning and gradually assimilate to having less structure, more independence, and a healthier relationship with food, stress, emotions—and with us—upon returning home. We know these next steps will be the most difficult for her.

The weeks pass quickly, the snow falls perpetually, and the air in Rochester remains cold and damp. While Emilee is in Residential Treatment, we have weekly counseling sessions over the phone with her and her therapist. Sometimes Emilee asks Matthew to participate in the sessions. Though she's compliant, it's evident she's not thrilled to be there.

While Emilee is in Denver, much is changing at home. My mother becomes even more despondent, and she is admitted to a Cardiac Intensive Care Unit in Rochester. Around this same time laxatives are found in Em's supervised apartment, and she is also caught exercising. Soon after, Emilee learns she is being sent back to residential care. She is furious about this demotion.

Three days later, Emilee calls home. Jack and I share information about my mother's condition with Emilee, and she expresses her sadness and concern. "I want to see Grandma," she says, her voice cracking.

"Emilee!" I plead. "You've made so much progress. You need to stay! Grandma wants you to stay. We all want you to stay!"

But Emilee signs papers to leave treatment against medical advice. She's been in treatment for two and a half months, and this time the Center cannot force her to stay longer. Despite our best efforts to persuade Emilee to remain in Denver, she makes arrangements to fly home the following day.

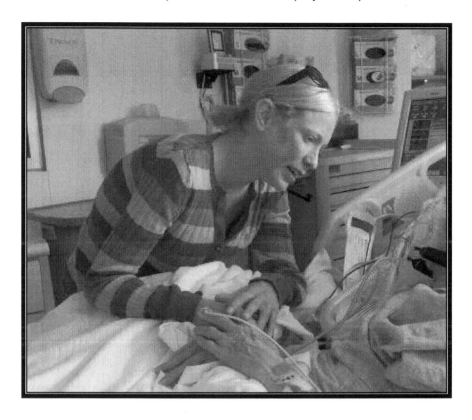

JACK
MAY 2015

It's dark outside when Linda and I make the drive to the airport. Throughout the day we've discussed how we will handle Emilee's return home, and have come to the realization there is nothing more we can do. We agree to welcome our daughter with open arms and hope for the best. We've missed her terribly, but to say we're disappointed she's left treatment against medical advice is a gross understatement. Trish and Mark join us at the airport, and while we wait for Emilee's flight to arrive Linda holds Duncan in her arms. He has looked out the window for her every day since she's been gone. "Emilee is coming home!" I tell him, and at the mention of her name his ears perk up, his tail wags furiously, and his eyes widen as he closely watches each person walking through the terminal door.

Moments later, Emilee walks up the ramp and through the glass door. She has color in her cheeks, and her face has filled out. She hasn't looked this healthy since she got out of alcohol treatment, three years earlier. Duncan becomes so excited Linda can hardly contain him, and in a split second he's leaping into Emilee's outstretched arms, licking her face, and yelping with joy.

"Hi, buddy!" Em says as Duncan wiggles in her arms. "I missed you so much!"

On the drive back home to the suburbs Linda and Emilee talk a mile a minute, and I find myself deep in thought. Six years ago, we were trusting of and still naïve about treatment for eating disorders, especially the insurance company guidelines. Since then we've learned treatment is just a beginning, and comprehensive follow-up care is critical for long-term success. This has been, by far, Emilee's longest treatment ever, and now that she's back home she's set up with a continuum of care and support. Weight restoration is the first step—but it does not mean cured.

The next morning Mark and I pick up Linda's father at the nursing home, and the entire family meets at the hospital to visit Linda's mother. It occurs to me, over the last few years, our families have spent a great deal of time gathering in hospital rooms. Dorothy's private space in the Cardiac Intensive Care Unit is big enough to accommodate a large number of people, which is good, as up to twelve or more of us sometimes visit at the same time. The nurses are lenient with us, not enforcing visitation rules. They know how important family is to Dorothy, who is now confined to bed with an IV in her arm. A large bi-pap oxygen mask over her nose and mouth makes it impossible for her to eat or talk. As we wheel Carmen into the room, Dorothy's eyes light up. We position his wheelchair next to her and help him stand. Linda pulls back the mask, and Carmen leans over to give his wife a kiss.

"I love you, Dot," he says, sitting back down in the wheelchair.

A few minutes later Emilee comes into the room, dressed in a pink striped sweater and grey slacks. She has a little makeup on, and her blonde wig is pulled back so that her hair is off her face. Emilee looks like the granddaughter Dorothy remembers.

"Hi, Grandma," Emilee says, bending to kiss her grandmother. "I'm so glad to see you!"

"I've been worried about you," Dorothy says. "I want you to get better."

"I'll be okay," Emilee reassures her.

The nurse comes in and tells us Dorothy has to put the mask back on for a while.

"Could I have some ice cream first?" Dorothy asks the nurse, who returns quickly with a tiny cup of what appears to be vanilla. Emilee spoon-feeds her grandmother and chatters about her memories of their bingo experiences at the Sons of Italy, Thanksgivings in Geneva, and other family stories, all of which make Dorothy smile. Watching them together makes me remember Emilee's goodness, compassion, and gentle nature—gifts she's always possessed—and I think, *This is who she is, this my daughter*. I find myself praying for two miracles.

Unfortunately Dorothy's condition worsens, and the doctors tell us further treatment is futile. The palliative care team comes into the cardiac ICU to break the news to Dorothy, and she tells the family she wants us all to stay with her.

When her doctors tell Dorothy there is nothing more they can do, and the medication isn't working, she is transferred to the hospice unit on another floor. They assure her she'll be kept comfortable, that she will just go to sleep. Dorothy indicates that she understands. A short time later she receives the Last Rites, and afterward Reverend Mary prays with the family.

Soon it's time for Mark and me to bring Carmen back to the nursing home. Due to his dementia, we're not sure he fully grasps what's happening, but when I tell him we're taking him back he nods then turns towards Dorothy. The whole family watches him as he rises from the wheelchair, leans over the hospital bed, and gingerly pulls back his wife's breathing mask. "This kiss will last for eternity," he says, pressing his lips against hers. There's not a dry eye in the room.

It's been a grueling time for the entire family. By 10 PM everyone is finally gone, except Linda and me. I'm scheduled to work the next day, and Linda tells me to go home and get some sleep. "It may be days," she says.

"I can sleep in this chair," I insist.

Linda shakes her head. "You'll sleep better at home. Plus, this whole thing is stressful for Emilee. You need to be there for her."

Reluctantly, I agree.

In the parking garage, alone in my car, I let out a long sigh, close my eyes, and start to cry. Then I think about the little children in the hospice unit. The ones in wheelchairs being pushed by their parents.

I feel so grateful to have been blessed with Emilee and Matthew.

"Dear God," I pray out loud. "Whatever happens, I thank You for the last thirty-four years."

LINDA

After Jack leaves I'm glad it's just the two of us, my mother and me. Sitting in the chair beside her bed I speak to her, and even though she isn't conscious I feel she can hear me.

"I can see myself as a little girl, sitting next to you on our nubby beige couch. You are holding my hand. 'Honey,' you said to me. 'You were such a beautiful baby, with your big blue eyes, and your round little face. I was nervous about being a new mom, but we did just fine together. And look at you now.' I remember you pushed the hair away from my face and told me, 'You're my best helper'."

I lean back in the hospital chair and wipe away the tears. Memories of our family flash through my mind.

When Ellen was three years old, my mother lifted her out of the bathtub, and as soon as she was dried off, my little sister bolted out of our house, naked. She ran all the way down our street to our grandmother's house a block away. She was fearless, fun, and always had a twinkle in her eye. I sensed my mother was sometimes overwhelmed by her energy. 'I can't take my eyes off of your sister for an instant,' my mother always said. 'She's as quick as lightning.'

When our brother Mark was born five years later, our parents brought him home from the hospital and my mom set him down in the handmade white wicker bassinette. The same bassinette that my mother and all the babies in our family have slept in. Ellen and I observed the adorable, tiny, redheaded baby. "Can we send him back to God?" Ellen asked. Meanwhile, I was delighted. I thought my mother had my brother just for me. I was eight years old and, to me, Mark was better than any baby doll. From the time he was a few months old I walked him up and down our street in the baby carriage, and when he was around six months old I began picking him up and carrying him around the house. Even though my mother scolded me, I didn't stop until I slipped down three steps with him in my arms. He was fine, but that frightened me. From that point on I was careful—about everything. I was dependable, nurturing, and careful.

As we grew older and moved into adulthood, my mother was always the calm voice of wisdom and reason for Ellen, Mark, and me. She's been there for all of us, for every situation, never judging. Just loving us. I can't imagine not being able to call her to talk to her.

After a time I notice my mother's face is red and hot, and I place cool compresses on her forehead. A little while later I put my hands on my mothers' body, using gentle Reiki touch. I pray, recite the rosary, and hope she can feel my presence, my love, and God's peace as she transitions from this world to the next realm.

"You've been a wonderful mother!" I tell her tearfully. "We'll be okay because of you. I promise."

In the morning my brother comes into the room, bringing coffee. As we stand over our mother, sharing stories of happy times, I notice how much space there is between her shallow breaths. "She's leaving us, Mark."

We tell our mother how much we love her. Our faces are wet with tears when I reach for my cell phone to call Ellen, who is en route to the hospital. I hold the phone to our mother's ear so Ellen can say goodbye, too.

***

LINDA

A week after my mother's funeral Emilee is sitting on our deck, looking stylish and healthy in khaki shorts and a purple t-shirt. I notice slight curves beneath her clothes, and her exposed arms and legs are thin but no longer stick-like. The sun is shining and feels warm on our backs as the songs of the Eagles band surround us.

Jack brings out a tray with a pitcher of iced tea, cheese, and crackers, and sets it on the table underneath the navy blue umbrella. The dogs are sleeping on the deck, Duncan right next Emilee's feet.

Jack pours the iced tea into our glasses. "You've made so much progress, Em. We're afraid you're going to slip backward if you don't have more support. Are you sure you won't reconsider the out-patient program here in town?"

"Transitioning and re-entry can be difficult," I say.

"I don't want to ruin the day, but I told you I'm not going to any treatment centers." Emilee's eyes dart from me to Jack. "Promise me you'll never force me into treatment again."

Jack's eyes meet mine. We have talked about Dr. Lee's assessment, and it weighs heavily in the back of our minds. We're hoping for the best and have agreed to make the most of our time with our daughter. We don't know what more we can do. Reluctantly, we tell her, "We promise we won't force you into treatment again."

"That's good, because I'd kill myself first."

***

For a time, Emilee seems to be doing okay. She adheres to her meal plan and keeps her weekly appointments with Hanna, her eating disorder therapist. However, as summer turns to fall, and fall to winter, Emilee begins to isolate—complaining of nausea, headaches, and stomach pain. Despite our effort, support, and pleading, her weight loss is obvious, and the downward spiral continues.

Nine months after Emilee returns from Denver, while the rest of the country is focusing on the upcoming presidential debates, Emilee is hospitalized, stabilized, and released. The following week I bring her to a nephrology follow-up appointment. The doctor monitors her kidney function, which had improved some after she returned from Denver, but is now back to Stage 4, one level away from requiring dialysis. I ask the doctor about the possibility of inserting a feeding tube, in hopes that weight gain and better nutrition might improve Emilee's condition.

The nephrologist tells Emilee about a procedure called a jejunostomy (sometimes referred to as a 'J-tube'). He explains that this temporary tube would send nourishment directly into her small intestine, to bypass her stomach. "It would allow you to be nourished without the nausea you're experiencing now, and it may also alleviate some of the anxiety you feel when you eat. You'd still be able to eat and drink by mouth when you chose."

Emilee has always been proud that she's never needed to be tube fed in any fashion, but now she takes some time to consider this option and makes an appointment for a work-up. Unfortunately, after more assessment, the doctors decide she isn't a good candidate for the jejunostomy, fearing she won't follow through with dispensing the proper amount of nutrition into the feeding tube as she begins to gain weight.

Emilee seems almost relieved when she learns about their decision. She turns to me and says, "I just want to go to sleep, like Grandma Dorothy did."

***

JACK

As temperatures rise and the trees and flowers bloom, Emilee receives a letter from her attorney, Mr. Melcher, about an upcoming court appearance. It's been a long and arduous four years for Emilee since her DWI. On the day she is scheduled to appear, she dresses in black dress slacks, a white blouse, and a tastefully tailored gray blazer. Though she is wearing make-up and is dressed professionally, her clothes hang on her frame. There is no camouflaging the fact that she is extremely thin.

When Emilee stands before the judge, outwardly she appears calm. Linda and I know otherwise. We've learned our daughter is a master at hiding her true feelings. When the judge tells Em he is releasing her from probation, she lets out a sigh of relief and thanks him.

Outside the courtroom, Emilee's face lights up with a smile. "I'm so glad this is finally over," she says. "I can get the Smart Start off my car, stop paying probation fees, and put this behind me. It's cost me a fortune."

As a family we continue to encourage Emilee to eat, drink her protein drinks, and share meals with us. Nevertheless, we observe Emilee becoming weaker by the day, isolating in her townhouse. Emilee complains of migraines and nausea, and is usually only functional early in the day. Linda stops at her townhome each morning and is able to coax Emilee into going to a local diner for breakfast a few times each week. Once there, Em orders the same thing each time, an egg over-easy and toast. "The waitresses and patrons stare at us," Linda tells me one night. "I'm sure they think that Emilee is battling cancer." I often think about the tremendous empathy and outreach that Emilee would receive if she did, in fact, have cancer.

Linda and I worry about Matthew, too. Emilee's illness has hit him hard, and though he tries his best to keep his sister engaged—making plans to take her to her favorite places, to the store, or out for lunch—she cancels most of the time. Matthew is quiet by nature, but lately he shares his feelings of sadness and frustration about his sister's condition with us. He has the same cloud of worry hanging over him that we do, and there's no bounce in his step anymore. We worry about Matthew and Emilee, and Matthew worries about Emilee, Linda, and me. We are afraid of losing our daughter, and Matthew fears the loss of his sister, and although our entire family is supportive—visiting Emilee, calling her, bringing her homemade soup, and perpetually checking on us—the three of us feel very alone.

LINDA

For years, no matter what, Emilee always calls me as soon as she wakes up, usually between 6 and 7 AM. One morning, it's nearly 8AM and Em still hasn't called, so I pick up my cell phone. She has trained me well, my daughter, and I'm immediately worried when my call goes right to voice mail.

I call again.

Voicemail.

With the phone tucked under my chin, I dial and redial. I try to stay calm as I pull a fresh fruit salad out of the refrigerator, but inside I'm frantic.

Something is wrong, I think to myself. *I know it.* Jack offers to come with me, but I know it's too late for him to get coverage. "She's probably okay," I tell him, trying to override the gnawing feeling in my stomach. "Go to work, and I'll call you when I get to Emilee's." We pull out of the driveway in tandem.

A few minutes later, I park my car and hurry along the wet sidewalk to Emilee's front door when something catches my eye. There, on the edge of the sidewalk, next to the porch step, I see Emilee's cellphone. The shattered case is filled with water from the overnight rain. I fumble with the key to her door, not knowing what's happened to our daughter or what I'll find inside. My hands shake with fear, but eventually the key stills enough for me to guide it into the lock. Running up the stairs, I shout Emilee's name.

She isn't in her bedroom.

Duncan whines in the crate beside her bed, which is unusual because he usually sleeps with her. On the rare occasion he doesn't, the first thing she does is let him out of the crate in the morning. Frantically I search every room, including the basement, hollering my daughter's name. She is nowhere to be found. My chest is tight, and I can hear my heart pounding. As I walk back into the living room I notice the wooden blinds are askew, and the couch is a little out of place, too, having been moved away from the wall.

I'm just about to call Jack when my phone rings, startling me.

"Mom," a voice whispers. "It's me. I'm in the hospital."

JACK

Walking into the Intensive Care Unit, Linda and I see Emilee lying in bed and hear the beeping monitors all around us. There are IV tubes in her arms, and a heart monitor is strapped across her chest. She is weak as a kitten and white as a ghost.

Emilee tells us she fell on the way to the bathroom, but this time she couldn't get up. "I couldn't feel my legs. I dragged myself across the floor to get my phone." She points to the rug burns on her legs. "The EMTs had to come through my living room window," she tells us, shaking her head in disbelief.

A young doctor wearing a starched lab coat and round glasses comes into the room and speaks with us. He tells Emilee her blood glucose was twenty-eight when she was brought in, and explains that normal blood glucose should be around 100. "You're lucky to be alive, young lady," he says, raising his eyebrows.

Emilee nods her head and seems unfazed.

Another physician suggests we look into palliative care. Days later, Emilee is interviewed by a team and is subsequently discouraged from pursuing this level of care because of her young age. We're baffled and can't understand why they'd discourage her.

We know the drill. Our daughter is going to be discharged as soon as she is stabilized—and she is.

CHAPTER THIRTY-THREE • PRECIOUS TIME

JACK

When Emilee is released from the hospital Linda and I make it clear to her that she can no longer stay in her townhome alone, and she doesn't disagree. We hire a nurse to help out a few mornings a week, and another family friend, Jan, a former hospice employee, volunteers to help us. Linda is there most of the day and sleeps there each night, in a twin bed in the bedroom adjacent to Emilee's. I am there each day and stay over many nights, sleeping next to Linda in the tiny twin bed.

Matthew does all he can to help his sister, his mother, and me, while family from near and far rally around us. Close friends call and offer their support. Linda prepares simple meals for Emilee— homemade soup, smoothies, anything she wants—anything her stomach will tolerate. Yet after a month, her condition deteriorates even more. Over time Emilee develops bedsores, and it becomes increasingly difficult to keep her comfortable. We soon realize she requires a greater level of care than we can provide. The care manager from Dr. Shay's office sets up a hospice evaluation for Emilee.

One a sunny July afternoon, a nurse and a social worker arrive at Emilee's. They fill out paperwork and evaluate Emilee to see if she might be a candidate for hospice care. Emilee tells them she'll call them when she's ready. Though Linda and I would welcome the help now, we respect Em's decision to wait.

A few days later, Emilee is worse. Her skin is gray, and her breaths are shallow. We call the nurse, who quickly returns to examine Emilee and makes some phone calls. She tells us Emilee has been approved for care; she's reached out to a hospice center that has a bed available. "Or you can take her to the hospital, where she'll have to go through the emergency department. She'll be 'fast-tracked' into palliative care, and then admitted into the hospice unit."

Emilee decides she wants to spend one more night in her home, with Duncan. "Tomorrow morning, I'll go to the hospice at the hospital," she says. "They took such good care of Grandma Dorothy there."

Concerned about Emilee and us, Uncle Tom and Aunt Mary Lou, a registered nurse, drive from Alfred to see what they can do. Aunt Mary Lou is like a sister to Linda and, seeing our distress and Emilee's discomfort, she offers to stay the night and help us attend to Emilee. The fact that she is a nurse is comforting to all of us.

That night, Linda is so worried about Emilee she sleeps in Emilee's bed, right next to her. I toss and turn in the twin bed across the hall, and Mary Lou sleeps on the couch downstairs. No one gets much sleep, but we're relieved to know Emilee will soon receive the level of care she needs and will be kept comfortable.

LINDA

The next morning, we arrive at the hospital and wait for the Palliative Team to meet with us. When the doctor comes into the emergency room bay he sees Emilee, writhing in pain on the bed, and looks at us with confusion. "Why did you bring her here?" he asks.

Jack and I are stunned by his question.

"We're doing what we were told," I say. "She's been evaluated and approved for hospice." I think to myself, *This has to be a misunderstanding,*

The doctor shifts his eyes from Jack to me. "You should never have brought her here."

"What do you mean?" Jack asks.

"This is a treatable disease," the doctor says, in a quiet, condescending voice.

Jack takes a step towards the doctor. He is too close, and for a moment it looks as if he might grab the doctor by the throat. "A treatable disease?!" Jack says sarcastically, his face turning red. "Our daughter has been in and out of hospitals and treatment centers for years," he shouts. "How's that treatment working? She weighs fifty pounds!"

Jack is getting angrier by the minute, yelling out, and causing a scene. Mary Lou takes Jack by the arm and guides him down the hallway toward the exit.

Standing across from the doctor, at the foot of Emilee's bed, I realize I have to explain more of the situation to the doctor. "Emilee has major kidney damage, heart damage, colon damage, bone pain, chronic headaches—she's in constant pain," I tell him. "She's near death, and she's decided not to fight anymore. I'm not asking you to euthanize her. I would never do that. We're just asking you to keep her comfortable, so she can pass naturally and without pain."

The doctor shakes his head. "You shouldn't have brought her here," he says, leaning back on his heels.

Normally I'm a levelheaded, calm person, but suddenly I'm the one who is shouting. "I've been in this hospital so many times, begging for more comprehensive care and follow-up for my daughter. I've advocated for her for years, right here in this hospital. And time after time she's deemed competent to make her own decisions and released, regardless of the fact that each time she leaves she's worse. I love her, and I don't want to lose her, yet I don't want her to suffer anymore. It's not fair to her. It's not my decision, it's hers, and she's already made it." I shake my head and look at him with disgust. "I can't believe you won't help us to let her die with dignity and free of pain. We were told to come here. This is insane!"

"I'll make some phone calls," the doctor says.

A nurse takes me aside and speaks to me in a hushed tone. "If I were you, I'd take her and leave right now."

I don't know what she means or how to respond. Is she being sarcastic, or trying to be kind? Does she know something I don't?

My head feels as if it will explode as I retrace my steps back to Emilee's bedside to hold her hand.

Eventually Emilee receives a psychiatric evaluation, and is it determined she is mentally sound enough to make an end-of-life decision. A doctor from the hospital's Ethics Board comes down to talk with us. I call Jack on his cell phone, and he returns to the unit. As we stand in the ER hallway, the doctor tells us they can treat Emilee's pain while her case is being discussed upstairs. Five arduous hours later, the doctor tells us the hospital's hospice program could be compromised if Emilee is admitted into the unit. "I assure you," he says, "no one in this city or state will accept her into hospice. You can take her to another state or country, and they might be able to help you."

The nurse was right, I think to myself. *We should have left hours ago.*

The doctor tells us to go home and keep doing what we've been doing with our make-shift homecare.

Jack protests, "This is really not right! We don't have the expertise to help her with all she needs."

We don't understand what's happening, but we don't argue. Exhausted, we leave the hospital with our daughter. Back at the townhouse Jack carries Emilee upstairs to her bedroom, and I follow behind. I watch my husband gently lay our daughter back into her bed and cover her with a burgundy comforter.

The next day a nurse comes to the house to evaluate Emilee for hospice again, and one hour later I receive a telephone call saying Em's been denied any type of nursing care let alone hospice care. "We can send someone out to determine if she'd be a candidate for physical therapy," a receptionist tells us over the phone.

Physical therapy? The response is ridiculous, and feels like salt being thrown on our wounds. My daughter can hardly breathe, and is experiencing organ failure. I think about Emilee upstairs in bed. She could die tonight, or it could be a slow, painful death. I call the care manager at the doctor's office and explain the latest developments.

"This doesn't make sense," she says. "I'll make some calls, and get back to you."

A short time later she calls me back, unable to get an answer as to why Emilee is being denied care, and neither can the doctor. Then the office manager says something chilling. "I know everything about Emilee's case is documented, but you might want to call your attorney just to be sure. If Emilee were to die tonight, I'm not sure what might happen."

By the time I push the 'end' button on my cell phone, my head is spinning. The day is warm, and I've been able to take these calls outside on Emilee's deck so she won't overhear all the craziness that's unfolding. It feels cozy and safe out here, and I'm grateful for the tall wooden fence providing privacy. I look at the colorful flowers bordering the fence and the back of the garage. Emilee and I planted them on a warm day in May, much like this one. Suddenly, I realize that she won't see the perennials when they come up next year—not the lavender, not the daisies, not the coneflowers. My eyes fill with tears and they roll down my face.

Back inside, I look in on Emilee. I'm not sure if she's awake or asleep, and from my place in the hallway I see her put something in her mouth then stuff something inside her pillowcase. When I confront her, she confesses she has been self-medicating to manage the pain. Reaching inside the pillowcase, I retrieve the tablets.

"I ordered them online," she says.

Just a week before, Jack and I scoured the house to make sure there wasn't any medication not currently prescribed. The hospice nurse and social worker told us that this was something that needed to be done before hospice care could begin.

When Jack comes home, Jan is at the house. She has stopped by with some fresh cut wildflowers, and while I search for a vase Matthew walks through the front door carrying a few bags of groceries. The four of us sit down in Emilee's living room, and I begin to explain what's transpired—the denial of nursing and hospice care as well as the tablets I found Emilee taking.

Jan looks concerned. "Okay, the way I understand it, if Emilee dies and she's not under hospice care, an autopsy could be ordered," she says. "And if something shows up in her system that's not been prescribed, it's possible you could be implicated."

Jack, Matthew, and I sit very still on the couch, trying to absorb what we're hearing. Jan is a close friend we trust. As a former employee at a hospice home, she raises issues about things that we don't know anything about. *Could this be true?*

JACK

After Jan leaves I call our attorney's office and get his voicemail, stating he'll be out of town for a few days. After discussing our options, I make a decision. "Emilee is not going to suffer and die upstairs under my watch," I say. "We can't take the chance of being held responsible for her death. If anorexia is a "treatable disease", we'll take her to the hospital and have her treated. I'll call 911."

Linda and I walk up the stairs to tell Emilee we're breaking our promise.

When the ambulance arrives, we're not surprised when Emilee refuses to go to the hospital. The EMTs try to reason with her, to no avail. A sheriff's deputy arrives. He walks up the stairs and into Emilee's bedroom. After conferring with the EMTs, he tells Emilee she has to go to the hospital. "If you don't go willingly, you leave me no choice but to mental health arrest you," he says.

She still refuses.

The EMTs carry Emilee down the narrow stairway in a special chair she's strapped into for safety. She's angry with us and crying softly, but she doesn't fight. Matthew waits at the bottom of the stairs and gently touches his sister's arm as they near the front door. From the top of the stairs Linda and I watch the scene unfolding, our faces wet with tears and our hearts heavy, knowing that we have to break the promise we made to our daughter that we'd never force her to go to the hospital again. We are distraught.

I tell the EMTs to take Emilee to a different hospital. *Maybe a new set of doctors will see how ill Emilee is, and understand what she needs.*

Matthew takes Duncan back to our house, and Linda's sister, Ellen, arrives as the ambulance pulls away. "What's going on?" she asks. We explain the crazy events of the day, and she opens her purse and pulls out three plastic rosaries. "For some reason, I threw these in my bag," she says. The three of us sit on the couch, pray, and say the rosary. We certainly can use some divine guidance right now.

Afterward, Linda and I head for the hospital. When we arrive we find Emilee in an emergency room bay, hooked up to monitors, with an IV in her arm. The hospital lighting makes her appear ghastly, even worse than she did at home. I didn't think that was possible.

"You told me you'd honor my wishes!" she shouts. "I don't want treatment!"

"We can't be held responsible for your death," Linda says. "I'm sorry."

I motion for the doctor to step outside the bay. Standing across from me, I notice how young he is. I think to myself, *He must be fresh out of medical school.* I fill him in on the events of the last two days and tell him she can't go home. Stepping closer, I say, "We can't be held responsible for our daughter's death."

"I can assure you she's not going anywhere," he says firmly.

When we walk back into the bay, Emilee asks us to leave. She's angry with us, and we decide to leave because she's so distraught.

We say goodbye to Emilee. Linda leans over to give her a kiss, but she turns her head away. Walking out of the unit and down the hall we can't decide if we're doing the right thing in leaving, but at least we know she's where she needs to be.

Later that night, feeling the need to go back to the hospital, we call to check on our daughter's condition. The cardiologist from the Intensive Care Unit tells us Emilee has been deemed incompetent to make medical decisions regarding her health. "She's stable, being treated, and resting comfortably. She needs to sleep. Get some rest yourselves. There's no need to come back tonight. I'll call you if there are any changes."

LINDA

At the crack of dawn Jack and I are back at the hospital, waiting to be granted permission to enter the cardiac intensive care unit. Sitting in the waiting room, I think to myself, *We can't be the first people to go through this*, and for the first time, I pull out my cell phone and conduct a Google search, typing *severe and enduring anorexia and hospice care*. I read many articles, and learn that, though it is controversial, in extreme cases of anorexia, where numerous treatments have failed, palliative and hospice care has been provided.

I don't want my precious daughter to die. I can't imagine my life without her. But I see her suffering, day after day, week after week, year after year, and I see no end in sight.

LINDA AND JACK

Several days later, after being nourished and hydrated, Emilee forgives us for sending her to the hospital, and we start fresh, grateful we have more time together. She receives another psychiatric evaluation and is, yet again, deemed competent to make her own decisions.

Emilee also meets with a palliative care doctor who takes a great deal of time reviewing her long history, talking to psychiatry, former and current doctors, as well as the hospice team. After her meeting with him, Emilee informs us, "The meeting went well. He's nice, and he really listened to me. We talked for a long time. You'll like him."

A nurse tells us we'll get to meet him tomorrow.

Emilee is right. Dr. Herbert is a kind and gentle man, and shares that he's just a little older than Emilee. He concludes that hers is indeed a very complex case, because of the disease, how long she's

258

suffered, the number of treatment centers she's been to, the damage that's been done to her body, and the fact that she's only 35 years old.

"I empathize with all she's been through, and all you've been through with her."

Standing in front of the nurses' station, he explains that it's difficult to make this diagnosis, and some may considerate it controversial. But after extensively reviewing her history, conferring with others who've treated her, and after talking with Emilee, he tells us he's confident in his diagnosis. "Emilee hasn't responded to treatments in the past, and I believe she will not respond to further treatment." He looks down at the floor for a moment. When he raises his head, his brown eyes focus on our faces. "Emilee has a terminal mental illness: Recalcitrant Anorexia Nervosa," he says in a quiet, yet firm voice.

We think to ourselves, *Emilee has known this. She knows her body and how sick she is. We've known for a while. And finally someone in the medical community, a doctor, understands and isn't afraid to agree with the fact she wants no more treatment—that enough is enough!*

JACK

The next day Emilee meets with a wonderful social worker named Erica. Emilee is accepted into a home hospice program, affiliated with a different nursing service. A wheelchair, a hospital bed, along with other essential items, are delivered to her townhouse. Her living room becomes her bedroom.

Emilee posts on Facebook that she is under hospice care. Friends from high school and college reach out to her through social media, phone calls, and visits. Most have no idea she's been ill.

One hot, summer morning, Emilee announces that she'd like to go to the Park Avenue Festival, and we are thrilled to comply. Park Avenue is one of Rochester's favorite neighborhoods and, during the festival, the entire street is lined with food trucks, performers, artists, music, and vendors of all types. Shops and restaurants are crowded with people as thousands of people pack the area during the two-day festival. The event is like Christmas in August for local business owners. On this particular Sunday the air is warm, the humidity is low, the sun is shining, and the sky is a brilliant blue. We pack the wheelchair into the back of our SUV and drive to the festival with our daughter.

"I'm tired," she says, "but I'm glad to be doing something outside that's...normal." Even her townhome no longer seems 'normal' with the hospital bed and all the medical paraphernalia strewn throughout—a constant reminder that our daughter is dying.

Pushing Emilee in her wheelchair down the tree-lined sidewalk toward the festival, people move out of the way, and I smile and nod as we pass them. *They probably assume she is a cancer patient,* I think to myself. Instantly, my mind rewinds to our vacation in Cape May, twenty years earlier, when the sight of a father pushing his disabled adult daughter up a ramp and onto a deck overlooking the beach brings tears to my eyes. How ironic it is, that today I'm pushing my own daughter in a wheelchair. But there are no coincidences. I know that now.

LINDA

By the end of the following week, Emilee is weaker. I help her into the bathtub, give her some privacy, and when she's ready to get out she calls for me to come and help her. Bending over her frail little body, I tell her to put her arms around my neck. As I slowly straighten up, she rises to her feet. We have our technique down to a science now, but it's taken us a few times to figure out this maneuver. After she's dressed, I help her down the stairs and into the hospital bed in the center of her living room.

The patio door slides open, and Jack walks into the house.

Emilee is feeling terrible, and I give her some ginger ale. Em calls for Duncan, and he jumps up on the bed and snuggles next to her, as close as he can get.

"I can't imagine how I'll go on without you," I say to Emilee, sitting on the edge of the bed, my eyes filling with tears. I pull a tissue out of the flowered box on the end table and wipe the tears running down my cheeks. I try to stop, but I can't. "Your father and I took the eating disorder seriously right from the beginning, but we never dreamed it would take your life. There are so many things we would do differently, knowing what we know now."

Emilee covers her face with her hands. She complains of a headache and asks me to stop talking, but I can't help myself. There are things that need to be said. "We've tried so hard. I'm so, so sorry."

Jack sits down on the couch and extends one hand toward Emilee. She takes it, and their eyes lock. Neither speaks.

Tears well in her eyes. "I've had migraines, neck pain, and nausea every day, for months and months. All my organs are shot. I'm tired," she says, leaning her head back into the pillow. "My body is done."

"Dad, there is nothing you could have done," Emilee says, squeezing her father's hand. "Trust me; there's nothing either of you could have done."

It's heart-wrenching watching someone you love so deeply, suffer. We try and keep Emilee comfortable, but she moans each time she moves. We keep our voices soft and the house quiet as the day slips away and becomes night. We know we're losing time.

JACK

Emilee's condition worsens and soon she's unable to move without tremendous discomfort, making it almost impossible for her to use the bathroom, even with the walker or wheelchair to assist. Her bedsores are worsening, despite being treated by the hospice nurse. Emilee insists she wants to remain in her home, but Linda and I are afraid.

Early the next morning Emilee's social worker, Erica, and a nurse arrive at Emilee's townhouse. The nurse takes Emilee's vitals and inputs the numbers into her laptop, and Erica takes a damp cloth and gently washes Emilee's face and hands. I can see that Erica understands Emilee's pain isn't being managed with the medication available in the home hospice setting. After a few minutes she steps outside to make a phone call, and when she returns she leans over Emilee's hospital bed. "Would you like to go to the Hildebrandt Hospice Care Center, Emilee?" Erica asks. "It's a beautiful place, and they will be able to manage your pain better there. Your parents can be your parents—not your caregivers. They can stay there with you."

Emilee listens intently, and I can see she is considering things.

"Can Duncan come to visit?"

Erica smiles and promises that he can.

"Okay," Emilee says quietly, "I'll go."

CHAPTER THIRTY-FOUR

The ELIZABETH G. & JENNIFER J. HILDEBRANDT HOSPICE

CARE CENTER

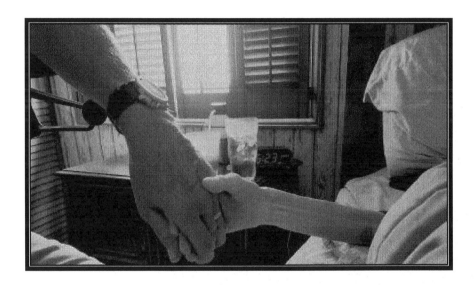

LINDA

Our very long and exhausting journey has finally brought us to this place of peace. As Emilee is wheeled out of the ambulance, I wait at the entrance of the Hildebrandt Hospice Care Center. It's raining—a soft, warm summer rain. I don't have a coat or umbrella, and although raindrops fall on my skin I don't feel them. Flowers and trees wrap around the entrance to the building, and as the double glass doors swish closed behind me I'm comforted by the gentle sound of cascading water. Just inside the expansive entryway, a tall waterfall framed in stone welcomes me into this sacred-feeling place. I wonder how many people have crossed this threshold just as we are. I say a silent prayer for those who have come to this place.

A large photograph on the wall catches my eye, and I instinctively put my hand to my heart. It's a photograph I first saw many years ago. Jennifer Hildebrandt was a friend and a client of mine. Her daughter and our son, Matt, were in the same class and played soccer together. During an appointment in my salon several years ago, she showed me a photograph very dear to her; a picture of herself and her mother-in-law, both battling cancer at the time. In the photo, both women were smiling, sitting in rocking chairs on a wooden porch. Jenny told me she hoped they could do something good to help other families someday. Today, I stand under the life-like version of this photo and remember trimming Jenny's hair, one last time, in her kitchen, while an oxygen tank hummed in the background. She expressed worries about leaving her family. "I'll keep praying for your children, Jenny," I said. And I have.

Today, I think, *I pray for Jenny's children because she couldn't be here for them. Now, my child will be cared for in this beautiful place that bears her name.* The serendipity of this moment comforts me. I believe we are all connected; there are no coincidences. When life is painful and seems out of control, serendipitous moments like this assure me we're tiny pieces of a master's mosaic. We are all drawn together magnetically, perfectly. No trial, no struggle has been wasted.

JACK

I meet a doctor with a gentle voice, a nurse with a kind smile, a social worker with compassionate eyes, and I instantly feel genuine warmth and tranquility of these surroundings, quelling my anxiety and fears. Never in my life would I have ever imagined I would be coming to a hospice center to be with one of my children. The hospice team tells me how grateful and honored they are to have the privilege of caring for Emilee. I am overwhelmed by their words and tell them how thankful we are.

The nurse offers to take me to Emilee's room and, on the walk there, I notice a large collection of stones in different sizes and colors spread out at the base of the waterfall. I ask what they are. The nurse explains the stones are meant for people to write on, to honor a loved one. I stop and look at a few. Some have just a name or a date, others bear short inspirational messages. Still others have little pictures of hearts or suns drawn on them. One stone stands out from the rest, as someone has meticulously penned the word "LOVE" on it in silver ink.

"What a wonderful idea," I say, making a mental note to pick a few blank ones for our family and friends to write on.

When I arrive at her room Emilee is propped up in bed, Linda at her side. When she sees me she smiles, and I lean over to give her a kiss, holding back my tears as best I can. A doctor knocks softly on the door, enters the room, and asks permission to examine Emilee. When he's finished, we step into the hall. He asks if we have any questions.

"How long do you think she has?" I ask.

"It's hard to say," he says, placing a hand on my shoulder. "Maybe two weeks."

I take Linda's hand and squeeze it.

"Thank you for letting us care for Emilee," he says. "She's helping us learn how to better care for someone with such a severe eating disorder. We've never had anyone like Emilee here before."

Wow! I think to myself. *He's thanking us for the privilege of caring for our daughter. That's never happened before.*

Emilee's first night is restless, and she moans deeply each time they turn her. The doctor takes us aside the next morning and tells us he doesn't think Emilee is able to absorb much of any medication that's being administered orally, due to her colon being so damaged. This makes sense to me, as the last few years Emilee has complained about the medications prescribed to help her sleep and deal with pain didn't help that much. After hearing the doctor's comment on this, it makes me realize she's suffered more than anyone understood.

"Subcutaneous injections aren't working because Emilee has virtually no body fat," he says. He goes on to explain that hospice centers prefer not to use IVs. Yet, in order to keep Emilee pain-free, he tells us he'll need to insert an IV and increase her pain medication. "She'll be in a deep sleep," the doctor says. "She won't be able to communicate with you." He pauses to give us a moment to make sure we understand what he's telling us. "Is that okay with you?"

There really is no decision to be made. I reach for Linda's hand.

"Doctor," I whisper, "we don't want her to suffer."

LINDA

Over the next few days, family and friends converge on the Hildebrandt Center to comfort and support us and to see Emilee. Though our dear friend Doctor V. passed away several years earlier his wife, Madaline and their daughter, Laura, visit. Before leaving, Laura asks to see me privately. We go to a comfortably furnished family room and sit down. Laura leans in close to me and tells me about a conversation she had with Emilee about a week ago. It was a very special visit, in which they reminisced about old friends, good times, hurts, grief, and life's disappointments. Laura reaches for my hand, an impassioned look on her face, "We shared a lot that day," she says, "and Emilee told me she wants her story told."

"Really?" I say. "She never mentioned that to me. But we'd always hoped she'd tell her story."

I remember how much Emilee loved to write; she expressed herself so beautifully, from the time she was young. I saved boxes filled with letters and cards in her handwriting, and she shared her journal entries describing the painful experience of her failed marriage, starting over, owning a home, and her desire to get healthy.

"She hasn't written much the last few years," I say. "She's been too sick."

We look into each other's tear-filled eyes. "I just thought you should know. She wants her story told."

JACK

When Father Jim comes to visit, he sits at Emilee's bedside and talks to her about being at peace. There is no response, but I'm certain she can hear his words. Other people visit; the nurse picks up on Emilee's agitation, even though she is sedated and sleeping, and asks the room be kept quiet.

The next day, it's apparent that the end is coming much sooner than the doctor originally thought. Now only immediate family and closest friends are allowed in Emilee's room. Emilee's friends, Kelly and Jeff, hold vigil with us.

The following evening, Linda and I advise those who are still present to go home and get some rest. Matthew stays with us a few hours longer, but he's exhausted. We tell him to go home and get some sleep, assuring him we'll call if anything changes. We step out of the room and give him some time alone with his sleeping sister. When we return, Matthew is saying goodbye to his sister. He kisses her on the cheek, and whispers in her ear, "I love you. I'll see you tomorrow."

In the middle of the night, a nurse informs us it appears Emilee may pass within the next few hours. I call Matthew and lean in close to Linda while holding the cell phone up to Emilee's ear, so Matthew can say goodbye. I never had a sibling, and I can't imagine how difficult this is for our son, but I know they love each other and how much they've supported each other their whole lives. He is losing his sister and his touchstone. My heart breaks for him.

MOTHER AND DAUGHTER • AUGUST 19, 2016
LINDA

Before sunrise, I briefly leave Emilee's side to use the bathroom. I wash my hands and splash cold water on my face. Returning to the room, I look at my daughter sleeping peacefully. My eyes shift to Jack, and I'm relieved to see he's finally asleep on the convertible bed.

In the still of the night, I remember part of my conversation with Reverend Mary earlier that day, when she came to deliver last rites. As I accompanied her down the long hallway, past the indoor waterfall, we found ourselves standing by the glass-paned entry door. We glanced out at the sunny day and admired the trees and gardens surrounding the entryway. For many weeks, Reverend Mary visited Emilee at her townhouse and in the hospital. Emilee obviously felt comfortable with her, sharing openly about her life, her illness, and her impending death. Most of all, Emilee was comforted by the pastor's reassurance of God's love for her, His precious child. Nothing she ever did, Reverend Mary told her, would ever change that fact.

"I want to share something with you," Reverend Mary said. "Once, when I visited Emilee at the townhouse, she told me you crawled into her bed with her one afternoon, and the two of you just talked and talked. She told me she could always talk to you, but that particular day was very special."

I think about all the times I've crawled into bed with Em when she wasn't feeling well. I wasn't sure which time she was referring to, but on one occasion, after a very moving conversation, I asked her for something of hers, something special, to remember her by. After thinking a moment Emilee got of bed, returning with her purse in hand. She smiled at me and pulled out a half-dollar-size finger rosary, and a four-leaf clover encased in a clear, hard plastic shell.

"Here," Emilee said, handing me both items.

"I keep these with me all the time," she said. "I got the four-leaf clover when I was in White Plains."

I was surprised to know Emilee kept a finger rosary in her purse, and I was intrigued about the four-leaf clover—from a treatment center, no less.

So many times along this crazy journey, I was sure I'd lost my daughter. I pictured anorexia as an evil entity that took Emilee by the hand and led her down a long and winding road, further and further from us until she was so far away we could barely see her. But when Emilee handed me the finger rosary and the four-leaf clover, I thought even if she couldn't break free from anorexia's grip, she held onto a rosary and a four-leaf clover for the things they represent: faith, hope, love, and luck. I believe these things kept her alive, against all the odds. Perhaps she knew how desperately I'd need the same things once she was gone.

I look at my precious daughter, so small and child-like, asleep in the bed. I realize our time together is coming to an end. My throat is tight, and tears stream down my face. As I walk towards the recliner next to the bed, I remember another scene from long ago. It's the day Matthew was born, and I'm propped up in a bed, wearing a flimsy blue hospital gown. Little Matthew is sleeping contentedly next to me. I call my mother, at home with Emilee, to ask how they're faring.

"How did everything go?" my mother asks.

I tell her everything: How this time, it was quick labor. Matthew, with big brown eyes and brown hair, looks just like Jack. "He has a curl on his forehead that looks like Superman's," I say.

In the background, I can hear Emilee's little two-year-old voice asking for the phone.

"Emilee misses you terribly," my mother says. "She's cried a lot, but she's helping me now. She knows where you keep everything."

I ask to speak to her and, during the momentary pause, I picture Emilee's little hand holding the phone next to her curly blonde head. "Hi, honey," I say. "Daddy is going to get you and bring you to the hospital in a little while. You'll get to meet your baby brother. And then, we'll all be coming home tomorrow. You're going to be a great big sister!"

On the other side of the line, Emilee is trying hard not to cry. "Mommmmmy," she weeps. "Mommmmmy!" She calls out for me over and over again, utterly inconsolable, and I can do nothing but listen helplessly as she stutters out her words. "I want you to...ho... ho... hold me. I need you to ho...ho...hold me."

Suddenly, I know exactly what to do.

I quietly pull a folding chair across the floor and prop it up against the upper part of Emilee's bed. I inch myself over to Emilee, getting as close as possible without disturbing the catheter, the IV, and oxygen. My body is half on the bed and half on the chair, and I curl myself around my precious daughter's tiny body. I cradle all fifty pounds of her in my arms, and gently stroke her round head and beautiful, angelic face. We've tried so hard and for so long, Jack and I, to help her, to save her, but we couldn't do it. I take a few deep breaths and begin to sing to her, the way I did when she was a child.

As I drift off to a light, dreamy sleep, a slideshow of memories plays in my mind: Emilee as a baby, as my helpful toddler, making push cookies, playing with her little brother, and caring for her Curious George, and Tiffany. I see Christmas celebrations, family reunions, her first solo bike ride sans training wheels, Jack jogging next to her, holding onto her seat—making sure she doesn't fall. I see Emilee playing with Matthew and with Kelly, always with a twinkle in her eye, and I can hear their giggles. I see Emilee growing and becoming independent, self-assured, and quietly proud of her report cards and accomplishments. I see my daughter standing tall, her violin tucked under her chin, her long fingers dancing on the neck of the violin as she guides the bow across the strings. My ears savor the rich notes and the masterful way she makes her instrument sing. And then, I see a beautiful, compassionate, professional woman, always there to listen and help a friend, family member, or customer. In my dream, I tell Emilee, "These memories I have of you, of how you used to be, is still who you are."

Suddenly, I feel my heart lurch as if it's been ripped out of my chest. I gasp and bolt upward, instantly awake.

"Emilee?" I turn my head toward my daughter, who appears to be sleeping. I'm worried my jolt might have hurt her or detached something important. When I touch her, I'm relieved to find she's warm. In the darkness, I feel for her face. My fingers touch the oxygen cannula resting on her cheek; it's still in place. As my eyes adapt to the dark room, I notice how white her face is. I hold my hand under her nose and in front of her mouth to see if she's still breathing. A slight bit of air floats across my fingers. She's still alive. The clock reads 6:00AM, the time she called me each morning. *How I wish I could hear her soft voice just one more time.* My heart aches, and a dull pain radiates across my lower back. I can't continue to lie in that awkward position. I manage to get out of the bed and attempt to stand up straight. Jack is awake and has moved from the convertible bed to the recliner chair next to Emilee's bed.

"Are you okay?" he asks in a whisper.

I nod and drag the folding chair to the opposite side of the bed, so I can reach Emilee's hand and see her face. I kiss my daughter and tell her how much I love her, and wrap my fingers around hers. I stand up next to the bed and touch my daughter's head.

She is still.

Too still.

I put my hand by her nose and mouth and wait to feel her breath on my hand.

I wait for a long time.

When I realize Emilee isn't breathing, my knees give way. I steady myself against the bed. Suddenly a strange vibration hits me like a wave, pulsating from my core to the tips of my fingers and toes.

I've never felt anything like this before, I think to myself, but then I remember after Emilee was born when I had the labor shakes, and the way my lower body shook so violently. This feels strangely similar. As the vibration subsides, I feel an ache in my heart and an overwhelming sense of emptiness.

271

"Jack," I cry out. "She's gone!" My legs feel week then buckle.

Jack rushes to my side, and together we stand over our daughter, tearfully stroking her face and reciting prayers.

I think to myself, *Emilee's beautiful spirit was trapped inside a broken shell of a body for such a long time.*

As Jack squeezes my hand, I consider the jolt I felt in my chest and wonder if it could have been her soul leaving her body. I decide that's what it was. "You're free now, Emilee," I say to her.

And I believe she is.

CHAPTER THIRTY-FIVE • CLOSURE

JACK

Linda and I didn't know if we could endure a funeral with calling hours, or if we should have a small, private service for the family. We'd talked about it with Emilee, and she said it was up to us. Ultimately, we decide we must honor her life and help others understand her illness.

On the morning of August 25, 2007, one day after my fifty-fifth birthday, Linda and I were preparing for Emilee's wedding day.

Exactly nine years later, on August 25th, 2016, one day after my sixty-fourth birthday, we were preparing for her calling hours.

It's difficult to fathom a more stark contrast of emotions. A few days before Emilee's service Linda, Trish, and our friend Sue travel to the Lake Ontario shore and gather hundreds of stones. At calling hours, we encourage people to choose a stone and select a colorful marker to write a little message for Emilee—just like at The Hildebrandt Hospice Care Center.

Hundreds of people patiently stand in the long line to pay their respects. Relatives from near and far surround us. Emilee's high school and college classmates are here, as well as teachers from kindergarten through high school, including her first violin teacher. Even the babysitter who inspired Emilee to play the violin stands in the long line and brings a scrapbook with pictures of Emilee. And then I see Adam approaching us. His eyes are red. He's obviously been crying. I think to myself, *It must be especially hard for Adam to be here.* His parents stand behind him in line. I know Emilee would be touched that they came. And so are we. We appreciate everyone's presence and the happy times we're reminded of. Many of these people knew Emilee before she became so sick. Their presence and compassion give us the strength to get through five extremely emotional hours. I keep looking up to heaven. *"Look at all the people you touched during your thirty-five years!"* I tell her.

Father Jim and Reverend Mary preside at the funeral. Reverend Mary's eulogy captures Emilee's spirit perfectly. She shares some of the stories about Emilee's life, one in particular about the young girl in middle school who ate lunch alone until Emilee sat with her. Emilee hadn't seen Karen since graduation, and Reverend Mary asks if she's in the church today. A hand goes up in the back of the church. Linda and I are stunned when we see that Karen is present. This incredible support gives Linda and me the strength and courage to stand up and speak about Emilee's life— the good times. We want the funeral to be a celebration of her life. It's also an opportunity to bring awareness about the unrelenting disease that caused Emilee's death. We know we've made the right choice, and we hope Emilee can see the outpouring of love from everyone who came to say goodbye.

The morning after the funeral, I have a hard time opening my eyes. When I do, it takes me a while to focus and read the time on the clock. Lying there, limp on the bed, I feel as though the life has been sucked out of me. Never have I felt so exhausted. Linda is still sleeping, and our two dogs, Abbie and Gracie, are also sleeping, curled up at the foot of the bed. Duncan prefers his independence and lies in his bed in front of Linda's nightstand. He's wide awake, wagging his tail furiously, ready to start the day. Slowly I get out of bed, pick him up, and place him in bed with us. Looking into his innocent brown eyes, I begin to cry.

Duncan licks Linda's face, stirring her awake.

"What time is it?" she asks.

"It's early," I say, wiping my tears away. I kiss her on the cheek and tell her I'll make the coffee and let the dogs out.

These past years have been difficult, to say the least, and the last months have been agony. Nothing about this time seems real, and on this morning it is still hard to accept that Emilee is gone. I imagine that feeling will last forever.

When the coffee is nearly done brewing Linda walks into the kitchen, yawning. "I'm exhausted," she says.

I walk toward her, wrap my arms around her, and we bury our heads in each other's shoulders. No words are spoken, and we stand there in a long embrace, wondering how we'll be able to go on.

The coffee maker beeps, and the dogs run through the opening in the screen door and into the kitchen. All three of them jump up to say good morning. We look down at them. Their innocence makes me a bit jealous. Nothing will ever be the same, but we have to gather the strength to go on and hope our faith and God's grace will guide us. I pour two cups of coffee and carry them outside to our deck. On this August morning the sky is bright blue, the air is warm, and the sun is shining. Sitting at the table, I notice how quiet it is. The trees are still; no leaves stirring, not a breath of wind. *So peaceful*, I think to myself.

As we gaze out at the backyard a blue jay sweeps by us and lands at the bird feeder, and we watch the smaller birds scatter. I think back to something Kelly shared with us the day after Emilee passed. Her daughter, Caiden, asked if Emilee spelled her name with two Es at the end.

"Yes," she replied curiously. "Why do you ask?"

Caiden walked over to the bookcase and pulled out a book of birds from grammar school, one that Kelly had forgotten about. Leafing through the book, Caiden stopped on a page that illustrated many different birds. She pointed to a blue jay. Kelly looked closer. Above the blue jay, a single word was written: *Emilee.*

There is no doubt it is Emilee's signature.

Before Emilee died, she posted a photograph of a blue jay on Facebook. It was perched on a tree limb, looking off in the distance.

Jack and I look at each other, and back at the blue jay lingering at the feeder. It stares at us for what seems like minutes.

We feel it is a sign; she wants us to know she's okay. With tears streaming down our cheeks, we both smile and say, "Hi, Emilee."

LINDA

It's spring 2019, two and a half years since Emilee has passed. It seems like just yesterday, and at the same time it seems forever ago. It's my day off and I need to keep busy, so I decide to clean the whole house, top to bottom. I make it to Emilee's room by mid-day. I can't be in this room without feeling her so I come in here often, just for that reason. I begin dusting the blinds, and I think about how neat and orderly Emilee was. But then I smile when I remember how she didn't like to dust. Looking outside the double window, through the slats, I see the spot where the beautiful silver maple tree once stood, tall and strong, with its thick trunk and sturdy branches inching their way towards the sun. The tree was much smaller when we moved here in 1978 and, through the years,

276

it grew and sheltered us from the hot sun of many summers, providing beauty as well as being a haven for countless birds and squirrels.

Not long ago we finally decided to have it taken down, and although it looked healthy on the outside, to our surprise the arborist told us the tree had been decaying on the inside for a very long time. "It was just a matter of time before the tree would have come down on its own, splitting down the center," he explained. I didn't think about it much at the time, but today I think how strange it is that a tree could be so damaged at its core, and for such a long time, yet the damage could be entirely camouflaged by its beautiful leaves and its height. From our vantage point, there was no damage visible; we just saw and appreciated the tree's beauty.

And then I think of Emilee.

I remember the early years. All the love and laughter she brought into our lives. I wonder about the things we couldn't see, things she was feeling but didn't share. I understand now, each day and everywhere Emilee went, she carried a heavy, invisible suitcase filled with shame, emotional pain, and regret. Counterparts of her illness. Eventually, the negativity of those emotions took its toll and weighed her down, ultimately exhausting her.

Linda, John, and *Emilee* Mazur

EPILOGUE

LINDA

I lost an essential part of myself the day my daughter died, and the hole in my heart can never be filled with anything else. That part of my heart was uniquely Emilee's. I have moved forward because my family depends on me, and I have purpose because of them, but Emilee always moves forward with me. She told me once, shortly before she died, that she'd never leave me. I dream of her nearly every night, and it's such a comfort. A few times since Emilee's passing, just before dawn, I stir in my sleep and I feel a gentle vibration running through me. Initially, I'm frightened something's wrong, but now I believe it's Emilee's energy running through me. The tether will never be broken.

The decision to write this book was a difficult one. As parents, we instinctively want to protect our children, and we didn't want Emilee's life to be judged by people who didn't know her. Our family and closest friends were the only people who knew the whole story. Yet Laura's words kept resonating in my ears: "Emilee wants her story told."

After Emilee passed Jack and I went through her writings and journal entries, obtained medical records and notes from the hospitals and treated centers she had visited, and we began journaling. We thought about writing a fictional story that could still educate people, but we soon realized the truth, as difficult as it would be to write, would be much more powerful.

I know that Emilee did her best, and I hope others can understand that she was afflicted with the most deadly mental disorder. After a time it ruled her mind, her organs began to fail and, ultimately, anorexia took her life. We find comfort knowing that Emilee was able to connect with old friends in her last weeks, and we're grateful family was present. We're comforted she was finally provided hospice care and allowed to pass naturally, without pain, and with dignity. It's such a joy to hold your child for the very first time, and so heart-wrenching, when you hold them, knowing it will be the last time.

Would I do things differently as Emilee's mother, knowing what I know now? Yes, I'd do dozens of things differently, and a million just the same. But I'll never have that chance. Emilee taught me so many things. I've learned more from Emilee and her journey than from any other person or experience in my entire life. I've learned love is truly the most important thing. I've learned that sometimes people who appear strong and capable are struggling, too afraid or unable to let their loved ones know. Emilee taught me to trust my instincts, to trust my heart and my gut, and from that point on I don't have regrets. Every single person experiencing a crisis is dealing with a unique set of circumstances. No one has walked their exact walk, and no one should judge it. In the end, we're accountable for our decisions and our actions, and we have to live with those decisions for the rest of our lives. As sick as Emilee became, and despite all the situations we went through with her, she knew our love for her never wavered. She knew we wouldn't abandon her, and she understood just how much we loved her every single day of her thirty-five years.

It's impossible to understand why some things happen the way they do. When I tap into my spiritual side, I believe each person comes into this world exactly when they're supposed to, and they leave this world when their soul's purpose is accomplished. Perhaps Emilee's purpose was to enlighten all of us about anorexia, bulimia, mental illness, and addiction. As hard as she fought, maybe it wasn't her battle to win. And maybe she knew we'd carry on the fight in her honor, to try and help others.

Two months after Emilee lost her battle, Jack and I became community advisory board members of the Western New York Comprehensive Care Center for Eating Disorders (WNYCCED). This organization supports individuals with eating disorders and their families by providing services that insurance doesn't cover, such as parent and peer mentoring, and life coaching provided by those who have lived eating disorders. WNYCCCED also educates medical professionals, as well as school counselors, teachers, and coaches through project ECHO-a web-based video conferencing technology. Dr. Mary Tantillo, Director of the WNYCCCED Board and a renowned expert on eating disorders has embraced us, as has the Board. We are honored to be part of this outreach. Jack and I advocate locally and in Albany for the grant that funds the Center.

Jack and I have come to learn that social connection is a vital part of healing from an eating disorder. The sicker a person becomes the more they disconnect from family, friends, and life in general and, as important as family and friends are, sometimes they're not enough. New connections with people who can see the individual through the disease can provide encouragement and help those who suffer to begin to believe in themselves again. It takes a village of family, friends, counselors, care managers, social workers, dieticians, and doctors to keep those afflicted interested in life, encouraged to try new experiences, and stay on a healing path.

There is some progress being made in the fight against eating disorders since Emilee was first diagnosed in 2008, but we have a long way to go. When twenty-one year-old Anna Westin died after her insurance company denied in-patient treatment coverage for her anorexia, her mother, Kitty Westin, became a fierce advocate in the fight against eating disorders. Kitty was a driving force behind The Anna Westin Act, signed into law by President Barack Obama on December 13, 2016, four months after Emilee passed away. The Anna Westin Act mandates insurance coverage for advanced eating disorder treatment, as well as education about eating disorders for health-care providers.

We couldn't save our daughter, but we're confident her story may help others. In order to do so, it was imperative to be honest about Emilee's journey, and what we lived through with her, as difficult as it was to revisit some of those dark times. It is our sincere hope that people will learn about eating disorders, anxiety, and addictions, help erase the associated stigma, and have compassion for the people who suffer, as well as their families.

JACK

During the three years of writing and editing our manuscript, Linda and I have read our story probably hundreds of times. Each time, we're struck with the realization that ours is just an ordinary family whose everyday ordinary issues, somewhere along the way, turned into something closer to everyday chaos.

Sadly, Emilee's story is not unique. For years, Linda and I watched powerlessly as our intelligent, compassionate, talented and beautiful daughter—with so much promise ahead of her— suffered tremendously, declining physically and mentally, more each day. We know that people reading this book can insert their own name or the name of a family member suffering from an eating disorder, another mental illness, or another type of addiction. We understand that the frustrations we experienced with the medical system are the very same ones many others share, especially with someone who is considered to be an adult and deemed competent to make their own medical decisions, when it should be obvious they aren't able to take care of themselves.

When the Health Insurance Portability and Accountability Act (HIPAA) was signed into legislation back in the 1990s, it was believed these regulations would improve the health insurance systems by ensuring the confidentiality and privacy of protected health information. Unfortunately, current HIPAA laws prevent parents from being involved in the care of their sick adult children, which may interfere with the doctor administering the care that their patient needs. This is especially problematic when a patient's decision-making abilities are compromised by a disease that affects the brain and causes that person to make poor choices that might threaten his/her overall health.

Linda and I often think about the medical care our daughter received and are dismayed at how she fell through the cracks of our current medical system. We wonder if Emilee would have been better served if we'd sought out an integrative, collaborative, medical team that embraced and utilized eastern and western medicine methods, as well as holistic practitioners. We believe a more personal and integrative approach, one that treats the whole person throughout their illness, on all levels—physical, mental, emotional, and spiritual—would have been more effective.

When Emilee was hospitalized it seemed she was often seen as a series of symptoms to be managed, not as an individual. We wish she could have received care before the black and white HIPAA laws were enacted, before the mammoth insurance industry dictated medical care, before small hospitals were gobbled up and became part of a large conglomerate. While we understand we can't go back in time the ideals of compassion, empathy, and treating patients as whole individuals, from the heart, with the best interest of the patient at the forefront, should continue to be the gold standard.

During Emilee's early hospitalizations, Linda and I trusted the medical community to help us care for our daughter. What else could we do? Where else could we go? Yet, as the hospital visits occurred more frequently, our frustration with the system morphed into anger because we saw how overwhelmed, impersonal, and imperfect the system has become. During these visits, Emilee was seen by different groups of doctors; she received no continuity of care and, as a result, she became just another face and another patient number in the system. Decisions were made based on which insurance she had, and what her insurance company would cover.

In Emilee's case, over three-quarters of a million dollars was spent on various treatment centers and hospitalizations. Emilee accrued deductibles and co-insurance payments totaling tens of thousands of dollars. Linda and I believe if Emilee had been approved for longer in-patient treatment and follow-up comprehensive care when she reached out for help in 2010— before the eating disorder became unmanageable and alcohol became an issue—she would have had a significantly better chance of finding recovery.

We still question ourselves and the decisions we made, occasionally spiraling into self-doubt. During those times, friends and family members tell us we were wonderful parents and maintain our daughter's death was not our fault; we did all we could. We want to believe that, but we still carry the burden of guilt of parents whose daughter is no longer here. We wish we could hear her voice, see her face, and hold her close. We miss her immeasurably. Our hearts will be forever broken. We find some peace because she is no longer suffering, and trust we will be with her again.

The most difficult part of Emilee's story is the ending—the end of her life. Of course, we wanted Emilee to live and get better, but she knew. And we reluctantly accepted the fact that it wasn't going to happen. When anorexia becomes severe and enduring, where years of medical treatments fail, when organs are damaged and failing, and doctors have nothing new to offer, we believe patients should have the right to stop treatment. A cancer patient with stage four cancer, who's exhausted all treatment and refuses further treatment, is not questioned when they stop treatment. They are welcomed into palliative and hospice care. Linda and I are eternally grateful to have found a doctor who understood our daughter's suffering and provided her with a diagnosis, which ultimately helped us get her placed into hospice care. We urge the medical community and insurance industry to understand the importance of early intervention and comprehensive treatment, so that end-of-life decisions never have to be part of the conversation.

Twenty-three people die from eating disorders every day. These statistics do not include people with eating disorders who commit suicide, have heart attacks, or suffer kidney failure as listed causes of death. Despite these statistics, doctors receive little or no training about eating disorders in medical school. Linda and I are doing our best to make sure this changes. We've been invited to sit in on psychiatry residents' classes, hoping some compassionate souls will specialize in eating disorders and the co-morbidities that come with it. We advocate for eating disorder awareness, increased education for medical professionals, better insurance coverage, and comprehensive care for individuals who suffer, as well as increased funding for research.

LINDA AND JACK

As we wrote this book, we wondered many times how people might feel as they read our story. Would they feel compassion? Would they understand? Would they be open-minded? Would they see the problems within the medical system and the insurance companies? Would they learn something about an illness about which they knew little? Would they judge Emilee? Would they judge us?

These days, we're less worried about what people think about us. More than anything else, we want people to understand that eating disorders affect individuals biologically, psychologically, and socially. They are diseases of disconnection, and the more affected a person is by the disease, the more disconnected they become from themselves and from the people in their lives. They feel judged by a society that doesn't understand their disease, and they feel intense shame for having the disease. Understanding, connection, and compassion are essential elements of healing which serve to foster hope and enhance the quality of life for anyone going through a difficult time, and this maxim holds true for eating disorders.

It is our hope the proceeds from this book will help us to create a gathering space here in Rochester, New York. We envision a place separate from the medical community, which would be a peaceful, comfortable space that will make a difference in the lives of adult individuals suffering from eating disorders and those who care about them. This would be a supportive place where people would feel safe and be able to share their feelings, socialize, make new connections, deepen existing ones, participate in activities, and stay engaged in life. A place where those suffering from eating disorders can be seen as people first.

The strength Emilee displayed throughout the years of her battle with the eating disorder, and the courage she showed at the end of that battle, gave us the strength to write this book. It is our tribute to our daughter. Doing something to help change the lens through which the disease is viewed and treated helps to lift the edge from our grief. People often ask what they can do to help someone they know or suspect may be suffering from an eating disorder, a mental illness, or an addiction. Reach out to them. Remind them you care about them, encourage them to talk about their feelings, and tell them you hope they seek help. We will never fully recover from the sadness of losing our child, but if Emilee's story can prevent just one individual from the same fate, then all the time, effort, and tears spent writing this book will have been worth it.

ACKNOWLEDGMENTS

It's not possible to thank all the people who reached out to Emilee and to us by name, but we have to tell you the tremendous impact your presence, hugs, meals, cards, phone calls, and empathy had on us. Your actions and prayers sustained us through the darkest of times. We are blessed and thankful for our cherished extended family, our dear friends, and Emilee's treasured friends. Your tender acts of loving-kindness are tattooed on our hearts, forever.

We are especially grateful to our wonderful son, Matthew. In writing this book, Matthew was the voice of truth when our timeline became blurred. His devotion to both of us and to Emilee has never wavered, and his love keeps moving us forward. Matthew, we are so blessed to have you as our son, and we thank you from the bottom of our hearts, for being you.

A special thank you to our local family, who held our hands and dried our tears through the years, and encouraged us as we wrote this book: Ellen and Al Lanio, Mark and Trisha DeBacco, and our precious nieces and nephews, Taylor, Tim, Paige, Molly, and Drew. Emilee loved you all immensely, and so do we.

We are grateful to the medical professionals who cared for our daughter during her illness. A special thank you to Panorama Internal Medicine. We extend a deep and heartfelt thanks to Dr. Joel Shamaskin, and to Care Manager, Patricia Montemale, Dr. Richard Kreipe, Dr. Helena Boersma, Dr. Jennifer Guadiani, and Dr. Adam Herman.

To the entire staff at The Elizabeth G. and Jennifer J. Hildebrandt Hospice Care Center. We are eternally grateful for your understanding and for the tender, loving care you gave to Emilee and to us. A special thank you to Dr. Jeffrey Allen, Erica Fragnito, and Theo Munson.

We are thankful for the prayers and support from Father Jim, Reverend Mary, Reverend Myra, and from the Spiritus Christie Community.

When we began writing, we had a vision for how the story would be told; from the perspective of a mother and a father. And Emilee's writing had to be included. After working on our book for one year, I serendipitously met our talented editor, Renee Schuls Jacobson. Renee's understanding of how patients sometimes fall through the cracks of our medical system, along with her ability to pull more out of our hearts and memories, tells me this was not a random meeting. She will remain a precious and forever friend.

A few weeks after Emilee passed, our friends, Judy and John Henderson, insisted we spend some time at their family place on Canandaigua Lake. The first pages of this book were written looking out at that beautiful lake, and the first draft of the book was completed two years later, looking out at that same lake. We thank you for your kindness, your friendship, and your generosity.

Kevin Mahoney helped provide technical support, encouragement, and special friendship. Thank you, Kevin.

We thank Kim Huther, of Wordsmith Proofreading, for proofreading this book.

We are grateful to Richard Hartmetz of Starry Nights Publishing, for his skill in publishing our book—beautifully.

For a time, we were part of a small writing group. We learned a great deal from each of you. Thank you, Jennifer, Andrew, Elizabeth, and Denise.

We are grateful to our beta readers for giving their precious time to the manuscript. Your insights and skills helped to shape this book. Thank you Michele Kaider-Korol, Deena Hucko, Danielle

Mora, Kristin Neufeld, Barbara McGlynn, Marge Volpe, Mark DeBacco, Matthew Mazur, Ellen and Al Lanio, and Paige Lanio.

We extend a heartfelt thank you to Emilee's closet friend, Kelly Boyer. Thank you for all you did for Emilee and for us. And warm thanks to Debbie, John, Pam, and Doug, for the kindness you showed to our precious daughter.

NINE TRUTHS ABOUT EATING DISORDERS

Truth #1: Many people with eating disorders look healthy, yet may be extremely ill.

Truth #2: Families are not to blame, and can be the patients' and providers' best allies in treatment.

Truth #3: An eating disorder diagnosis is a health crisis that disrupts personal and family functioning.

Truth #4: Eating disorders are not choices, but serious biologically influenced illnesses.

Truth #5: Eating disorders affect people of all genders, ages, races, ethnicities, body shapes and weights, sexual orientations, and socioeconomic statuses.

Truth #6: Eating disorders carry an increased risk for both suicide and medical complications.

Truth #7: Genes and environment play important roles in the development of eating disorders.

Truth #8: Genes alone do not predict who will develop eating disorders.

Truth #9: Full recovery from an eating disorder is possible. Early detection and intervention are important.

The "Nine Truths" have been translated into multiple languages and were produced by the Academy for Eating Disorders in collaboration with Dr. Cynthia Bulik, PhD, FAED, who serves as distinguished Professor of Eating Disorders in the School of Medicine at the University of North Carolina at Chapel Hill. "Nine Truths" is based on Dr. Bulik's 2014 "9 Eating Disorders Myths Busted" talk at the National Institute of Mental Health.

A number of other organizations have worked to disseminate the "Nine Truths" including:

Families Empowered and Supporting Treatment of Eating Disorders

National Association of Anorexia Nervosa and Associated Disorders

National Eating Disorders Association

The International Association of Eating Disorders Professionals Foundation

Residential Eating Disorders Consortium

Eating Disorders Coalition for Research, Policy & Action

MultiService Eating Disorders Association

Binge Eating Disorder Association

Eating Disorder Parent Support Group

International Eating Disorder Action

Project HEAL

Trans Folx Fighting Eating Disorders

Facts About Eating Disorders:
What The Research Shows

Eating Disorders Affect Millions of Americans:

- At least 30 million Americans suffer from an eating disorder in their lifetime.[1,2]
  - Eating disorders are the 3rd most common chronic illness among adolescent females.[3]
- Eating disorders do not discriminate: male and female, young and old, all economic classes and race/ethnicities are affected.[1]
  - 0.9% of American women suffer from anorexia in their lifetime.
  - 1.5% of American women suffer from bulimia nervosa in their lifetime.
  - 2.8% of American adults suffer from binge eating disorder in their lifetime.
- Eating disorders affect large numbers of US military personnel.[4]
  - In a study following active duty military personnel over time, 5.5% of women and 4% of men had an eating disorder at the beginning of the study, and within just a few years of continued service, 3.3% more women and 2.6% more men developed an eating disorder.

Eating Disorders Are Dangerous:

- Every 62 minutes at least one person dies as a direct result from an eating disorder.[5]
- Anorexia has the highest mortality rate of all mental disorders, with a mortality rate of 5% per decade. Young people ages 15-24 years with anorexia have 10 times the risk of dying compared to their same-age peers.[6,7]

Eating Disorders Are Treatable:

- Eating disorders can be successfully and fully treated; unfortunately only about a third of people with an eating disorder ever receive treatment.[8]
- Among adolescents with an eating disorder, fewer than 1 in 5 have received treatment.[8]

Insurance Does Not Adequately Cover Eating Disorder Treatment:

- According to a survey of 109 specialists, representing nearly every inpatient eating disorders program in the United States:[9]
  - 1 in 5 eating disorder specialists believe that insurance companies are indirectly responsible for the death of at least one of their patients.
  - 96.7% of eating disorder specialists believe their patients with anorexia nervosa are put in life threatening situations because of health insurance companies' refusal to cover treatment.
- TRICARE provides healthcare coverage for over 9.5 million active duty service members and their families.[10]
  - Unfortunately, TRICARE restricts access to needed treatment, denying coverage of treatment from freestanding eating disorder centers.

References

1. Hudson, J. I., Hiripi, E., Pope, H. G., & Kessler, R. C. (2007). The prevalence and correlates of eating disorders in the national comorbidity survey replication. *Biological Psychiatry, 61*(3), 348–358.

2. Le Grange, D., Swanson, S. A., Crow, S. J., & Merikangas, K. R. (2012). Eating disorder not otherwise specified presentation in the US population. *International Journal of Eating Disorders, 45*(5), 711–718.

3. Kalisvaart, J. L., & Hergenroeder, A. C. (2007). Hospitalization of patients with eating disorders on adolescent medical units is threatened by current reimbursement systems. *International Journal of Adolescent Medicine and Health, 19*(2), 155–165.

4. Jacobson, I. G., Smith, T. C., Smith, B., Keel, P. K., Amoroso, P. J., Wells, T. S., Bathalon, G. P., Boyko, E. J., & Ryan, M. A. (2009). Disordered eating and weight changes after deployment: Longitudinal assessment of a large US military cohort. *American Journal of Epidemiology, 169*(4), 415–427.

5. The Eating Disorders Coalition for Research, Policy & Action thanks Scott J. Crow, MD, and Sonja Swanson, PhD, for their diligence and dedication in researching and compiling these latest statistics on the mortality rate. September 25, 2014.

6. Smink, F. E., van Hoeken, D., & Hoek, H. W. (2012). Epidemiology of eating disorders: Incidence, prevalence and mortality rates. *Current Psychiatry Reports, 14*(4), 406–414.

7. Fichter, M. M., & Quadflieg, N. (2016). Mortality in eating disorders – Results of a large prospective clinical longitudinal study. *International Journal of Eating Disorders, Epub ahead of print.*

8. Swanson, S. A., Crow, S. J., Le Grange, D., Swendsen, J., & Merikangas, K. R. (2011). Prevalence and correlates of eating disorders in adolescents. Results from the national comorbidity survey replication adolescent supplement. *Archives of General Psychiatry, 68*(7), 714–723.

9. Anonymous. (1999). *Glamour magazine exclusively investigates managed-care organizations who refuse treatment for anorexics.* Retrieved from http://www.thefreelibrary.com/Glamour+Magazine +Exclusively+Investigates+Managed-Care+Organizations...-a055122563

10. TRICARE, Defense Health Agency, Military Health System. (2014). *Eating disorder treatment.* Retrieved from http://tricare.mil/CoveredServices/IsItCovered/EatingDisorderTreatment.aspx

RECOMMENDED READING

Understanding Teen Eating Disorders
Warning Signs, Treatment Options, and Stories of Courage

Chris E. Haltom, Cathie Simpson, and Mary Tantillo

Sick Enough
A Guide to the Medical Complications of Eating Disorders

Jennifer L. Gaudiani

MD, CEDS, FAED

· Made in the USA
Lexington, KY
02 November 2019